T0387834

China Economic Transition Research

China has experienced radical economic and societal change since the initiation of the reform process in 1978. These changes have greatly affected various aspects of people's livelihoods and inspired scholars to reconsider the relationship between planning and the market in China.

This book is a collection of fourteen papers by Zhao Renwei, the former director of the Institute of Economics of the Chinese Academy of Social Sciences. First, the author discusses his views on the relationship between planning and the market in Chinese society before subsequently going on to examine the changes in economic systems of the intervening decades, using examples and economic models, and then drawing conclusions for policy.

The book will appeal to students and scholars interested in China's social and economic reform.

Zhao Renwei is a member of the Chinese Academy of Social Sciences (CASS), president of the Cairncross Economic Research Foundation, former director of the Institute of Economics CASS and former chief editor of the *Economic Research Journal*. He has been a visiting scholar at St. Antony's College of Oxford University, Columbia University, University of California, Riverside (UCR), University of Duisburg and All Souls College, Oxford, since the 1980s. He has won the 1st, 2nd and 6th Sun Yefang Fiscal Science Award.

China Perspectives

The *China Perspectives* series focuses on translating and publishing works by leading Chinese scholars, writing about both global topics and China-related themes. It covers Humanities & Social Sciences, Education, Media and Psychology, as well as many interdisciplinary themes.

This is the first time any of these books have been published in English for international readers. The series aims to put forward a Chinese perspective, give insights into cutting-edge academic thinking in China, and inspire researchers globally.

Titles in sociology currently include

Living Conditions and Targeted Aiding Mechanisms of the Urban Underclass in China
Zhu Li, Mao Feifei

The Way to a Great Country
A Macroscopic View on Chinese Population in the 21st Century
Tian Xueyuan

Social Structure and Social Stratification in Contemporary China
Lu Xueyi

Social Construction and Social Development in Contemporary China
Lu Xueyi

Economic Transition and People's Livelihood
China Income Distribution Research
Zhao Renwei

Economic Transition and People's Livelihood
China Economic Transition Research
Zhao Renwei

For more information, please visit www.routledge.com/series/CPH

China Economic Transition Research

Zhao Renwei

Routledge
Taylor & Francis Group
LONDON AND NEW YORK

CHINA SOCIAL SCIENCES PRESS

This book is published with financial support from the Chinese Fund for the Humanities and Social Sciences.

First published in English 2020
by Routledge
2 Park Square, Milton Park, Abingdon, Oxon OX14 4RN

and by Routledge
52 Vanderbilt Avenue, New York, NY 10017

Routledge is an imprint of the Taylor & Francis Group, an informa business

© 2020 Zhao Renwei

Translated by Zhang Xiaotong

English Version by permission of China Social Sciences Press.

British Library Cataloguing-in-Publication Data
A catalogue record for this book is available from the British Library

Library of Congress Cataloging-in-Publication Data
A catalog record for this book has been requested

ISBN: 978-0-367-41697-3 (hbk)
ISBN: 978-0-367-81575-2 (ebk)

Typeset in Times New Roman
by Apex CoVantage, LLC

Contents

Figures

Table

Part 1

Planning and market

1 On the relationship between planning and market in a socialist economy

Currently, the Party's work priority is shifting towards socialist modernization. In order to adapt to such a change and to ensure the steady development of our national economy, it is important for us to take stock of the experiences and lessons from the construction of the economy over the past three decades and to seriously reform the management system and its operation and methodology. In order to carry on this reform task, there are many impressively large theoretical and practical issues, which we need to study and resolve. One of the all-encompassing issues of socialist economic management is how to handle the relationship between planning and the market. This article represents a preliminary exploration of this issue.

I. Inevitability of combining planning with the market in a socialist economy

An established perception in the study of socialist political economy holds that since the socialist economy is a planned economy and a capitalist economy is a market economy, a socialist economy is therefore incompatible with the market. This perception would mean the socialist planned economy is a simple and absolute denial of the relevance of the market. Although in China the existence of production of goods and the law of value in a socialist economy have gradually been recognized, the roles of production of goods, the law of value and the market mechanism are still considered as incompatible with the role of planning. It is believed that in areas where planning works, the market mechanism does not work; and vice versa. According to this view, the superiority of socialism cannot be reflected in the use of the market, but only in the restriction or rejection of the market. Socialism can show its superiority by giving planning a greater role and restricting the role of the market. Regarding the market as inherently incompatible with the nature of a socialist economy had a number of negative consequences for our economy. For example:

Production is divorced from demand. Since there is a one-sided emphasis on planning and little attention to the market, what, and how much, businesses produce mainly reflects the mandatory top-down plan and targets but is not designed to take account of society's actual expectations. Theoretically speaking, planned production and production needs should match. However, under socialist conditions, in the absence of a market mechanism, a unified planning center actually cannot faithfully reflect the ever-changing demand for millions of different products. The result would inevitably be that goods produced according to top-down plans would not be what the market wants, and would result in inventory building-up, whereas what the community needs would remain in short supply. Moreover, most products are purchased and distributed by the state in a centralized way, and most production materials needed by businesses are allocated under the national plan. Producers and consumers have no direct relationship, nor do they meet face to face. As a result, the producers do not know the needs of consumers, while consumers have no impact on production at all. The failure of planned targets to actual needs means that there cannot be a flexible response through the market mechanism, and therefore no timely correction can take place. Hence the long-term divorce of production, supply and distribution cannot be resolved.

Planned prices are divorced from reality. Since the objective requirements of the law of value are ignored during the pricing process, subsequently the planned prices of many products will diverge from their value over a period of time. Under such price conditions, the operating results of businesses by value, profits and other indicators cannot reflect the true operating conditions of these businesses; profit and loss arising from non-rational price factors cannot help distinguish the strengths and weaknesses of the businesses. Planned prices seldom factor in changes in supply and demand and tend to remain fixed for a long period of time. When goods are in short supply, price adjustment mechanisms to encourage supply increase and demand control are not used, and instead, quotas and vouchers are used to restrict supply, so that vouchers then start to play a role as a complementary currency, resulting in de facto different values for the same product.[1] This method of limiting supply by using vouchers is also known as "planned supply" and seems to reflect the nature of the socialist planned economy. This is a method that any besieged garrison commander would resort to, and not necessarily a feature of a socialist planned economy. Of course, a socialist planned economy in certain circumstances may well use production restrictions and price controls at times. However, such an approach offers no economic incentive for raising scarce products. Rather, it consolidates and enhances the unfavorable conditions of producers of such goods, leading to the reduction of both production and supply. Therefore, this approach is unable to resolve the divergences between supply and demand, but rather further exacerbates the gap.

We now turn to the system for supplying and allocating finance in China. Not only is the role of the market in production and exchange of products ignored, but mobilization and allocation of financing is likewise ignored. This is most apparent in the centralized collection and management of revenue and financial expenditure. In the past, business revenues in China included net corporate income and basic depreciation, which were paid into the state coffers in whole or for the most part; businesses had to apply to the authorities for permission to spend on production expansion, welfare improvements, etc. The state provided all fixed assets and most of the working capital free of charge. Businesses did not assume any financial responsibility for the way they use such resources, regardless of favorable or unfavorable operational circumstances and profits or losses. Businesses received large amounts to fund their payroll, and shared in "the same big pot", while workers depended on "iron rice bowl". Since there were no material incentives for obtaining profitable operating results, business accounting became a mere formality, purely for bookkeeping purposes, rather than giving incentives to collective workers to promote positive effects on production. In this case, although the authorities issued a number of administrative orders and appeals, businesses and their workers had little lasting motivation from within the businesses to reduce excessive use of production inputs, improve product quality and widen product ranges to meet the needs of consumers, and thus delays and wastage became long-term problems.

There has been a tendency towards self-sufficiency in the organizational structure of businesses. The socialist economy is based on large-scale socialized production, where there are wide-ranging relationships of specialization and collaboration between businesses, regions and sectors. Especially with scientific and technological progress, production specialization and collaboration further develop. However, ignoring market relations and treating large-scale socialist production with operational modes better suited for small-scale production drove many businesses towards self-sufficiency rather than specialization and collaboration. Thus, China's industrial businesses tend to be either "small yet complete" or "large and complete", and many businesses not only take on non-core functions but even become self-sufficient communities. Of course, this situation is not entirely caused by internal reasons. The imbalance of production, supply and demand, breaches of contract by partners, and collaboration uncertainties and various other reasons often drive businesses to undertake non-core activities themselves. However, the underlying cause from the perspective of society in general is rejection of the market.

All of the cases mentioned here indicate that ignoring the role of production of goods and the law of value and market mechanisms is in fact not conducive to a socialist planned economy. An important feature of the socialist planned economy is to organize properly and to maintain an appropriate proportion of the national economy, and to balance production and demand. Lenin said: "to consciously and regularly maintain balance is in effect to practice planning".[2] However, in a socialist economy, the exclusion of the market mechanism tends to separate supply, production and sales and makes it difficult to strike a balance between production and demand; if the planned prices of various products violate the law of value for a long period and price ratios between various products are unreasonable, it would tend to make the production of these products fail to meet the objectively required percentage. Another important feature of the socialist planned economy is reducing the waste of resources of living labor and materialized labor. Of course, reducing labor time and pro rata allocation of labor time are interrelated. Marx pointed out: "The saving of time, like the planned distribution of labor time in the various sectors of production, remains the primary economic law, on the basis of collective production. It becomes a law even to a much higher degree."[3] However, under socialist conditions, if we deny the commodity-money relationship, refuse to use the law of value and do not adopt accounting based on economic principles, this will inevitably lead to high wastage, low quality and low efficiency, and we will thus fail to maximize output with minimal use of labor, which is an essential requirement of the socialist planned economy.

In practice, it is vitally important for us to acknowledge the fact that the market does exist in a socialist economy and should be actively utilized for the development of the planned economy. There have been two periods of fast growth in the past 30 years or so in the process of building socialism in China – "the First Five-Year Plan" and "the Three Year Adjustment period" – when the law of value was deliberately observed and the role of the market was acknowledged. As a result, cooperation between rural and urban areas was good, the development of agriculture, light industry and heavy industry was proportional, and stake-holders paid proper attention to economic accounting and economic results. However, China also suffered two major setbacks. We must note that it is both a major harmful practice and an untenable theory in a socialist society to deny the positive role of money and commodities and regard planning and market as incompatible.

It is true to say that the socialist economy based on public ownership of means of production is an economy based on development plans. However, this does not deny the relevance of the market; it does oppose spontaneity and anarchy in production – a basic characteristic of all economies with private ownership of the means of production. The market economy, in contrast to the natural economy where there is only distribution of goods among people and no relationship between commodities and money (a basic characteristic of the self-sufficient society with its doors closed to the outside world) is *not* unique to economies of private ownership. A market economy, based on social division of labor and cooperation, is *not* necessarily spontaneous and anarchic, depending on the nature of ownership. In a situation of socialist public ownership, it is possible that market economic relations, subject to people's deliberate regulation, can be used in the service of a socialist planned economy. Assuming division of labor and socialized production, the relationships in a market economy may have something in common, not necessarily contradictory, with a socialist planned economy characterized by socialized mass production. Therefore, in a socialist society, the planned economy, compatible with a market economy regulated by people's conscious awareness, only goes against the laissez-faire market economy and the natural economy.

Two major misconceptions have long accounted for the unbalanced emphasis on planning and ignoring of the market: one equating the market with laissez-faire, especially with the capitalist economy's state of anarchy; the other confusing a planned economy with a natural economy. The former view has become a weapon to be used by those opposing the market as a symbol of capitalism; the latter has become a false theory seeking to replace the socialist planned economy with a natural economy. Shielded by these two outdated views and calling upon the seeming pros of a socialist planned economy and cons of a capitalist market economy, much bad practice running counter to socialist economic development and the people's interests has occurred: the one-sided administrative method versus market-based economic management; the "will of officialdom" versus the objective laws of economics; patriarchal rules versus people's autonomy; the Feudal Yamen system applied in the natural economy versus the scientific management practiced in socialized mass production, etc. Such misconceptions and bad practices are deeply ingrained in Chinese society where the commercial economy remains underdeveloped and 80% of the population still engage in farming. The historic mission now facing us is to develop the commercial economy by observing the laws of economics for the benefit of achieving the four modernizations (industrial, agricultural, defense and scientific modernizations). It is imperative to destroy the aforementioned deep-rooted traditional views before we can utilize the commodity-money relationship, properly handle the planning-market relationship and change the ideas and systems incompatible with the laws of socialist economic development.

Breaking away from these stereotypical concepts and bringing together planning and market, we need to further investigate issues such as the relationship between commodity and money and why there is a market in a socialist society. Many economists have tried to explain these issues by recalling the fact that there are always two juxtaposed forms of ownership of means of production in a socialist economy. In the view of the authors, the commodity-money relationship between the two forms of ownership is important for the development of a socialist economy. This is particularly true in the current situation where China, with a large majority of rural population and a collective form of ownership dominating agricultural production, must pay more attention to the role of commodities in the two forms of public ownership and respect the autonomy of the producers of commodities in collectively-owned work units. However, we cannot see the essence of the problem by simply assuming that the coexistence of the two forms of public ownership is able to explain why there a commodity-money relationship exists and why there is a market in the socialist economic system, as this would mean that the commodity-market relationship does not fit into the core of public ownership – ownership by the whole people. This explains why there is a necessary relationship between commodities and market only where there is exogenous influence of ownership by all the people and not from within. Some ideas prevalent among economists actually derived from this "external reason" theory. For example, the means of production allocated from within the system of ownership by the whole people no longer constitute commodities but are mere shells (the shell theory). Another example is the law of value, which cannot adjust production, has been replaced by the law of planned and proportional development (the substitution theory). The law of value, as well as price, profit, cost, interest and other categories of value, is used only as an optional accounting tool (the tool theory) and is not an objective economic mechanism. It should be noted that all these opinions, which claim to reflect the experiences of all socialist countries, do not conform to the reality of each country and will, if further followed, in practice inevitably become increasingly dangerous.

The special relationship between people in terms of their material interest in a socialist society helps explain the existence of commodities and market in a socialist economy characterized by ownership by the whole people. Where there is public ownership of means of production, eliminating exploitation and the rivalry between people based on material interests, people's material interests will still differ from one another because people have disparities in capacity for work and contribution to society and regard it as a mere means for making a living, unlike the people at the communist stage of development where work becomes their primary need. Moreover, the disparities in material gains may be apparent not just between the individuals but also between enterprises owned by the whole people. Different enterprises with different production outcomes (because of better management, not because of some objective advantageous factors) may lead to material benefits different from other enterprises and employees. If this were not the case, it could well hamper the development of the enterprise. Therefore the enterprises owned by the whole people (those with a relatively independent accounting mechanism) must compensate each other and trade with one another through the equivalence principle; and unless they do so, this could result in the denial of disparities and the disruption of relationship vis-à-vis employees in their material benefits. This special relationship between employees and enterprises constitutes a direct cause for commodity and market to exist in a socialist economy (of course predetermined by division of labor and socialization of production). Such a commodity and market relationship is deeply rooted in the disparities between people's material interests. The economic enterprise category corresponding to this relationship is by no means an optional tool or a mere shell; it is an objective economic mechanism with practical content. People's labor, the so-called direct social labor in a situation of socialist public ownership, assumes that the individuals' labor has been freed from the laissez-faire market ownership. In practice, in the socialist phase, only by working for sustenance are individual employees able to relate to all the social means of production. Therefore, this principle of exchange at equivalent value has to be followed between employees and enterprises. The direct socialization of labor has to be represented by a planned market, i.e., a well-planned allocation and rational use of social labor must be achieved through the market mechanism, which reflects the special relationship between enterprises and employees in material interests in the socialist phase.

The relationship between planning and market is not mutually exclusive, nor a forced combination decided by external factors. Rather, it is an intrinsic integration determined by the nature of a socialist economy. If the fundamental identity of people's material interests, resulting from the socialist public ownership of means of production, serves as an objective basis for the practice of management according to plans, the disparities in material interests constitute the immediate justification for the existence of the market in a socialist economy. This convergence and divergence between employees' interests form, in reality, the objective basis for harmonizing planning and market despite the apparent contradiction. It has been found that overemphasizing planning, ignoring the market, may cause people to see only the agreement in their fundamental interests rather than differences, only the whole picture of interests rather than their local and individual interests. This is not conducive to motivating enterprise and worker activity. However, if the role of the market is excessively emphasized with planning ignored, this would mean that ordinary employees may well act blindly and chaotically. Therefore, it is important for planning and market to be integrated in theory and in practice so material benefits for enterprises and employees can be properly balanced and building socialism in China can be speeded up.

II. On how to use the market in a socialist planned economy

The previous analyses indicate that planning and market, which are not mutually exclusive, must be combined before the superiority of socialism can be fully expressed. In terms of the relationship between planning and market, neither planning nor market is separable from each other. So far, the main tendency when dealing with this issue has been an excessive concentration on planning rather than the market. To address this problem, the first priority should be how to both develop the commodity economy and utilize market mechanisms in a socialist planned economy.

Without the activities of individual producers in the market, there will not be any growth in the commercial economy and the market mechanism will not function. The term economic entity in the context of the socialist market, besides the collectively owned enterprises, mainly refers to those owned by all the people (socially owned in some countries), providing consumer goods and means of production to the market as well as purchasing various kinds of means of production. For the market to work, a certain degree of autonomy must be given to the enterprises owned by the whole people who will then be able to treat each other as relatively independent producers. If they continue to be confined to a state of no power and no responsibility, the market will never be utilized. Therefore, the problem is closely linked to the need to expand enterprise authority.

Concordantly, in a planned economy, it is equally important for the market to provide economic leverage and mechanism for the value categories such as supply and demand, price, cost, profit, credit, interest rates and taxes, so that each enterprise's performance is related to its employees' material interests, which is precisely the substance of economic management. The market cannot be used unless economic levers and mechanisms work correctly; in other words, unless proper attention is paid to the economic benefits for enterprises and individuals, and not only an administrative approach to management is applied. Solving this problem therefore means adopting an economic approach to economic management.

To sum up, using the market in a planned economy requires not only the expansion of an enterprise's authority but also the unrestricted application of economic methods and means to the full in management. Such action aims to allocate rationally and make economic use of the material, financial and human resources according to the needs of society. Consequently, this issue is closely linked to the delegation of management power and the application of economic methods is how to allocate and use these resources in order that the market mechanism works better.

A.   The allocation and use of material resources: it is an issue of production, supply and sales

In this regard, market mechanisms should be improved – production subject to sales determines supply to meet the needs of the market. What to produce, and how much? By what standard can we determine this? In what way will the products be sold? How and in what way are the means of production supplied? In the last section, we mentioned that the mode of production at present basically follows a prescriptive plan from the government; products are sold by unified purchase and sales (state monopoly over the purchase and marketing of the enterprise's products), and the means of production for the enterprise are supplied through uniform distribution and planned allocation. These methods often result in disconnection between production and the needs of society and leave the purpose of socialist production unachieved. The purpose of socialist production is to satisfy social needs, and this determines what and how much to produce. This is a fundamental principle of the socialist economy. Production according to state plans is fundamentally consistent with production according to social needs, but in practice they are different. State plans mainly consider the needs of the country as a whole and by and large only reflect the needs of society while the various needs of different parts of society do not receive a flexible response. Nor is it possible to consider the specific technical production conditions for every single enterprise. To solve the problem and meet social needs, in particular in terms of quantity, kind and quality of the product, a production plan should not be established using the prescriptive targets from the government, but rather, within the state plan, it should be defined by signing various contracts such as manufacturing and marketing contracts and purchase and sales contracts in accordance with the specific needs of the market and the particular situation and interests of the enterprise. Accordingly, materials, for consumption and production, must be made available through the market except the few for which there is a shortage and not available within a sufficiently short time, which need to be handled by the state supply and demand agencies in coordination. The old practice of resorting only to the state-owned commercial departments or material agencies regardless of the market situation is to be avoided. The means of consumption should be circulated by combining commercial marketing and industrial self-marketing, in order to meet consumer needs and to produce according to sales. Likewise, materials should also be circulated by phased commercialization, which directly links production to sales, or via a middleman, so as to meet the needs of the producer and supply according to production. To compensate for insufficient supply, enterprises may work together or invest separately to increase production. These methods, which aim to resolve the problems that may occur during production, supply, and sales by improving market mechanisms, are essential to achieve the following objectives: eliminating unwanted goods, avoiding the coexistence of overstocking and scarcity of goods, enhancing product quality, reducing costs, improving colors and variety of products, and increasing the producer's interests as well as safeguarding consumers' rights.[4]

B.   The allocation and use of financial resources, namely, financial and capital management

In this regard, the market mechanism is to be improved through financial self-management and accountability of enterprises, and by introducing the principle of enterprises paying interest on funds made available by the state and making investments based on expected yields. In the past, in financial management, funds were basically collected and allocated free of charge and uniformly by the state for investment in capital construction of enterprises and for working capital. This disconnected an enterprise's financial performance from its collective interest and the workers' individual interests, resulting in indifference and feelings of irresponsibility towards the rational and effective use of the state funding, while encouraging bargaining, fighting for funds, materials and foreign currency when making development plans. The over-reliance on the state's administration of financial management was not conducive to effective investment and accurate calculations. To address this aspect of the problem, the market mechanism needs to be enhanced within the guidelines of the state's unified plans, with particular reference to the transition from the centralized model of unified revenues and expenditure to a model of financial self-management and accountability relying on bank credits. A truly financially independent enterprise is one that does not pay any profit to the state after paying its dues (the taxes, fees and principals and interests on loans assuming a reasonable allowance for price and taxation). Any remaining revenue is supposed to be at the disposal of the enterprise subject to the state decrees and policies. For example, it can be used for investment in expanding production and improving staff's income and collective welfare. As an interim method, after paying its due taxes and profits to the state, the enterprise would be able to retain a certain proportion of profits as the enterprise funds, part of this as staff incentive and for collective welfare, and for tapping the potential of the enterprise, corporate renovation and reformation, along with basic depreciation funds and maintenance funds.

From free to paid usage of funds, the state shall impose some proportional taxes on those state-financed fixed assets. This payment or usage tax, coupled with the profit retention system, enables those enterprises where funds were better utilized and management of performance was better, to retain more money from even greater profits, whereas less profitable enterprises would enjoy fewer benefits or even none. Charging compensation for usage of funds is therefore beneficial for encouraging the enterprise and workers to tap potentials of every kind, strive to save funds and make the best use of the funds occupied.

In a comparatively independent financial system, the capital construction and part of working capital shall not be entirely sustained by state financing. Apart from the funds for production and development drawn from the corporate net income and retained profits, the capital investment in construction shall be mostly funded by bank loans, and the working capital shall be entirely acquired through bank credits. Before investing and lending, the bank, following state planning, should apply an optional loan system, taking account of the effectiveness of investment in all relevant sectors including sub-programs.

In an independent financial system, an enterprise would no longer act irresponsibly and indifferently, as its development chiefly depends on the profits it has retained from revenue and bank loans (with principal to be reimbursed and interest to be paid). Such a system requires a conscientious and careful approach. Moreover, leverage from bank interest is important since it can be used to mobilize temporarily idle funds in society and to control investment credit, encouraging the enterprise to strengthen its economic accounting and speed up its cash flow to improve effective use of funds. To this end, the funds' supply and demand must be regulated to benefit production and circulation of commodities and a policy of differential interest rates needs be adopted so that the bank can make timely adjustments to the rates, in an attempt to change the old policy of long-termed fixed rates or declining interest rates.

C.   *The allocation and use of labor resources*

To improve the market mechanism, merit-based recruitment should be introduced, which allows a degree of free choice and the regulation of supply and demand of labor force using economic principles. In the past, labor, material and financial resources were simply completely allocated purely by administrative means, and the allocation of labor resources was least subject to any market mechanism. Allocation of labor resources by the labor authorities based on planned targets was able with difficulty to meet the need for a labor force in some sectors and enabled some people to solve their unemployment problem. However, administrative allocation alone had many problems. Enterprises often were unable to recruit workers to meet their own needs, while individuals in many cases were unable to choose their careers according to their own interests and talents; it was the labor authorities who determined the allocation of jobs, almost inevitably resulting in a "square peg in a round hole" situation. This was obviously not conducive to the rational use of labor resources and to mobilizing the enthusiasm of people, nor was it conducive to the implementation of economic accounting systems and improving the efficiency of economic activities. Problems, such as a mismatch between education and career, long-distance separation of couples and a certain number of unemployed workers, still exist. Of course, such problems are the result of disruption and destruction caused by the ultra-left ideologies represented by Lin Biao and the "gang of four". However, these problems are closely linked to the lack of a market mechanism for labor resource allocation. Strange phenomena, such as backdoor recruitment and nepotism in the allocation and use of workforce, are not only incompatible with the nature of the socialist economic system, but can also be considered as artifacts of feudalism, which are even more retrograde than capitalism and almost unknown in the capitalist commodity economy.

To eliminate the various unreasonable practices in allocation and use of labor resources, and to let everyone make full use of their talents, the principle of merit-based recruitment and a combination of planned allocation and free choice should be introduced. Within the scope permitted by national laws and guided by state planning, enterprises should have the right to recruit the workers they need through labor authorities based on the enterprises' requirements for production techniques while respecting the principle of merit-based recruitment. They should also have the right to return any surplus workforce to the labor authorities, who could then reallocate this workforce to the desired enterprises, or organize training and make suitable arrangements. The living costs of unemployed workers should be covered by a social insurance fund. On the premise that individual interests are subordinate to collective interests, there should be a certain degree of free choice of jobs. It should be noted that freedom to choose a career is an important part of everyone's freedom of development. Just as the founders of the theory of scientific Communism have pointed out, the free development of each is the condition for the free development of all.[5]

In the socialist stage, especially in our country where productivity is relatively low, it is impossible to grant full freedom of job choice, which can happen only at the Communist stage. However, socialism recognizes that each individual has the natural privilege of acquiring revenue based on his/her labor capacity, and in the case of the implementation of the principle of distribution according to work, the costs of simple reproduction and even expanded reproduction (including upbringing, education and training) are borne to varying degrees by individual workers and their families. Therefore, we must acknowledge that each worker has a certain degree of ownership of their labor and allow people to have some freedom of career choice. This encourages better implementation of the principle of work allocation according to personal ability and based on the actual job requirements, and the development of individual talents and the society as a whole.

Of course, a certain degree of freedom of career choice does not mean that uncontrolled flow of labor force among enterprises and sectors and between urban and rural areas should be allowed. To control mobility of labor, we should use mainly economic means rather than administrative or legal means. For example, we can encourage workers to stay longer in particular enterprises by offering them long-term service allowances; we can adjust the wage gap between regions and take measures to improve living conditions to take account of the actual situation so as to stabilize the population of workers in remote areas. Moreover, in the light of the needs of domestic and foreign markets, we can make advantageous use of our labor-abundant and low-wage conditions and adopt flexible approaches to employment, such as exploring the possibilities of development of a wide range of services and considering the development of various forms of labor export. This would not only help to find a solution for the problem of unemployment, but also help to improve market supply, increase foreign exchange earnings and improve production technology.

Thus far, we have discussed the use of market mechanisms in the socialist planned economy in respect of production, supply and sales of commodities as well as allocation of labor, material and financial resources. It should be noted that, in the context of market mechanisms, two wider issues are worthy of our attention – price and competition. We will now briefly discuss these two issues.

The issue is about price. For a long time, people denied the role of the law of value in regulating socialist production and considered the economic means associated with the law of value as mere computing tools or methods to facilitate accounting. They advocated long-term fixed prices, and turned the policy of relatively stable planned prices into a policy of long-term price freezes. However, changes in the economic landscape lead to objective changes in various factors which affect product prices; prices cannot remain unchanged indefinitely. Artificially freezing prices detaches prices from objective reality, in contradiction to objective law and its requirements. For example, any change in labor productivity results in a change in product value, which is a fundamental causal factor in determining price movements. It is a well-known fact that changes in labor productivity vary between sectors. Labor productivity in China at this stage is growing faster in the industrial sector than in the agricultural sector. However, long-term fixed prices are making it difficult for the relative pricing of different products to reflect changes in labor productivity for such products and the changes in their value. The current agricultural product price scissors are not actually entirely the product of history. The price ratio between industrial and agricultural products should be seen in relative terms, and where industrial labor productivity grows faster than agricultural labor productivity, freezing the original price relationship means the expansion of price scissors. Another factor affecting the price is the relationship between supply and demand. However, fixed prices without fluctuations cannot reflect the changes in supply and demand. Many products suffer long-term imbalance between supply and demand, which cannot be adjusted by price changes alone. For some products suffering losses because the prices are too low, keeping their prices fixed by offering financial subsidies can help ensure stable production and people's livelihood for a period; but this approach is fundamentally incompatible with the improvement and development of production and management, as it is after all a stopgap measure. Only through taking fundamental measures, such as increasing production and supply, can we fundamentally resolve the contradiction of supply falling short of demand. In the past, freezing prices came at a high cost – people spent a lot of time waiting in line with purchasing vouchers, and what they received was a substandard equality of distribution, rather than rapid growth of production and supply. This creates a vicious circle: the fixed price and limited supply are imposed on a product, thereby eliminating the necessary stimulus for production and thus resulting in a more serious shortage in its supply. A large number of cases have proven that, if prices are unreasonable, it will be difficult to achieve the planned targets. For many products, the current price is increasingly at odds with the value. This had a negative effect on the development of some sectors, particularly agriculture, raw materials and fuel industries, and has also affected the balance of relations between agriculture and the light and heavy industrial sectors.

If we want to change this situation, we should not only continue to regulate product price relations between major sectors in the spirit of the Third Plenary Session of the Central Committee of the CPC in 1978 on narrowing price differentials between industrial and agricultural products, but also allow enterprises some flexibility to change the planned prices of their products. We should acknowledge that price is an integral part of market mechanisms. Allowing prices to float within certain limits, which helps to balance supply and demand and promotes increased production, is a manifestation of the use of market mechanisms in accordance with the guidelines of national planning. Of course, allowing prices to float within a certain range does not mean total elimination of price controls. Regulations of changes and fluctuations in prices are in fact inseparable from the national planning guidelines. For a small number of major consumer goods closely related to the life of the masses, and the major means of production that is highly influential on the cost of production, the state must be able to set the prices and impose price controls for a given period.

Furthermore, the basis for price formation is linked to the measurement of economic performance of various sectors. This issue will not be discussed here in detail. We support using the profit margin on capital as the benchmark to measure production and operational performance of an enterprise or a sector. To achieve this, we need to set the sales price based on production price, which is the premise for allowing price comparison. This is the only way production and operation of enterprises or sectors using different materials, technological equipment and different levels of investment capital can be measured to uniform standards, so that the production and operating conditions of different enterprises or sectors are reflected in the actual profit margin on investment capital of such enterprises or sectors. This is the only way for us to achieve the objective standards we need in order to decide where to invest our capital and how best to allocate the social workforce, and thereby create more favorable conditions for the development of a socialist economy.

The issue is about competition. In a commodity economy, competition is always present. Competitions to a certain degree and price fluctuations to a certain degree are interrelated and have interdependent causes, and both are integral parts of market mechanisms. Competition cannot exist without fluctuating and differential prices; conversely, without competition, fluctuating and differential prices cannot be truly achieved, the law of supply and demand cannot function properly in the market and the law of value can hardly be implemented.[6] In a socialist planned economy, we must allow a degree of competition in order to be able to use market mechanisms in allocating physical, financial and labor resources. Unless we have competition, we cannot reach a balance of production, supply and sales in line with market needs, nor can we decide where to make capital investments in accordance with investment results, or allocate workers on the principle of merit-based recruitment.

Competition is very easily associated with capitalism. In fact, competition is not peculiar to the capitalist economy. It exists in all kinds of commodity economies. Competition appeared as early as in the slave society with the development of commodity production and exchange. In the feudal society, the craft guild system restricted competition, which would not have been necessary without the existence of competition. Guilds gradually disappeared as capitalism developed. In the capitalist society, competition became universal along with the generalization of commodity relations. Historically, competition in a capitalist commodity economy not only played a negative role; it also promoted the extensive development of the productive forces of capitalism. Commodity production and exchange are objective reality under the socialist system, so to deny competition is to deny the objective existence of the commodity economy and to deny the law of value. In socialist society, enterprises operate in the market and treat each other as commodity producers, and the material interests of enterprises and their employees are affected by such factors as whether or not the quality and diversity of their goods are welcomed by the market and consumers, and whether or not and to what extent their unit labor costs in the production of commodities are above or below the socially necessary labor costs. Competition between enterprises plays a positive role in improving production technology, operation and management, labor productivity, product quality and diversity, and in reducing all kinds of consumption. Competition enables enterprises' operating performance to be tested in the market, enables consumers' demand for cheap and diverse commodities to be satisfied, and promotes the forward development of social productive forces. Striving for more material benefits is an internal driving force for the development of enterprise production, while competition between enterprises is an external pressure to develop enterprise production. If we do not allow competition and adhere to monopoly, we will see declining diversity and quality of goods, and growing wastage in production and circulation. In short, competition results in progress, while monopoly leads to stagnation and retrogression. This also applies to socialism in a certain sense. We should allow a certain degree of competition not only between enterprises owned by the whole people, but also between collectively owned enterprises, between collectively owned enterprises and enterprises owned by the whole people within certain limits, and in local shopping markets within the limits prescribed by law. Competition not only can increase the supply of cheap goods in the market and the income of farmers, but it also encourages enterprises owned by the whole people to improve their operational, management and service quality.

Of course, competition in a socialist market is fundamentally different from competition in a capitalist market, and the most fundamental reason is that competition under the socialist public ownership system is based on the common fundamental interests, while competition under the capitalist private ownership system is a life-and-death struggle between fundamentally incompatible basic interests. Socialist competition does not exclude cooperation but rather is based on cooperation and is integrated with cooperation. Therefore, competition must be subject to regulation by socialist laws and national planning guidelines. Only in this way can socialist competition encourage enterprises lagging behind to catch up with more advanced enterprises and such enterprises to become even more advanced, while avoiding the disastrous results caused by capitalist competition, such as anarchy, polarization of rich and poor, and unemployment.

There are similarities and differences between socialist competition and socialist emulation, the traditionally used term. Both are means to encourage lagging enterprises to catch up with more advanced enterprises and to become even more advanced. However, socialist emulation is not necessarily linked to the material interests of participants and does not eliminate lagging participants, whereas capitalist competition is closely linked to the material interests of competitors and does eliminate lagging competitors. Competing enterprises running a long-term deficit without good reason, unable to meet market needs and maintain simple reproduction, must be eliminated to safeguard the overall interests of society as a whole, and those responsible for the closure of enterprise must be investigated and held liable for their negligence or misconduct. Employees of such enterprises, which are shut down, should be redeployed by the labor authorities to other enterprises to avoid unemployment, which is an inevitable consequence in such a situation under the capitalist system. Redeployment would have consequences for the income of such employees compared with the incomes of the employees of normal enterprises, and their material benefits are inevitably affected by the elimination of their enterprises. That is why we say competition is a powerful economic incentive for all employees to care about the fate of their enterprise.

In short, market forces in a socialist planned economy can play an active role in a wide range of fields. Market mechanisms can serve socialist construction in such aspects as production, supply, sale of goods, management of capital, and allocation of labor force. Competition and price fluctuations within certain limits are necessary for market mechanisms to operate. Market mechanisms, if used properly, will help to achieve planned targets and reasonable and effective use of various social resources, and to satisfy a variety of social needs.

III.   Strengthening economic development planning under market mechanisms

In the process of China's socialist economic construction, there has long been a tendency to neglect market forces and reject the use of market mechanisms to serve the socialist planned economy. If we accept this tendency, we cannot allow the market to play an active role or create a positive combination of planning and the role of market in the socialist economy. Moreover, in order to reconcile the relationship between planning and the market, we should also take care to prevent and reject the tendency to exaggerate the role of the market while ignoring and even denying the role of planning. It should be noted that such a tendency has emerged in both domestic and foreign studies. For example, some describe the planned economy as a bureaucratic economy and think it is a matter of choosing between market and bureaucracy, while others equate planned management with mere administrative management and have a negative view of the planned economy.

In this regard, those who hold planning and the market to be incompatible in the planned socialist economy and who deny any possibility of combining planning and the market lie at two extremes: supporters of planning who reject the market hold that following national planning to the letter is inherent to a socialist economy; whereas those supporting the market while rejecting planning hold that the needs of society can only be reflected through the needs of the market and that planning is just so much red tape, hindering the satisfaction of market needs. The latter view is clearly wrong. We can neither underestimate the importance of planning in the socialist economy nor ignore the guiding role of national or social planning, especially when reviewing the role of the market in the socialist economy. Planning and guidance using market mechanisms are irrelevant to purely bureaucratic management, characterized by simply implementing administrative instructions and working at the will of higher officials. The planning we are talking about here is subject to adjustment, implemented with the support of market mechanisms and totally different from red tape.

Why do we need to strengthen the guiding function of planning in the implementation of market mechanisms? This is because the market under the socialist public ownership system is quite different from the market under the capitalist private ownership system. The capitalist market works blindly within the anarchy of production. As Marx pointed out, "the essence of bourgeois society consists precisely in this, that a priori there is no conscious social regulation of production. The rational and naturally necessary asserts itself only as a blindly working average."[7] There is indeed a market under the socialist economy, but the essential feature of the socialist economy is not anarchy, but rather the conscious social regulation in respect to the reproduction process, known as social regulation according to a definite plan. Engels pointed out,

> With this recognition, at last, of the real nature of the productive forces of today, the social anarchy of production gives place to a social regulation of production upon a definite plan, according to the needs of the community and of each individual.[8]

From the point of view of the practice of socialist development, this social adjustment according to a definite plan under the socialist system is also applicable to market forces. Therefore, the market in a socialist economy cannot be run in a laissez-faire manner without the guidance and regulation of national planning. We need to develop the socialist commodity production vigorously and enhance the role of market forces in the service of socialist construction; but we are not libertarians, and so we cannot let the "invisible hand" of Adam Smith control our economic development; because such an "invisible hand" depends on bourgeois egoism, whereas in the socialist economy, individual interests and partial interests are integrated with and subordinate to overall interests, and the relations between these interests can be properly treated only by regulating through national planning or social planning. Therefore, the development of the socialist economy cannot be achieved solely through market forces, without national planning guidance.

For example, choices made by individual consumers according to their own preferences and choices made by individual producers according to their own interests do not necessarily coincide with the overall interests of the society. The free decisions of market players do not necessarily lead to economically reasonable allocation and use of the society's labor, financial, and physical resources, nor do they necessarily meet the requirements of social development. In the process of accelerating industrialization and socialist modernization, we often expect a dramatic change in the short term in the industrial structure and allocation of productive forces. If we allow market players freely to make decisions and to act freely, we cannot possibly achieve in the short term such a dramatic change in the industrial structure and allocation of productive forces. These issues of overall importance in the development of the socialist economy cannot be resolved by market mechanisms alone, and we must rely on national planning or social planning for such a far-reaching change. Without national planning, it would be a very slow process and extremely difficult to achieve the reasonable allocation of productive forces and the economic development in remote and lagging areas through market forces alone.

Another example in the socialist economy is that objective conditions cause income disparities in various production enterprises: for example, natural conditions, market and sales conditions and equipment conditions. If such an income disparity is left to market forces alone to regulate, without intervention of national planning, it will lead to excessive widening of the gap between the material interests of the different enterprises, which is contrary to the socialist principle of distribution. From a wider perspective, socialism should oppose both excessive income disparity and egalitarianism, and rather should promote differential development to counter any tendency towards egalitarianism at a time of transition. This would enable some people to get rich first so that they can then drive common prosperity, and help build an environment supporting everyone in moving forward. This being so, we need to widen income disparity at certain times while narrowing it at other times (the long-term trend should be to gradually reduce it), and such changes cannot be achieved solely by market forces without national planning.

However, economic activities deemed advantageous in the local context but disadvantageous in an overall context or vice versa need to be regulated through social planning. For example, environmental protection and public hazard elimination will increase spending and reduce revenue of individual production enterprises, so that these issues cannot be properly addressed by market forces alone. Another example is product standardization. This is undoubtedly beneficial to the improvement of production and labor productivity as well as to the rational use of resources; but some enterprises may be resistant to product standardization, because they would thereby risk losing their favorable technical positions under market competition. Unless competition between syndicalist-style cooperative enterprises is subjected to unified social control, we will be unable to avoid anarchy and other consequences even where there is public ownership of the means of production. Therefore, in order to prevent the negative effects of competition, we need to implement unified regulation through social planning while allowing some freedom for competition to play a positive role.

In short, in order to ensure economic development towards socialism, provide balanced economic development of all sectors and regions of the country, safeguard the public interests of society as a whole and properly handle material interest in relations between all parties, it is essential for us to strengthen the regulatory role of national planning while still maintaining the use of market mechanisms. Somebody once made a vivid metaphor on the relationship between planning and the market: planning is like looking at the scene from the top of the mountain – we see the whole scene rather than the details; while the market is like viewing the scene from the foot of the mountain – we see the details rather than the whole scene. There is indeed some truth to this metaphor: decisions made by the state economic planning authority tend to focus on the overall interests of society as a whole, while decisions made by individual commodity producers and consumers tend to focus on their individual and partial interests. In the socialist community, the principle of balancing the relations among national, collective and individual interests requires the state to make overall plans by taking all relevant factors into consideration. Therefore, to strike a successful balance in relations among national, collective and individual interests, we should insist on the guidance provided by unified planning while allowing market mechanisms to operate.

So, how can we strengthen the planned regulation of the national economy while also allowing unified planning to play the guiding role? The answer very much depends on how people understand the planned economy. As mentioned earlier, a long-standing popular point of view was that a socialist planned economy meant systematically issuing top-down mandatory targets. However, some people even thought the socialist planned economy was more powerful when the plans were mandatory for more sectors and included more targets. Based on this understanding, they interpreted "strengthening unified planning and centralized leadership" as meaning a concentration of power over enterprise management as well as over financial, physical and labor resources. Centralizing power over affairs which should be handled by local governments and enterprises ties the hands and feet of local governments and enterprises and is clearly harmful to the development of the socialist economy. Furthermore, the excessive concentration of administrative power has been criticized in the resolution of the Third Plenary Session of the 11th Central Committee of the Communist Party of China. The socialist planned economy does not mean mandatory planning or concentration of power over financial, physical and labor resources; what counts most is whether effective measures can deliberately be taken in accordance with the prior scientific forecast to ensure the balanced and progressive development of all social and economic aspects including the rational use of social labor. To take mandatory planning as the only hallmark of a planned economy and concentration of power over financial, physical and labor recourses as the key component of the strengthening of planned management is to misunderstand the planned economy (another misunderstanding being a rejection of market mechanisms). Therefore, subject to the premise of acknowledging the necessity to combine the role of planning and the role of the market while making active use of market mechanisms to serve socialist construction, what, then, should we do to strengthen planning-based guidance?

First, we should focus our efforts on research and development of long-term plans, especially the Five-Year Plan, to address the strategic issues of national economic development and to determine the main national economic development targets and key ratios, such as those between accumulation of national income and consumption, scale of capital construction, direction of capital investments, key construction projects, the level of development of important industrial and agricultural products, and the standards of living. Yearly targets should be set in the Five-Year Plan. The annual plan should be adjusted on the basis of yearly targets, emphasizing exploration and development of policies and measures to implement the plan. We should progressively restrict the scope of mandatory plans and ultimately abandon the mandatory production targets required of enterprises. National plans should aim to predict the development of the national economy and play a guiding role in respect to the economic activities of local enterprises, without being binding upon them except for a handful of very special and important areas. Enterprises should independently develop their own plans depending on market conditions and their individual capabilities, with continuing reference to the requirements of national plans. The significance of national planning should not be underestimated, since enterprises do not have a clear picture of the general trends of the national economy but make their plans based on market conditions, which are closely linked to the overall picture and the general trends of the national economy. The information in national plans is vital for enterprises so that they can maximize the accuracy of their assessment of market conditions. The more scientific and realistic national plans are, the more reliable the guidance is to enterprises for their economic decisions and actions. This would further enhance confidence of enterprises in national plans while raising their prestige; whereas subjective plans imposed by higher officials, even if mandatory, enjoy no prestige at all among enterprises. We have paid a heavy price in this regard. That is why it is so important for the national economic planning authorities to try their utmost to study and develop scientific and reliable national economic plans to guide the economic activities of enterprises. This task is more challenging than ever.

If the authority of national plans is to be improved, they need to be better integrated with enterprise plans, so that national plans would be based on coordination between national and enterprise plans. This coordination should be bottom-up, covering all levels, and should aim at a balanced resolution at each level. Problems such as the appropriate balance between production and sales, and financial cooperation and labor coordination, which can be resolved through interaction and economic agreements between enterprises, need not necessarily be submitted to the higher authorities for resolution. Only insoluble problems would be submitted to the higher authorities for resolution. Such an approach not only enables enterprises to stay clear of unnecessary administrative interference, but also allows national economic planning authorities to avoid cumbersome administrative burdens and concentrate on research and development into guidelines and policies, while continuing to coordinate developmental tasks important for the overall national economy.

To ensure the coordinated development of social production and the achievement of the targets specified in national plans, we must allow economic policies and measures to play a guiding role in economic activities. These policies mainly include price policy, tax policy, credit policy, investment policy, income distribution policy, foreign trade policy and foreign exchange policy. The state adopts such economic policies to encourage the emergence of sectors conducive to meeting social needs, while restricting the emergence of sectors not conducive to meeting social needs, and at the same time guides the economic activities of enterprises in support of the achievement of predetermined targets in national plans. For example, in order to overcome the difficulties caused by the development of our raw material and fuel industries lagging behind our processing industries, and to accelerate the development of raw material and fuel industries, we must encourage these industries through economic policies, such as preferential loans, price adjustments and tax cuts. On the contrary, however, we may need to restrict the development of the general machine tool industry by measures such as restricting loans, raising interest rates and taxes and lowering product prices. Using adjustments through economic policies, we should urge enterprises to arrange their economic activities along the lines suggested in the national plans, even if decisions of enterprises are in their own economic interests. Using economic policies to guide economic development and economic means to achieve the targets of national plans is inseparable from market mechanisms. In other words, economic policies serve as a bridge between national planning and market mechanisms.

When implementing these measures, we also need to improve the legal system, introduce strict economic legislation, establish the system of supervision by the masses and the system of social supervision, establish and improve the banking supervision in order to coordinate market relations and promote the development of the national economy. These issues will not be discussed in detail in this article.

The relationship between planning and the market in the socialist economy is highly complex and involves many aspects of socialist economic management. Such problems cannot be solved overnight. They require certain conditions and steps to be resolved. At present, we need to spend time improving the relative ratios of certain components in the national economy, moving forward with the reform of the economic system, continue the reorganization of existing enterprises and substantially improve the quality of economic management. It is important to implement the necessary reforms during this process of adjustment and reorganization, while exploring the right way to achieve further reform. Only through the process of adjustment, reorganization and reform can we gradually find the appropriate and correct approach to the relationship between planning and the market.

(In collaboration with Liu Guoguang, *Economic Research Journal*, Issue 5, 1979)

Notes

1 Marx pointed out: "a double standard of value is inconsistent with the functions of a standard". "Where two commodities function as legally valid measures of value, it is always one of them only which actually maintains this position." Central Compilation & Translation Bureau. (1972). 马克思恩格斯全集 [Karl Marx and Frederick Engels] (Vol. 23, comments on p. 114 and p. 115). Beijing: People's Publishing House. Didn't many of our price coupons become valuable coupons?
2 Central Compilation & Translation Bureau. (1955). 列宁全集 [The Collected Works of Lenin] (Vol. 3, p. 566). Beijing: People's Publishing House.
3 Karl Marx. (1975). 政治经济学批判大纲 [Grundrisse] (Vol. 1, p. 112). Beijing: People's Publishing House.
4 See Huang Fanzhang. (1979). "消费者权利"刍议 [On Consumer Powers]. *Economic Management*, 2.
5 See Karl Marx & Friedrich Engels. (1972). 共产党宣言 [Communist Manifesto]. In Central Compilation & Translation Bureau (Eds.), *Selected Works of Marx and Engels* (Vol. 1, p. 273). Beijing: People's Publishing House.

6 As Engels put it, only through the fluctuations of competition, and consequently of com-modity prices, does the law of value of commodity production assert itself and the deter-mination of the value of the commodity by the socially necessary labor time become a reality. Central Compilation & Translation Bureau. (1972). 马克思恩格斯全集 [Karl Marx and Frederick Engels] (Vol. 21, p. 215). Beijing: People's Publishing House.
7 Central Compilation & Translation Bureau (Eds.). 马克思恩格斯选集 [Selected Works of Marx and Engels] (Vol. 4, p. 369). Beijing: People's Publishing House.
8 Central Compilation & Translation Bureau (Eds.). 马克思恩格斯选集 [Selected Works of Marx and Engels] (Vol. 3, p. 319). Beijing: People's Publishing House.

2 Several issues on the relationship between planning and market

I. The issue brought about by the practice of socialist economic construction

A comprehensive reform of the economic management system requires us to study and solve many of the major theoretical and practical problems. One of the most important issues is how to correctly understand and deal with the relationship between planning and market.

There are different views on whether many of the problems in China's economy are related to the neglect of using the role of the market. The present problem is not that planning is playing a bigger role than the market, but that a large number of the factors outside government planning are disrupting what we have planned. They believe that in the first Five-Year Plan period (1953–1957) and the adjustment period of national economy in the early 1960s, the economic development speed was relatively fast. That's because we adopted a set of measures to strengthen the planning and management. Now as long as we make adjustment and rectification, and reinstate the previous system of planning and management, we will be able to adapt to the current needs of the transfer of the focus of our work. So there is no need to emphasize the use of the market and, therefore, no need to study the relationship between planning and market.

We must admit that these problems are the result of defects in the economic management system, one of which is the neglect of the role of the market. China's current economic management system was basically borrowed from the Soviet Union in the early 1950s. It played its role in China's economic recovery and development at the time. But its fundamental flaw lies in the concentration of the management authority – the enterprises lacked decision-making power in management and operation, the state planning controlled too much without flexibility, and the role of the market and the law of value was ignored. Later, some reforms were made to this system, but generally speaking, these reforms were focused on splitting the power between the central government and local authorities, and they rarely touched upon the relationship between the state and business, planning and market. Therefore, the current economic management system is not by nature different from the old one, and various problems brought about by the rigid control of national plan and by the lack of market mechanisms still have not been resolved. If this management system is not comprehensively reformed, we are bound to see a growing conflict between this system and the development of socialist modernization. Therefore, whether or not to carry out a comprehensive reform of this system is, in fact, the issue about whether we can really achieve the transfer of the focus of our work and whether we can speed up the realization of the four modernizations.

Among the four-word principle of "adjustment, reform, rectification and improvement" that we are implementing at present, adjustment is the center. Here, we encounter a problem, that is: whether or not the issue about the relationship between planning and market has only something to do with the economic system reform, but has nothing to do with the adjustment of the national economy? There is such a view: it seems that only when we are engaging in reform can we talk about the decentralization of management power and the playing of the role of the market, while in the adjustment of the national economy, we can focus only on centralization and unification and regulation through state planning. Of course, in order to do a good job in the adjustment of the national economy, necessary centralization and unification should be emphasized; otherwise, the disorder of major proportions of the national economy is difficult to adjust. However, if we do not pay attention to mobilizing the initiatives of all parties through proper decentralization of management authority and the use of market mechanisms, the task of the adjustment will be difficult to achieve. I would like to ask: can we make it when we want to change the situation of serious imbalance between various sectors of the national economy, so that industry and agriculture, heavy industry and light industry, raw materials and fuel industry and processing industry, develop in a coordinated manner only under the guidance of the national plan without using the economic lever of the price or adjusting the price relationship between various types of products? One more example: in our adjustment, we have to solve the problem of "closing down, suspending operation, merging with others or shifting to a different line of production" of a number of enterprises. Such a task, of course, should be done step by step in accordance with a plan. However, in making decisions about what enterprises should be "closed down, suspended operation, merged with others or shifted to a different line of production" and what enterprises should maintain and expand their production, they must be based on the management status of the enterprise, especially its product quality, variety, consumption, cost, and profit and loss, and be tested by the law of value and the market mechanism, and we must not simply resort to administrative orders to solve the problems.

Looking back at the lessons of the past, why were we always trapped in the vicious circle in our economic management: "rigid unified management, lackluster economy, loosened control, disorder, unified management again"? This is because we never effectively handled the dialectical relationship between planning and market, between centralization and decentralization. Using a simple approach of unified management to deal with disorder seems to be more labor saving, but it is difficult to jump out of the vicious circle through this approach. It is more laborious to use the approach where planning and market are combined and centralization, and decentralization are combined, so that we have a robust economy but not disorder, effective regulation but not rigid control. In the process of adjustment, we must prevent the reinstatement of the previous excessively centralized economic management system, so that we have to overhaul it once again in a few years' time. Instead, we must dovetail the adjustment with our reform. The four aspects of the tasks of adjustment, reform, rectification and improvement are related to each other, and they are promoting each other. We must make necessary reforms in the adjustment and must gradually establish a system combining regulations through both planning and market.

In short, the correct handling of the relationship between planning and market is not only related to the long-term direction of the economic reform itself, but also closely linked with the current national economic adjustment and rectification. This is an important issue the practice of economic construction raises for us.

II. The continuation and progress of the discussion about the issue of commodity production and the law of value under the socialist system

Since the founding of People's Republic of China, its economic circles have conducted long-term discussions about the issue of commodity production and the law of value under the socialist system. The current discussion on the relationship between planning and market is, in fact, the continuation of these long-term discussions over the years. Compared with the ones in the past, what are some of the new things in the current discussions, theoretically? It seems that at least the following three points are worth noting and further studying.

A. *Issues about the reasons for the existence of the relationship between commodity production and market under the socialist system*

In the past, many economists attributed this to the coexistence of two forms of socialist ownership, which was the view of the majority of the comrades in the heated discussions in 1959 and later adjustment periods. This view is of positive significance in overcoming the "communist wind" (characterized by extreme equalitarianism and other practices of a supposedly communist society) and "requisition wind" (transferring and using the means of production or capital of individuals or subordinate units without compensation) that violated the interests of collectively owned units or the interests of peasants since 1958, and in protecting the autonomy rights of units under collective ownership as a commodity producer. The main task at that time was to solve the relationship between the two public ownership systems and the management system within the people's communes. The attention of the theorists was on the commodity-money relations between different owners, and they did not direct their attention to the analysis of the commodity-money relations within the ownership by the whole people, which is understandable. Thus, the predominant view was that the very existence of collective ownership was the reason behind the commodity-currency relationship in the ownership by the whole people. This view is often referred to as "theory of external cause". In contrast to the past, the practical background of current discussions is to solve the problem of the whole socialist economic management system, especially the internal management system of the ownership by the whole people. People's attention has naturally shifted to the aspect of commodity-currency relations within the ownership by the whole people, and they realize that the aforementioned "theory of external cause" does not, in essence, adequately explain the existence of commodities and markets under the socialist system, and it cannot explain the internal market mechanism inside the ownership by the whole people; thus it cannot meet the requirements of the reform of the system of economic management of the ownership by the whole people. Although the economists have different interpretations of the reasons for the existence of the commodity-currency relationship and market mechanisms within the ownership by the whole people, for example, some interpretations focus on the nature of the relationship between labor and material interests; while other interpretations focus on the immaturity of socialist ownership by the whole people, namely on its difference from communist ownership by the whole people, and so on. But almost all of them have discarded the "theory of external cause" and have begun to explore the reasons for the existence of commodity-currency relations from the internal economic relations within the ownership by the whole people, which is certainly an advancement in theory. It involves the question of whether we admit that there is a market relationship within the socialist ownership by the whole people and whether we can take advantage of the market mechanism. If the problem of understanding and using the internal market mechanism within the ownership by the whole people is properly solved, the problem of understanding and using the market mechanism in the whole socialist economy will be easy to solve.

B. Whether the relationship between the law of planning and the law of value and that between planning and market is one being pieced together in plates, inversely proportional or mutually penetrative

In the past, the more popular view was that the relationship between planning and market was mutually antagonistic and mutually exclusive, believing that where the law of planning worked, the law of value and the market mechanism would not work; or that in the field where the planning could not play a role, the market mechanism would play a complementary role. As for what was the scope where the law of planning was effective and what was the scope where the law of the market was effective, the points of views were different. For example, some comrades believe that only the market trade belongs to the scope of market regulation, and that the rest belong to the scope adjusted by planning. Other comrades regard the scope of the market as slightly larger, and they think that in addition to market trade, purchase on negotiation also belongs to the scope of market regulation, while unified and fixed state purchase belong to the scope of planned adjustment. Still other comrades believe the scope of the market is even broader. They think that the commodity circulation between collective ownership and ownership by the whole people and that between various economic units of the collective ownership belong to the scope of market regulation, while the material circulation within the ownership by the whole people belongs to the scope of planned adjustment. Still others who regard the scope of the market as even wider believe that all the circulation of materials through the commercial sector within the ownership by the whole people also belongs to the scope of market regulation, while only the allocation of materials through the material allocation department belongs to the scope of planned adjustment.

Although these views have different interpretations of the scope of market and planning, they all see the relationship as one of inverse proportion, or as one of plates pieced together. According to this theory, there is no possibility of a combination of planning and market regulations, whether in the part considered to be regulated by market or in the one considered to be adjusted by planning. If there is really a combination of the two, it is in the sense they are two plates pieced together. In the present discussion, more and more comrades have given up this view, and they recognize that between planning and market of the socialist economy is a mutually penetrative relationship where they are interconnected. Planning adjustment cannot do without the role of the market, while market regulation must work under the guidance of the planning. For example, in the area that is generally considered to have the strongest degree of adjustment by planning, that is, within the ownership by the whole people, the unified distribution and allocation according to plan of products among the units should also stipulate reasonable prices according to the requirements of the law of value; and by using the economic levers, it can better adapt to the requirement of proportional development and being conducive to economic accounting. The organization of planned production and sales for a large number of consumer goods should make full use of the law of value and the market mechanism to make the planning more realistic and be in line with the needs of consumers. As for the production and circulation of those products through the market trade, it seems that they are fully regulated by the market, but in fact, they are also guided and affected by national acquisition plans of agricultural products.

Obviously, development from the theory of inverse proportion or the theory of plates pieced together to the theory of internal integration is further progress in the theory under current discussion. Only in this way can we effectively solve the problem of the combination of planning and market in the whole socialist economy, especially in the economy of the ownership by the whole people, and realize the full play of the market mechanism under the guidance of the planning, and at the same time strengthen the guiding role of national plans while market mechanism is fully utilized.

C.   Issues about the model of socialist planned economy

For a long time, we regarded the highly centralized economic management system borrowed from the Soviet Union in the early 1950s as the only model of the socialist planned economy. It seemed that only the issuance of mandatory plan targets by the country from top to bottom, the implementation of unified collection and allocation of financial funds and the practice of unified purchase and sale of materials could be called the socialist planned economy; other models were considered revisionism or any other heresy. Now our vision is expanded. In addition to the model of socialist planned economy of the Soviet Union under the leadership of Lenin and Stalin, there are other models of socialist planned economy. The degree and manner of combination of planning and market vary from one model to another. Some still focus on centralized planning and at the same time vigorously expand the power of enterprises and workers and take advantage of market mechanisms; others feature decentralized management, worker autonomy and a combination of market economy and social planning.

In the current discussion, although not everyone is fully consistent with the understanding of the regulation by planning and by market, more and more comrades have realized that the socialist planned economy is not limited to the only model that we have become used to. As long as we adhere to socialist public ownership and do not allow the phenomenon of some people exploiting others to occur, we can take a variety of models in which planning and market are combined in varying degrees. This is a further theoretical advancement: from the recognition of only one model of planned economy to the recognition of different models of planned economy under socialism. What model we will choose or try to establish bears on the direction of the reform of the economic management system. Of course, we should not copy the experience of other countries, but we should take the program suited to China's situation based on summing up our own experience, learning from the experience of other countries and comparing the pros and cons of various planning-market models. The times and conditions are now right for us to conduct the research and make selections as more and more people subscribe to the concept of "practice is the sole criterion for testing truth". We certainly can, through practice, find a new system of the management of socialist planned economy that is appropriate to our situation and that meets the needs of the realization of the four modernizations.

III. Issues about the use of the role of the market

How to use the market under the conditions of the socialist planned economy is a very broad issue. Here are some opinions about a few key issues related to the playing of the role of the market.

A. *We must recognize the position of socialist enterprises as a relatively independent commodity producer, and give them management authority they deserve to have*

The use of the market cannot be separated from the activities of various commodity producers emerged on the market stage. The main players of the socialist market, in addition to business units of collective ownership and individual consumers, are business units of the ownership by the whole people. These units not only provide the market with a variety of consumer goods and means of production, but also buy all kinds of means of production and consumer goods on the market. If the state conducts rigid control over these enterprises so that they are in a position where they neither bear responsibilities nor have rights, then the so-called use of the market is nothing but empty talk. Therefore, we should enable enterprises to carry out their own activities in the market, as relatively independent commodity producers, and give more decision-making rights to the enterprises. We should let enterprises do all that they can by themselves as far as possible.

B.   *We must make full use of economic means to manage the economy, and leverage the role of economic levers such as price, cost, profits, wages, bonuses, credit, interest, tax, etc., related to value*

In the presence of the commodity economy, whether or not the goal of the plan is realistic, whether or not the distribution of social resources is in line with the proportion of the needs of the society, the effect of the use of resources, namely the comparison between cost and effectiveness, should all be reflected through the value category and adjusted through economic leverage. Only by using value categories and economic leverage can we link business results with the material interests of corporate collective and individual employees, correctly handle all aspects of material interests and prompt enterprises to arrange their own economic activities from their own economic interests in accordance with the directions prescribed by the national plan. This is the essence of using economic ways to manage the economy. If we do not use these economic levers or pay attention to the material interests of enterprises and individual employees, but simply use the administrative approach to manage the economy, we are far from using the market, nor is it beneficial to the achievement of the goal of the plan. Of course, when we advocate economic measures, we do not deny the administrative approaches. The two should not be separate from each other. To improve the level of economic management, we must organically combine administrative approaches and economic methods, which is also the manifestation of combination of planning and market regulations in management methods.

C.   *Our prices must reflect the requirements of the law of value and the changes of objective reality*

Economic life is in continuous development and changes, and various objective factors affecting the price of various products are also constantly changing. If the price is made fixed for a long-term artificially, and the guideline of relatively stable price is changed into the guideline of its long-term freeze, it will make the price deviate from reflecting objective reality, which violates the objective economic laws. In the past, we made a great deal of effort and paid a great price to keep the price fixed. We adopted the methods of unified purchase, purchase by state quotas, fixed supply and other means to ensure the balance between supply and demand, which played a positive role in the past. We still have to use this approach for some time in the future, but this is not the approach that a socialist planned economy must always take. In fact, some socialist countries did not use these methods. Some used them in the period of scarcity, and abolished the practice later.

Obviously these methods are not necessarily linked to the socialist planned economy but are only temporary measures taken by the state when some products related to the people's livelihood are in short supply because of inadequate production. As an attempt to balance supply and demand, these methods, after all, are addressing the symptoms but not the root cause of the problem. If they are used for a long term in a large area, a vicious circle will result: when the state limited the price and quotas of a product, its production would remain stagnant because of the lack of necessary incentives, and supply shortage would become more severe, which would in turn force us to put further limits on the price and quotas in the acquisition and supply of the product. For the time being, we must still adopt this approach (limit the price and quotas in the purchase and supply of many important agricultural products and industrial products), but it must be understood that this is only an expedient measure.

To fundamentally solve the contradiction of demand exceeding supply, and to achieve production and demand balance and development in proportion of a variety of products, we must respect the law of value, so that the product price reflects its value and a reasonable price relationship is maintained, and the price can reflect the changes of the objective reality. To this end, it is necessary to give enterprises and local authorities some leeway toward the planned price of products; allow enterprises to negotiate prices among themselves; and implement a system where unified price, floating price and agreement price are combined. As price changes involve thousands of households, we must be very cautious. Price changes and the degrees of price fluctuations must be brought under the guidance of the planning. It is necessary for the state to conduct unified pricing and price control in a certain period of time for a small number of key consumer goods closely related to the life of the people and important means of production, which has a great impact on production costs.

D.   *We should allow a certain degree of competition*

In order to use market mechanisms under the planned socialist economy, we must allow a certain degree of competition. For example, the conduction of production and organization of supply and distribution in accordance with the needs of the market, the decision of investment of funds in accordance with the size of effectiveness, as well as the employment of staff on the basis of merit, all involve competition. Under the socialist system, enterprises compete with each other in the market in the capacity of relatively independent commodity producers, which is more effective than any administrative order in helping the enterprises to improve labor productivity, product quality, varieties and designs and management control and to reduce various consumptions. This competition allows the final results of business to be tested by the market, meeting consumers' needs for inexpensive but good products and promoting the development of the entire social productive forces. If we consider striving for more material interests to be an intrinsic motivation for the development of enterprise production, then the competition between enterprises is an external pressure for the development of enterprise production.

To sum up, in order to play the role of market regulation in the socialist planned economy, it is necessary to expand the authority of an enterprise as a relatively independent commodity producer by adopting economic means relevant to the law of value and the category of value. In this respect, it is necessary to allow price fluctuation within a certain limit and competition to a certain extent. Used properly, they will enable the market regulation to be conducive to the realization of the planned target, so that a variety of social resources will be used reasonably and effectively, and all kinds of social needs will be satisfied.

IV.   Issues about strengthening guidance of planning

Under the guidance of the state plan, the correct use of the market mechanism will enable social labor (materialized labor and living labor) to be used reasonably and effectively in accordance with the proportion of social needs. From this point of view, the directions of the effects of market regulation and planning adjustment are consistent. However, there is also an objective contradiction between them. Ignoring the coherence between them will make us refrain from actively using the market; ignoring the contradiction between them will lead us to relax our planned guidance to the market.

The reason why contradiction appears between planning and market regulations is that the objective basis for planning and market in a socialist economy is not the same. The objective basis for the implementation of socialist planning is the consistency of material interests among people brought about by the public ownership of the means of production. The objective basis for the existence of market relations is that there is still a difference in material interests between people in the socialist stage. This difference in objective basis makes planning and market solve problems from different angles. In general, national planning decisions often tend to view problems from the overall interests, while choices of various commodity producers and consumers in the market often focus on the interests of each individual or local parts of the country. Even under the conditions of socialist public ownership, the choices made by single consumers as the main body of the market according to their own preferences, and the choices made by single production units according to their own interests, are not always consistent with the overall interests of society. The result of the free decision of these market players and the distribution and use of human, financial and material resources are not necessarily economical and reasonable and may not be conducive to the requirements of overall social development. For example, in the process of accelerating the realization of socialist industrialization and modernization, it is often required that the social industrial structure and productivity layout be significantly changed in a short period of time; and if various single market players are left to make their own decisions and act out of their own will, the requirements for rapid change in the layout of industrial structure and productivity cannot be effected. Obviously, if we let the market do the adjustment freely without the coordination of a national plan, it will be very slow and very difficult to achieve the industrial structure changes and rationalization of the layout of the productive forces, especially when it comes to the development of the economy in remote and backward areas.

Another example is that in the socialist economy, there are differences in income of different production units due to differences in objective conditions (such as natural conditions, market conditions, equipment level, etc.) rather than subjective efforts. This gap in income, if left to the market to adjust and distribute without social intervention, will be widened between different units, eventually running counter to the socialist principle of income distribution. Some other things, which are beneficial from the local point of view but unfavorable from the overall point of view, or unfavorable from the local point of view but favorable from the overall point of view, cannot simply be adjusted by the market, but we should emphasize their adjustment through planning on the social level.

In this way, the unity and contradiction between market regulation and planning adjustment actually reflect the unity and contradiction between local interests, personal interests and overall interests in the socialist economy. In socialist society, the principle of dealing with the interests of the three is to give overall consideration, make appropriate arrangements, and make local and personal interests subordinated to the overall interests when the interests of the three contradict each other. Therefore, in the coordination of the interests of the three, both market regulation and unified planning guidance are needed, and in the event of a conflict between the two, market regulation must give way to planning adjustment. In this sense, when we are implementing the national economic management system where planning adjustment is combined with market regulation, we should give priority to planning adjustment, while giving full attention to the auxiliary role of market regulation.

The relationship between planning adjustment and market regulation shows that, despite the existence of commodity and market relations in the socialist economy, the essential characteristics of the socialist economy are, after all, planned economy. Some comrades believe that the socialist economy is essentially a commodity economy, and that it has not entered the stage of planned economy on the grounds that there still exist goods and markets. They deny that the socialist economy, in essence, is a planned economy. This view confuses the distinction between goods and markets under the conditions of socialist public ownership and those under the conditions of private ownership of capitalism, and regards them as the same thing, which is theoretically untenable. Also, this view will lead to the weakening of planning adjustment or even the cancellation of the planned economy, and thus it is harmful in practice. In addition, some foreign commentators describe the national economic management system where planning and market are combined that China will implement as a socialist and capitalist system, calling it "market socialism", "mixed economy", etc. This type of misinterpretation still does not jump out of the old frame that equates the socialist market with the capitalist market, and it is equally not worth refuting. In the reform of the economic management system, the Chinese people will unswervingly follow the path of the socialist planned economy, which cannot be stopped by any force.

(Coauthored with Liu Guoguang, and originally published in the ninth issue of *Hong Qi* in 1979)

3 Socialist planned economy and market mechanism

I. Planned development of the national economy is an important manifestation of the superiority of the socialist system

The socialist economy is a planned economy based on the public ownership of the means of production and was produced as an antithesis of the anarchic capitalist economy. The planned development of the economy is an essential feature of the socialist system that differs from the capitalist system and an important manifestation of the superiority of the socialist system. Such superiority not only is the scientific foresight of the founders of Marxism but also has been confirmed by the practice of some socialist countries, including China, and will certainly be further confirmed by future practice.

However, there is much interference by non-essential factors in real economic life, and the socialist planned economy itself has a development process. Therefore, in order to reveal the superiority of the socialist planned economy, we must first exclude these interference factors and explore essentially the pure model. At the same time, we must temporarily ignore the different models in socialist planned economic development and explore the general model.

So, what is the superiority of the socialist planned economy in essence?

A. It can achieve the planned development of economy in the whole society

We know that as long as there is a social division of labor, in any social production there are objective requirements for the distribution of social labor in a certain proportion. But under the capitalist system, because of the contradiction between socialization of production and capitalist private possession, the necessity of allocating social labor proportionally is achieved through a blind and spontaneous process; that is, through continuously breaking up the balance. As Karl Marx pointed out, "the crux of bourgeois society is that there is no conscious social regulation of production from the beginning."[1]

Only under the conditions of socialism with public ownership of the means of production can we achieve a planned distribution of social labor and maintain the balance of the national economy on a regular and conscious basis. It is true that, in the context of the growing impact of the socialist planned economy, modern capitalist countries are also preparing a wide variety of "plans". Not only are various monopolies strengthening their plans, but the capitalist countries are also strengthening the states' intervention in economic life, which has been glamorized as "planned capitalism". However, in fact, the strengthening of the internal planning of various enterprises and even monopolies does not change the anarchy of social production as a whole; on the contrary, because of the more intense competition among monopolies, the strengthening of planning within each monopoly organization can only lead to exacerbation of non-planning of the entire social production in capitalist countries. As for the state intervention of the economic life in capitalist countries, it can only play a limited role in regulating capitalist production within a certain range, and it would be basically impossible for them to adjust the entire social production through a unified plan. Only under the condition of socialist public ownership can we achieve the planned development of the economy in the whole society. The superiority of the socialist planned economy gives the society great capabilities to achieve common goals. Just imagine, if not for the superiority of the socialist planned economy, could the Soviet Union under the leadership of Lenin and Stalin achieve industrialization in the short term and integrate the powers of the whole society to achieve such a great victory in the fight against the fascist invaders? If not for the superiority of the socialist planned economy, could China lay the initial foundation of socialist industrialization in the 1950s and establish an independent and complete national economic system in the short period of time after that?

B. It can prevent all kinds of waste caused by the private capitalist economy and thus achieve greater efficiency

As we all know, the capitalist economy is an economy with amazing waste. The socialist planned economy can prevent this waste, not only because it has eliminated exploitation, thus removing the burden brought by parasitic consumption to the society, but also because it has provided objective possibilities for a reasonable organization of social reproduction and for making full use of human, material and financial resources. Under the condition of capitalist blind competition, capitalists pay attention only to the saving of their own capital, ignoring the waste of social resources. They often conduct predatory exploitation of material resources and excessively exploit the human resources. Many production and construction projects are the result of blind competition between private capitals, and whether or not they are reasonable and needed economically from the point of view of the whole society is not taken into account at all. In order to compete for the market, capitalist groups make advertisements that cover every corner of society, which exceed the necessary limits in providing consumers with information. This expense paid for extra advertising (not to mention some deceptive advertising) is a kind of virtual expense whether for the community or for individual consumers. In the socialist planned economy, all the above wastage can be prevented so as to obtain higher efficiency. The practices during China's First Five-Year Plan period and other years prove that under the circumstances, the planned economy runs relatively smoothly and waste is prevented. Socialism can completely achieve a higher growth rate in terms of total social products and national income and, on this basis, make the accumulation and consumption grow faster, thus achieving the goal of high growth rate of national construction and improvement of people's quality of life.

C. It can get rid of the economic crisis of overproduction

Under the capitalist system, the economic crisis of overproduction is inevitable. Since the crisis of the capitalist economy in 1825, especially since the Great Depression of 1929, bourgeois economists have tried their best to help the capitalist economy to get rid of the crisis, but as long as the basic contradictions of capitalism exist, the contradiction between the expansion of production and the demand by the masses with payment ability cannot be resolved, so the economic crisis of overproduction cannot be shaken off. Some people say, "Doesn't the socialist economy also suffer from serious economic disorders like underproduction? Didn't some economists argue that demand exceeding supply was the objective law of the socialist economy?" In fact, the socialist planned economy, by nature, is not naturally linked to the economic crisis of overproduction, nor is it indissoluble with serious economic disorders of underproduction. On the contrary, it is the objective requirements of the socialist planned economy to consciously maintain the coordinated development of various sectors of the national economy, to maintain the comprehensive balance between material, financial, credit, foreign exchange and other aspects. The socialist public ownership provides the possibility of the conscious maintenance of the balanced development of the economy.

In addition, the superiority of the socialist planned economy is manifested in many other aspects, such as in the guarantee of employment of the labor force and in the prevention of excessive income disparity, which are unmatched by the capitalist economy, and which I will not discuss in detail here.

Now comes the problem: since the socialist planned economy has so many advantages, why hasn't it given full play to these advantages in China's three decades of economic construction? Especially in the "two downs" of the two times of ups and downs, why was there serious imbalance and wastage? The two main reasons are: first, the interference of the "left deviation mistakes", which played a decisive role in causing the ups and downs in the economy in those three decades; second, the management system of the socialist planned economy was far from mature and perfect. Therefore, in order to give full play to the strengths of the socialist planned economy, in addition to preventing and eliminating interference, we must also improve our economic management system and explore to establish a better model of the planned economy. In the following passages, we will explore how to use the market mechanism appropriately in the socialist planned economy so that it can grow more smoothly, and so that the superiority of the socialist economic system can be fully exerted.

II. The planned economy containing market mechanisms is a historical trend

The issue concerning how the socialist planned economy should run – for example, whether the planned development of the economy means that all economic activities are to be decided by a unified center, and whether it will inevitably exclude the role of the market mechanism – is a long-standing issue with divergent views. However, practice and the theoretical exploration have shown clearly that the economy that excludes the market mechanism is not the ideal model of the socialist planned economy. A number of socialist countries are trying to use the market mechanism in the practice of planned economy, and China is also integrating planning and market in the adjustment and reform of its national economy. Many economists at home and abroad are also studying the issue of how the socialist planned economy with market mechanisms operates. We believe that although there are many problems needing further study and resolutions yet to be found for such a planned economy, in principle, it is correct. This came from historical experiences, and it is a historical trend as well.

It has been more than 60 years since people began to explore in practice the issue of how the socialist planned economy was run from the October Revolution, and it has been more than 30 years if we counted the first experience of some socialist countries established after the Second World War. From the historical experience, people's understanding about whether commodity currency relations or market mechanisms exist in the socialist stage has progressed step by step. The first step is the view that as soon as the proletarian revolution succeeds, the commodity-currency relationship can be eliminated immediately. The general bartering of economic relations in the Soviet Union's military communist period is in line with this step of understanding. The second step is to acknowledge that after the proletariats take over power, there will be a transitional period which is characterized by the coexistence of socialist and non-socialist components. In this case, the use of commodity-currency relations and market mechanisms is necessary. The case in which commodity-currency relations are used during the Soviet Union's new economic policy period and the period prior to the basic completion of China's three major transformations is in line with the understanding of this step. However, precisely because the commodity-currency relations are linked with the existence of non-socialist economic components, there emerged the tendencies of bartering of economic relations in the Soviet Union's agricultural collectivization in the late 1920s and early 1930s. After the completion of China's three major transformations, especially in the process of establishing people's communes, there were attempts to eliminate commodity-currency relations immediately. The third step is the acknowledgment that the economy of socialist collective ownership is a commodity economy, and that because of its existence, the whole national economy, including the economy by the whole people, has to use commodity currencies to carry out accounting and distribution. In other words, they admit that commodities and currencies, in form, do exist in the economy by the whole people, but they play the role of calculation. They do not admit that there exists in it the regulatory role of the market mechanism or the law of value. The long-term practices of the socialist economic construction of the Soviet Union during the Stalin period and China's socialist economic construction were all consistent with this understanding. The fourth step is that they think commodity-currency relations exist not only in the economy of socialist collective ownership, but also in the economy of socialist ownership by the whole people; that the role of the market mechanism cannot be excluded from the most important part of the socialist economy – the economy of the ownership by the whole people – and that it must be explained with intrinsic reasons. The economic reforms of some socialist countries in Eastern Europe after the death of Stalin and the economic reforms that China is going to embark on are in line with this understanding.

If the analysis just presented makes sense, then, in further analysis, it seems that the first two of the above four steps can be discarded, because, whether in theory or from a practical point of view, the most difficult is the move from the third step to the fourth step. As we all know, even in the third step, when the commodity-currency relations are linked with the socialist public ownership, they are only linked with the economy of socialist collective ownership. For the economy of the ownership by the whole people, the commodity-currency relations not only come into existence as a result of external factors, they are considered to be only a shell or tool, and they are still not regarded as an intrinsic economic mechanism; this in turn affects the commodity nature of the collectively owned economy. As commands and mandatory allocations are customarily used within the economy of the ownership by the whole people, the practice of "equalitarianism and indiscriminate transfer of resources" is also used in the collectively owned economy. Only until the recognition of the market mechanism within the ownership by the whole people, and of the status of the state-owned enterprises as a relatively independent commodity producer, is the autonomy of the economy of collective ownership recognized more thoroughly.

The socialist planned economy established in accordance with the understanding in step three described previously is, fundamentally, still an economy repelling market mechanism or lack thereof. We may call this model the traditional socialist planned economy, or the Soviet model in the period of Stalin's leadership. The disadvantages in the operation of this model have been known to more and more people. For example, regarding decision-making of economic activities, there is the tendency of centralization of a high degree. Complicated economic activities at different levels cannot be decided respectively by each of the main players concerned, but the decision-making comes from a unified center. This monolayer pattern in decision-making is often an important cause for bureaucracy and subjectivism. In terms of management method, it mainly uses administrative means to issue orders from top to bottom, without or rarely considering the use of economic means or bringing into play the driving force of economic interests to achieve the projected objectives of a program. As for the linkages of the various parts of the national economy, the vertical linkages are dominant and the horizontal linkages serve only as a supplement, and there is a tendency of self-sufficiency in various enterprises, regions and departments, which hinders the development of specialization and collaboration. In terms of economic computing and resource allocation, the physical form prevails, currency is only a tool of calculation and the value expressed by currency, such as the price level, does not constitute the basis for selection. In view of this, even the socialist planned economy established in accordance with the understanding in step three still did not draw a line between the socialist planned economy and the natural economy. As mentioned earlier, if this situation is studied in the long course of human socialist economic practice, it shows the immaturity of socialist development during the early stages.

As to why the planned economy in the early development period of the socialist economy has these shortcomings, people can give many explanations. I am not going to give a detailed analysis of the reasons one by one, but it would be useful for summing up historical experience to cite the following two reasons.

First, the situation came about under the historical conditions in which socialism first succeeded in countries where the level of productivity was relatively low. Both the old Russia and the old China were countries with small production dominant. All the things of the self-sufficiency of production, the physical form of economic ties and the simple administrative orders between the upper and lower levels, all of which are characteristics of a natural economy, have a long-standing historical tradition. To engage in socialist economic construction in such a situation makes the planned economy of the early socialist stages has, to a certain degree, some flavor of a natural economy. Although Lenin had warned in the early 1920s, "We must not be dominated by 'emotional socialism' which inexplicably despise commerce or by old Russian, semi aristocratic, semipeasant and patriotic emotions",[2] but later development showed that getting rid of this historical tradition was not an easy task. The model of socialist planned economy established under Stalin's leadership undoubtedly played an important historical role, but seen from the perspective of historical limitations, it still did not completely get rid of the influence of the "old Russian" ideas that despised commerce. As for China, in addition to copying the Stalin model, we were also under the influence of "old Chinese society's" ideas of despising commerce. This influence was most prominent in the two waves of denying socialist commodity production in 1958 and 1975.

Second, this situation also came about as a result of the specific environment in which some countries built socialism. We know that the socialist construction of the Soviet Union in the 1930s was carried out in the context of imperialist military encirclement and war threats. This objective situation forced the Soviet economic system to adapt to the special needs of the military affairs, thus becoming one of the reasons why the role of administrative orders in economic management is emphasized and the role of the market is ignored. Because of this, some economists call the economic system established under Stalin's leadership a quasi-war economic system. In China, there was the tradition of the military communist economy formed during the period of the revolutionary bases, before the establishment of the People's Republic, and in the relatively isolated international environment for considerably a long period in the late 1950s and early 1960s; the economic system had been under the influence of this tradition. People often regarded certain practices that had been adopted to meet the needs of a special time as general practices; for example, regarding the method of mobilization as the most effective way to serve as the primary method of managing the national economy and regarding the tendency of barter in economic relations as normality and making it fixed. This further deepened the misunderstanding that the planned economy was tantamount to a barter economy.

From summing up the above historical experience, it seems we have come to this general conclusion: there is indeed a process of gradual exploration about how the socialist planned economy works. During this process, we not only have to get rid of the influences of old historical traditions and other special circumstances, but also have to make continuous innovation in accordance with the principle that practice is the sole criterion for testing truth. Because of this, it is a process to bring into play the superiority of the socialist planned economy. At the same time, historical experience also shows that the superiority of the socialist planned economy is not manifested in the absolute exclusion of the market mechanism, but rather in the planned and appropriate use of the market mechanism. If we do not draw a clear line between the socialist planned economy and the natural economy and think that the socialist planned economy is by nature incompatible with the market mechanism, then it will be impossible to give full play to the great superiority of the socialist economic system or to promote the effective operation and rapid development of the economy. Therefore, to maintain and give full play to the strengths of the socialist planned economic system, we must put our foothold on the socialist planned economy containing market mechanism.

As for the issue about how to maintain and give play to the strengths of the socialist planned economy, a simple review of a debate in Western economic circles can serve as a reference. In the 1920s and 1930s, some anti-socialist economists in the West used some natural economic tendencies in the socialist planned economic theory and the bartering tendencies in Soviet economic practice to equate the socialist economy with public ownership with the natural economy, thus attacking the socialist planned economy by criticizing the inefficiency of the natural economy in organizing production and attempting to deny the right of survival of socialism. Economists who support socialism argue that while we should uphold socialist public ownership and economic planning, we must use some of the positive functions of the market mechanism. They believe that the combination of planning and market mechanisms under socialist public ownership can help achieve the most reasonable allocation of resources and the most appropriate scale of production, so that consumers get the greatest satisfaction; such a socialist economy is superior to the capitalist economy. Although these economists were not engaged in the practice of the socialist planned economy at the time, and the soundness of some of their arguments was debatable, the debate at least enlightens us on one point that not distinguishing the socialist planned economy from the natural economy will not only fail in helping maintain the superiority of the socialist economic system, but will give opportunities to those who oppose socialism.

III.   Flexible operation of the socialist economy

For a long time, some people have always been accustomed to linking the socialist planned economy with stereotype and even rigidness, and they seem to think that socialism has been like this since the day it was born. In fact, the reason why the socialist planned economy gives people such an impression is mainly the result of the exclusion of the market mechanism and the result of not clearly drawing a line between the socialist planned economy and the natural economy; in other words, these are not the characteristics of the socialist planned economy by nature.

As mentioned earlier, if the socialist economy is a planned economy with a market mechanism, in particular, if the market mechanism is allowed to enter[3] the sacred place of the economy by the whole people, then the socialist planned economy can be operated flexibly and efficiently.

In what areas is the flexibility of the socialist planned economy with market mechanism manifested? This is an issue with a very wide range; here I will talk only about a few major areas.

A.   Economic activities of enterprises

The use of market mechanisms cannot be separated from the activities of various commodity producers in the market, and within the ownership by the whole people; it is first inseparable from the activities of various enterprises. Therefore, the use of market mechanisms means that enterprises have a relatively independent status as commodity producers, and in this capacity they engage in all kinds of activities in the market. This is a key issue about the use of market mechanisms in the economy of the ownership by the whole people. When enterprises have such an identity and status, their own economic activities will have considerable flexibility and proactivity. For example, what and how much an enterprise produces is generally not prescribed by the mandatory goals through administrative orders issued by the state, but is determined by the enterprise itself after giving considerations to the market needs and its own interests and under the overall guidance of the national plan. Correspondingly, the sale of the products produced by the enterprise and the supply of the means of production needed for the production of the enterprise are, in principle, no longer purchased and sold by state monopoly and allocated by the commercial sector or the materials department. Either the circulation of means of consumption or that of means of production is realized through trade in the market. In this way, in terms of production-supply-marketing relations, it is conducive to the realization of producing according to sales, supplying according to production and combining production with demand. In terms of the allocation and use of financial resources, the former supply system of unified state control over income and expenditure is replaced by the independent finance management of enterprise and its sole responsibility for its own profits or losses, and the approach in which the state's funds are used freely by an enterprise is replaced by the practice that state funds are used by the enterprise at a cost. An enterprise has greater control over its financial income, and it also assumes greater responsibilities, which is conducive to making good use of funds and improving its effectiveness. With regard to the allocation and use of human resources, it is no longer completely undertaken by the state through administrative methods. Under the guidance of the state plan, an enterprise has the right to hire desirable employees based on the principle of selection on merit; it also has the right to transfer surplus employees to the units in need, or to organize training sessions for them and then put them in appropriate posts.

Of course, given China's actual situation, it takes time to achieve this. With regard to the use of market mechanisms in the allocation and use of human resources, there is still strong opposition, and the specific way of using the market mechanism needs to be further explored, which cannot be done very well in a very short time. Still, this is much better than the "unified job assignment" system or the "iron rice bowl" regarding labor and employment. The recruitment system advocated and tried out currently is, in fact, moving in the right direction.

B. Individual economic activities

The introduction of market mechanisms in the socialist planned economy also helps expand the freedom of individual economic activities. This is reflected in two aspects. One is that within the established income range, individuals have greater freedom of choice of consumer goods and labor projects; the second is that under the premise of obeying the general needs of the society, individuals have a certain degree of freedom of choice of jobs. For a long time, people regard some practices in respect of individual economic activities that deny the market mechanism; for example, the supply of consumer goods in kind and their rationing and the allocation of jobs by the superiors through administrative orders, as a manifestation of the essence or superiority of socialist planned economy; this, in fact, is a complete misunderstanding.

In the case of the rationing of consumer goods, this is a temporary measure that is taken in the event of short supply and is a measure that any social system can take in the event of a serious shortage caused by war or other special circumstances. This measure will certainly give people the basic guarantee of life, but it also creates a lot of inconveniences. Even within the established income range, consumers' needs and hobbies are vastly different. Some people would rather give up a sewing machine allocated to them and get a bike instead; some mothers would give up her meat in exchange for one more share of milk for her children. Obviously, the rationing system cannot meet diverse needs of the people. However, both the economic literature of the Soviet Union and that of our country have regarded the tendency of bartering in economic relations as a manifestation of the strengthening of socialist economic planning and affirmed and advocated the temporary measures that should be gradually removed as a strategic direction. It is gratifying that this misunderstanding has been largely eliminated in our country in recent years.

As for a certain degree of freedom of the individual in the choice of occupation, versus the aforementioned employers' hiring of employees based on the principle of merits, are two sides of the same coin. This freedom is needed to break the "unified job assignment system" in allocation of human resources. Only when there is such a freedom can we overcome many of the shortcomings brought about by the "unified job assignment system", stimulate people's enthusiasm, give full scope to the talents and improve the effectiveness of economic activities. Moreover, such a freedom is also the prerequisite to overcoming egalitarianism and achieving the principle of distribution "to each according to his work". It's hard to imagine that under the circumstances, the deployment and use of human resources rely entirely on administrative means without the incentives of wages or bonuses, or that we can implement the socialist principle of distribution properly. Past experience shows clearly that without the increase in labor remuneration that is closely linked to the freedom of choice of employment based on merits, even if periodical salary adjustment is conducted, the difference between employees' labor remuneration will be difficult to accurately and promptly reflect the difference in their contribution.

C. Socio-economic linkages

The socialist economy is based on the socialized mass production, and there exists a wide range of division of labor between enterprises, regions and departments. Under the conditions of socialism, this division of labor should be a commodity relationship that is realized through the market. However, in the socialist planned economy with rejection or lack of market mechanism, the economic ties of this division of labor have been repressed, and there is a tendency of self-sufficiency among various enterprises, departments and regions. The "large and comprehensive" and "small and comprehensive" situation in respect of enterprise structure has been common knowledge. In fact, not only are the enterprises like this, but various regions and departments are often like this. As some comrades have said, managing according to the departments means the establishment of various closed natural economic systems; managing in accordance with regions means to establish a closed natural economic system according to different regions. It is difficult to establish a collaborative relationship between the enterprises belonging to two different departments, even if they are geographically adjacent. Neighboring provinces, prefectures and counties all established their own complete economic systems regardless of their own conditions. The use of market mechanisms in the socialist planned economy asks us to break this state of mutual blockage and closed-door policy, and to promote the development of production by developing a broad division of labor and cooperative relations to invigorate the national economy. Enterprises, regions and departments should give play to their respective strengths and avoid their weaknesses in the collaboration system established and developed through the market, so that the entire national economy can be developed vividly and efficiently.

Of course, it is not easy to overcome the tendency of self-sufficiency, and sometimes we will encounter a variety of twists and turns. For example, some places, in the name of leveraging local strengths, engage in new regional blockage and departmental division and encourage small businesses to push out large businesses. In fact, this is contrary to the principle of developing social division of labor and giving play to the strengths. This also shows that we can break various blockades and develop comprehensive collaborative relations only by protecting competition, so that a more reasonable division of labor can be established between various regions and departments.

D. Price system

The use of a market mechanism in the planned economy cannot be accomplished without the establishment of a more flexible price system. If the relative stability of the price is understood as absolute freezing of price, then the price cannot be a market mechanism, and at best, it can only serve as a calculation tool. To make the price truly become a market mechanism, it is necessary to make the price reflect the requirements of the law of value and the changes in the objective situation and make it have a certain degree of flexibility. For example, the prices of various products must reflect the changes in labor productivity and value in order to have a reasonable price relationship between all kinds of products, which is conducive to the economic accounting of enterprises and the coordinated development of various sectors of the national economy. At the same time, the price must also reflect the changes in supply and demand. Although the planned price cannot fully reflect market fluctuations and changes in supply and demand, frozen prices completely regardless of the supply and demand can serve only as a short-term measure; turning it into a permanent measure that is used regularly will not be conducive to the improvement of management and production. In order to make the price system have a certain degree of flexibility, we must adopt different forms of pricing. For example, China is now considering a price system combining the three forms of price, namely, a unified price, a floating price and a negotiation price, which we believe is a good experiment.

IV. The conscious adjustment of the socialist economy

The focus of our discussion to this point is the flexible operation of the socialist planned economy, which is to draw a clear line between planning and stereotype and rigidness. But this is only one aspect of the problem; the other side of the problem is that the socialist planned economy is also an economy whose operation is controlled, that is, a clear line must also be drawn between flexibility and blindness and spontaneity. Only by drawing a clear line in this area can we reject the traditional thinking of equating the market mechanism with spontaneity, blindness and anarchy, and explain why the socialist planned economy with market mechanism is superior.

Why is such an economy not running spontaneously and blindly? Fundamentally speaking, it is determined by the socialist public ownership. Specifically, the topic can be studied from the following aspects.

A.   *From the perspective of decision-making*

As mentioned earlier, the introduction of a market mechanism to the socialist planned economy means that a single centralized decision-making is changed into a multi-level decision-making; that is, different levels of economic activities are to be decided respectively by the players at different levels, for example, by introducing market mechanisms into the economic activities of an enterprise means that the enterprise has a relatively independent decision-making power on its daily economic activities. The enterprise can decide by itself what to produce and how many to produce according to the information from the market, and it can choose the source of supply and sales direction voluntarily. The introduction of market mechanisms into individual economic activities means that individuals have relatively independent decision-making power over their own economic activities. Individuals can choose what kind of consumer goods to buy and what kind of work to do based on information from the market. So, in this multi-level decision-making situation, does it mean that the state or society has lost control of the entire economic activities, so that the whole economy is plunged into a situation of blind development? No. Under the socialist public ownership, there must be a certain degree of centralized decision-making, for example, the macroeconomic activities regarding the strategic issues related to the development of the national economy (such as the growth rate of the national economy, the distribution of national income between accumulation and consumption, the distribution of the investment funds between various sectors of the national economy and other issues) must be determined by the central authorities. In this case, the decentralization of the decision-making of corporate day-to-day economic activities and individual economic activities does not lead to the blindness of economic development, and it does not deprive the state of its control over the economic activities of enterprises and individuals. In respect of the economic activities of enterprises, the daily production, supply and marketing activities are decided by the enterprises themselves. Although they are given a certain degree of freedom, this freedom is not infinite. The fact that the macroeconomic activities are decided by the central authorities prescribes a general outline of the scope of the activities of the enterprise. Under the circumstances that there is a general provision over the size and direction of major investments and the proportion of accumulation and consumption, the enterprise can conduct free activities only within this range. In the case of personal choice of profession, although there is a certain degree of freedom, the state can still exercise an overall control through centralized decision-making over macroeconomic activities. For example, through the decision-making on investment, the state will exert influence over jobs that can be provided by different sectors, and individuals can only make free choices in this range; for another example, through the education program, the state will generally grasp the types of job that individuals can do, that is, what kind of work an individual can do is actually subject to the control of the national education program. Far-sighted planning officials will by no means simply dictate the specific jobs of each person through administrative orders; instead, they will keep a general balance on labor supply and demand. It is clear that the key to the orderly operation of a socio-economic system does not lie in the mandatory provisions of the minutiae of microeconomic activities, but rather in making scientifically sound strategic decisions on macroeconomic activities so that these decisions have really meaningful guidance on microeconomic activities. If we lack vision of the strategic issues of macroeconomic activities but are busy dealing with the ever-changing problems of microeconomic activities; if we don't have a practical medium and long-term plan but are busy "making plans all year round but only making a one-year plan", that will be a practice of attending to trifles to the neglect of essentials. Therefore, the introduction of market mechanisms into the planned economy and the implementation of multi-level decision-making are by no means to weaken the planned economy, but to make the planned economy more perfect. By doing so, it would be possible to get the state plan out of some of the cumbersome details, not only to make the lower-level authorities exert their initiatives, but to make the central authorities consider the big and long-term things. It is not weakening the planning, but strengthening it.

B. From the perspective of competition

The use of the market mechanism means there is competition, which is an undeniable fact. Even the refusal to use the concept of "socialist competition" by expanding the meaning of the "socialist emulation" will only lead to a semantic debate and cannot change the nature of things. The positive role of socialist competition has become a fact obvious to all in respect to promoting the improvement of business management, improving product quality, reducing costs, adopting advanced technology, and overcoming "eating from the same big pot" (getting an equal share regardless of the work done). No matter whether people like it or not, it is objectively promoting the development of productive forces. The focus and difficulty of the problem lies in expounding how socialist competition will not eventually turn into a blind and spontaneous force just as capitalist competition does.

The socialist competition is based on the public ownership of the means of production. It is a limited competition under the guidance of planning. What it needs to solve is the contradiction between the advanced and the backward among the people, that is, to encourage the advanced and to spur those that are backward, but unlike the capitalist competition, to implement the principle of "great trees keeping down the little ones." The socialist competition will not turn itself into a blind and spontaneous force because of the following characteristics:

First, this is a competition that has selection instead of bankruptcy. Where there is competition, there is selection; and only when there is selection, the advanced can be encouraged and the backward spurred in accordance with the principle of reward and punishment. But this kind of selection is by no means like the "collapse" and "bankruptcy" caused by the competition between capitalist enterprises, forcing those who are eliminated through selection to jump to their deaths or live on the street. It is true that the relevant personnel of the eliminated enterprises who fail their duties must be held accountable, but the state still has to give the eliminated a guaranteed basic subsistence. In other words, this elimination is to break down the phenomena of "eating from big pot" and "fighting a war of attrition", rather than to make some people jobless. For example, in the period of adjustment of the national economy, it is necessary to concentrate on resolving the problems of shutting down, stopping production, merging and changing products of a number of enterprises, which will be conducive to the later development of the national economy. Even during a period of normal development of the national economy, there will be problems, but they are not as prominent as the ones in the adjustment period. In the socialist system, the elimination manifested as shutting down, stopping production, merging and changing products is essential for the development of the national economy, and it is achieved by means of competition mechanism. Obviously, limited competition has become the means by which people achieve a planned and proportionate development of the national economy here, but it is not a spontaneous force.

Second, it is competition that has fluctuation instead of crisis. When enterprises arrange their own production, supply and marketing activities in the competitive conditions according to market information, a situation will inevitably occur; that is, some things are sometimes produced a little more, while some other things are sometimes produced a little less. In other words, the supply-and-demand relationship is not in an absolutely balanced state. We believe that such a moderate volatility is not only not a spontaneous, terrible thing, but an essential thing in the process of adjusting production to meet the demand. The issue is not to reject such a fluctuation, but rather to take advantage of such a fluctuation and conduct timely adjustments to ensure the planned development of the economy. We must not require that the socialist planned economy have an absolute balanced supply-and-demand relationship. In fact, the demand for absolute balance often brings about the loss of balance. It seems that the kind of state of production while backlogging and being in short supply at the same time has neither competition nor fluctuation, but it does not bring the socialist planned economy any benefits. Of course, since the socialist competition is carried out under the guidance of planning, such a fluctuation is bound to be controlled within a certain limit, and it will not lead to an economic crisis characterized by relative surplus of production as in capitalist countries.

Third, this is a kind of competition that features, to some degree, flow of labor force instead of competition of industrial reserve force. In the competition, some enterprises are eliminated. This, coupled with the selection on a merit basis of labor resources and a certain degree of freedom in choosing one's profession, there are free movements of laborers between enterprises, regions and departments. Some comrades believe that since employment is the result of the choice of both enterprises and individuals, it is natural that some workers are temporarily left outside the production process. This phenomenon can be called structural unemployment and should be made into one of the regulators of the socialist planned economy. We believe that if the socialist planned economy with market mechanisms does have structural unemployment, then this unemployment must be regulated in terms of quality and quantity. In terms of quality, it is fundamentally different from the capitalist industrial reserve force; that is, it should not make the unemployment of some workers the conditions that other workers are overworked and exploited. In terms of quantity, it should remain within the necessary scope of labor mobility, and should not, in particular, use the necessity of existence of structural unemployment as a pretext in defense of the disastrous damage caused by Lin Biao and the "gang of four".

C. *From the perspective of regulation*

Earlier we talked about the multi-level decision-making of socio-economic activities. It is known to all that the whole socio-economic life constituted by economic activities at different levels is an organic whole. Therefore, in the case of hierarchical decision-making, we must ensure that all levels of economic activities should be in close cooperation and contact. In the socialist planned economy that uses the market mechanism, this contact cannot be achieved through mandatory means, but through a series of regulatory means. In the case where macroeconomic activities are centralized and determined by the state, they will exert overall impact and control on the economic activities of enterprises and individuals as mentioned earlier, but the state can also exert specific impact and control over these activities through a series of regulatory measures. Through price, tax, credit and other means of regulation, the state can exert influence and control on the economic activities of enterprises, for example: reducing the price of the products whose production needs to be limited and raising the price of the products whose production needs encouragement; increasing taxes for the products whose production needs to be limited and reducing or remitting taxes for the products whose production needs encouragement; reducing interest rates and giving more loans to the enterprises that need to be developed and raising interest rates and giving less or no loans to the enterprises that should be restricted; and so on. What is more obvious, the state can exert influence over the individual choice of consumer goods and employment through price, wages and other means of regulation.

Although the use of such regulatory means is inseparable from the category of value, we should not think that this is only a market regulation, and it has nothing to do with the unified planning. In the socialist planned economy with market mechanism, the roles of the law of planning and the law of value are intertwined. Using these means of regulation not only reflects the requirements of the law of value, but also reflects the requirements of the law of planning. Regulatory means such as price, tax and credit will not be manipulated by individual enterprises, nor do they come into being blindly and spontaneously. They are formed under the guidance of planning. The use of these means of regulation reflects the use of market mechanisms under the guidance of the planning in respect of the connection between macroeconomic and micro-economic activities. In fact, whatever level of economic activity cannot be carried out without the involvement of market mechanisms, or without the guidance of national planning. In micro-economic activities, where market mechanism is thought to play a particularly significant role, they actually cannot deviate from the track of planned development; in macroeconomic activities, where planning is thought to be particularly influential, they involve elements like the various preferences reflected in the market; as for the means of regulation that links macroeconomic activities with micro-economic activities, it more clearly reflects the integration of planning guidance and market mechanisms. Therefore, the use of price and other means of regulation should not make us think that the social and economic life has been plunged into a situation of blind adjustment. Blind adjustment is a characteristic of uncontrolled economy based on private ownership. On the basis of the socialist public ownership, the use of these adjustment measures under the precondition that the state has overall control over the macroeconomic activities is based on the general social preference and the long-term socio-economic rationality. Its purpose is to make the micro-economic activities meet the requirements of the decision-making of macroeconomic activities as much as possible, which is not the same in nature as the use of similar means of regulation in the case of private ownership of production and decentralized decision-making for macroeconomic activities. Of course, this can be considered an indirect regulation. This indirect regulation is a concrete manifestation of market regulation under the guidance of the planning, so it is different from the post-regulation in the spontaneous economy; instead, it is a flexible form of prior regulation, or a supplement to the prior regulation.

Of course, the state can also strengthen the coordination between a large number of macroeconomic activities and the connection between the macroeconomic activities and micro-economic activities through organized coordination; guide economic activities through economic policies and ensure the smooth progress of economic activities through economic legislation. However, the use of such administrative means is inseparable from the above economic means.

Previously, we examined from a few different perspectives why the socialist planned economy which uses the market mechanism is not a blindly running economy. If we further examine the problem from the opposite angle, we can ask this question: in the case of a complete exclusion of market mechanisms, are we able to eliminate all the spontaneous factors in our economic life? The historical experience of various socialist countries proves that in the case where the economic relations are generally manifested by bartering and the market mechanism is severely restricted by act of man; for example, on the occasion where the means of production and consumer goods are generally rationed with the aid of administrative means, the rationing system is often accompanied by speculation, black market transactions, etc. Outside the channel of rationing of goods, an "underground" distribution channel is formed spontaneously, which shows that spontaneous factors are an inevitable companion of stereotype and rigidity. A few years ago, we pointed out that there was a semi-planned and semi-anarchy state in the national economy. This semi-anarchy, of course, is, to a large part, a direct result of the interference and destruction caused by Lin Biao and the "gang of four". However, many things are often not caused by a single factor. Suppose we ignore the aforementioned factors of interference and destruction, and further our study in relation to the economic system itself. We find that a certain degree of anarchy is precisely the result of turning planning into a rigid practice, a result of wanting to make unified planning and control over everything but failed to do so. In this sense, only the proper use of the market mechanism and the implementation of a good combination of the principle and flexibility in the planned economy can we avoid the coexistence of rigidity and spontaneity.

The inherent binding relationship between planning and market is fairly difficult in theoretical understanding and practical application. However, only by really overcoming this difficulty can we make the socialist planned economy with the market mechanism a flexibly operating economy, but not a spontaneously developed economy. From this point of view, the extent to which the superiority of the socialist planned economy is to be exercised will be decided by the extent of the internal integration between planning and market.

V. Planning, market and economic interests

Is planning and market just a tool for organizing and managing economy, and is it a reflection of economic interests? This question has not yet been adequately discussed and is often overlooked by people. In practice, however, there are many people who just consciously or unconsciously regard planning and market as a tool for organizing and managing the economy.

For example, some people say that both planning and market are good tools and means of organizing and managing the economy. Both capitalist and socialist countries can use them, and in fact capitalist countries today are increasing their use of planning, while the socialist countries are increasing the use of the market. Therefore, we do not see any difference between socialism and capitalism from the perspective of the use of planning and market.

Another example is that some people simply regard the problem of whether to use the market under the socialist system as a technical problem based on the assumption just stated. Among them, some people make the argument from the technical point of view that socialist countries certainly have to use the market. They say that there are tens of thousands or hundreds of thousands of social products. If different specifications or colors are counted, there will be more. It is absolutely impossible to include the production, distribution and circulation of all these products in the planning and to manage them well. Therefore, it is necessary to supplement the lack of planning adjustment with market regulation. Other people argue that socialism can live completely without the market from the technical point of view. They say that the problems like production becoming divorced from marketing and others in the economic life are all due to mismanagement of the planning, which has nothing to do with the rejection of the market mechanism. Therefore, the key is to strengthen the research and enhance the reliability of the planning instead of conducting any market regulation. There are similar views in foreign economic circles, and some economists believe that thanks to the development of modern electronic computing technology, it has become possible to collect and process economic data through a sophisticated electronic computer network to ensure the possibility of centralized planning. The centralized planning based on a complete information technology network can both prevent bureaucracy and subjectivism brought about by the lack of economic information or the timeliness of processing, and avoid the trouble brought about by using the market.

Although the views expressed are different, and some even have completely different conclusions, they have a common flaw: they notice only the pure technical aspects of planning and market but ignored the fact that they are a reflection of economic interests. We believe that both planning and market are of a dual nature. As a tool for organizing and managing the economy, both can be used by the socialist system or the capitalist system – although the extent and circumstances of their use are quite different; but as a reflection of the relationship of production or economic interests, they are fundamentally different in nature under the socialist system and under the capitalist system.

Under the capitalist system, the market reflects the economic interests between each of the private commodity producers who are separated from each other. Although a certain degree of "planning" at the society level can, to a certain extent, alleviate the contradiction between the individual producers of private goods, it cannot fundamentally eliminate the conflicts between their economic interests. Especially because the labor force is transformed into goods, it is impossible to eliminate the confrontation between the interests of capitalists and hired laborers. It is true that some western capitalist countries, especially after the Second World War, have indeed strengthened their intervention in the capitalist market economy, and some bourgeois economists have called this state intervention "economic planning" and this kind of economy featuring market regulation and state intervention "mixed economy". However, these state interventions or "planning", fundamentally speaking, serve the interests of private capital. This is a mitigation measure taken in the context of the sharpening of fundamental contradiction in capitalism and the deepening of the economic crisis. It cannot change the fundamental nature of the private capitalist market economy. For example, under the circumstances of capitalist market economy failure, economic recession and increased unemployment, the state's guarantee of the continued operation of the economy through deficit budget, direct investment and other means is to fundamentally safeguard the capitalist system of exploitation, and to ensure the capitalists' continued exploitation of workers; in the case of failure of some industries and sectors (such as agriculture), the state provides protection and support through price, tax, credit and other policies with the intention of coordinating the economic interest relationship between various capitalist groups; in the case of strong labor movements, the capitalist countries would adopt a series of welfare measures in order to alleviate the conflicts of interest between the working class and the bourgeoisie; and so on. However, these interventions or "planning" can only alleviate the contradictions of the capitalist market economy; they cannot fundamentally solve these contradictions in this economic system. The essence of the capitalist market economy is to safeguard the interests of private capital, where the interests of society as a whole are treated simply as sums of private interests, and no such issue as the individual interests being subordinate to the interests of the collective. No matter how many "planning" measures are taken, the capitalist market economy cannot completely stay away from the adjustment of the "invisible hand" in respect to operation, and in the relationship of economic interests, it is not possible to achieve the common goal of society.

Under the socialist system, the public ownership of the means of production makes the economic interests between people fundamentally consistent, which are the objective basis for the socialist economy to be able to implement the planning. However, due to the characteristics of the nature of people's labor in the socialist stage, it is necessary to maintain the difference in economic interests between people. This is the direct cause of the existence of the market in the economy of socialist public ownership. From the perspective of economic interest relationship, the relationship between planning and market in the socialist economy is exactly a reflection of the consistency and difference of economic interest relationship between people. Therefore, the appropriate use of the market mechanism, or the proper management of the relationship between planning and market in the socialist planned economy, requires us to coordinate the economic interest relationship between people according to the objective inevitability of the socialist economy.

The consistency and difference of economic interests among people in the socialist economy are mainly manifested in the economic interests of the state (the whole), the collective (the part) and the individual. In general, national planning decisions tend to focus on the overall interests, while the decisions of each commodity producer and consumer in the market tend to focus on local or individual interests. Thus, the use of market mechanisms in the socialist planned economy is necessary not only for the flexible operation of the socialist economic organism, but also for maintaining the differences in the economic interests of the people in the socialist economy, in particular for safeguarding the particularity of the interests of enterprises and individuals. Modern electronic computing technology displays an extraordinary ability in collecting and processing economic information, and we must make full use of this technology to improve the planning work to enhance its accuracy and timeliness. But we do not agree to the point of view that sophisticated electronic computing technology can completely replace the market mechanism. In fact, the shortcomings of single centralized decision-making lie not only in having difficulties in collecting and processing economic data, but also in the incompetence in respect to the coordination of economic interests. Even if the development of electronic computing technology can gradually help solve the aforementioned technical difficulties, with respect to the coordination of economic interests, we still need the market mechanism and multi-level decision-making. We cannot imagine that if we do not give enterprises and individuals the power to make decisions about their own economic activities based on market information, they can ensure their economic interests and coordinate the economic interests between themselves.

Of course, the fact that we point out the necessity of using market mechanisms and multi-level decision-making to protect the differences or particularity of enterprises and individuals in terms of the economic interests does not mean that we want to separate local and personal interests from the overall interests or put them above the overall interests. In the socialist economy, the overall interests are not the simple sum of personal interests and local interests; personal interests and local interests should be subordinated to the overall interests. This means that we must ensure the guidance of the unified planning in the implementation of the socialist planned economic system with market mechanisms. In connection with this, in the socialist economy under the ownership by the whole people, regardless of the extent to which the independent autonomy of the enterprise is expanded, its independence is always relative. While we admit that the enterprise has its own unique economic interests, we maintain that the interests of enterprises must be subordinated to the national or social interests; that is, the overall interests of the state or society come first, and the local interests of the enterprise come second. This shows that in China, the expansion of corporate autonomy is fundamentally different from the capitalist free enterprise system.

Of course, in the socialist economy, it is not easy to coordinate the economic interests between people by the proper management of the planning-market relationship. But we try our best in this regard. For example, the question of how to define the limits of competition is a comprehensive question involving how economic interests are coordinated, which needs further study. As mentioned earlier, under the conditions of socialism, as long as there is a market mechanism, there will be competition; as long as there is competition, there will be elimination. From the economic point of view, the essence of competition and elimination is to recognize the differences in economic interests between competitors (enterprises and individuals). We should overcome the state of "communal pot" and "holding the iron rice bowl" where there is no discrimination between good and bad, and no distinction is made between those meriting rewards and those deserving punishments. Only in this way can we stimulate the enthusiasm of enterprises and individuals to ensure the improvement of micro-economic efficiency. However, in socialism we must guarantee the basic economic interests of those who are eliminated in the competition. Only in this way can we stimulate the enthusiasm of all members of society to ensure the improvement of macroeconomic efficiency. The guarantee of basic economic interests and the maintenance of the economic interest gap between enterprises and individuals are clearly inseparable from the guidance of the state planning and subordinated to the overall interests of the society. In other words, competition is limited. As we have said previously, in order to break the blockade and monopoly, we must protect the competition; but in order to coordinate the economic interest relationship of all aspects, we must keep competition within certain limits. Therefore, we should explore to find a moderate (optimal) competition. The optimal combination of interests is conducive to the unity of macroeconomic efficiency and micro-economic efficiency and unity of efficiency and equality.

In short, in the socialist planned economy, the coordination of economic interests between the people cannot be achieved without the market mechanism. Only through the appropriate (moderate) use of market mechanisms, including competitive mechanisms, can we achieve the optimal combination of economic interests of all parties.

We have analyzed the superiority of the socialist planned economy in the general sense and have analyzed the superiority of the socialist planned economy with market mechanism from several different aspects. We would like to draw a conclusion as we make the following points:

1 How should the socialist planned economy with the market mechanism operate is a question that is still being studied both in practice and in theory. But experience has shown that the direction of this exploration is undoubtedly correct and is of great significance. The trend of history suggests that things have evolved from the question whether socialist planned economy should use market mechanisms to the question of how to use market mechanisms appropriately; that is, the problem has become increasingly focused on in what way and to what extent should planning and market be combined. This problem has never been faced by the traditional socialist economic model, where the market mechanism is fundamentally rejected or neglected. Thus, what we called superiority of the socialist planned economy with the market mechanism is not only in comparison with the capitalist economy, but also as opposed to the traditional socialist economic model. Therefore, the question of how to use the market mechanism in the socialist planned economy, in fact, also involves the choice of the optimal model of the socialist economy.

2 The use of market mechanisms in the socialist planned economy and the use of planning in the capitalist market economy do not mean that the two different types of socio-economic systems are converging (aggregating). In the case of coexistence of the two different socio-economic systems, it is unavoidable that each will absorb the methods and tools used by the other. However, this cannot fundamentally change the nature of different productive relations. As long as the capitalist ownership of the means of production does not change, it will be impossible for the market economy based on such an ownership to obey a common planning goal and to fundamentally get rid of the blindness of economic development; nor will it be possible to eliminate the confrontation of economic interests between people and to coordinate various aspects of economic interest relations, so that personal, local interests will be subordinate to social and public interests. People in favor of the "convergence theory" see only the changes in the phenomenon of economic life and do not recognize the nature of economic relations.

3 The use of market mechanisms in the socialist planned economy does not mean it is regressing or that socialism is inferior to capitalism, but it is an attempt to open up the socialist road of forward development. In China, a country where the level of productivity was relatively low and small production was dominant, we also need to overcome the impact of natural economy in our socialist construction. Obviously, choosing the model of the socialist planned economy with the market mechanism is an attempt to get rid of the backwardness and to move forward. Marxism is not dogma, and socialism is not something immutable. The socialist economy will continue to advance based on absorbing all the cultural achievements of humankind and summing up new practical experiences under the guidance of Marxism. "Regress

View" and "Inferiority View" are both manifestations of shortsightedness and lacking in faith.

(Edited by Dong Furen, *The Socialist System and Its Superiority*, Beijing Publishing House, 1981)

Notes

1 Karl Marx. 致路·库格曼(1968年7月11日) [To Rude Kugmann (July 11, 1868)]. In Central Compilation & Translation Bureau (Eds.), *Selected Works of Marx and Engels* (Vol. 4, p. 369). Beijing: People's Publishing House.
2 Vladimir Lenin. 论黄金在目前和社会主义完全胜利后的作用 [On the Role of Gold at Present and after the Complete Success of Socialism]. In Central Compilation & Translation Bureau (Eds.), *Selected works of Lenin* (Vol. 4, p. 580). Beijing: People's Publishing House.
3 Neither the "enter" nor the "introduction" mentioned elsewhere have the meaning of imposing on the economic process from the outside artificially, but they mean to use the market mechanism in accordance with the objective inevitability of the economy, as opposed against the practice of rejecting the market mechanism.

4 A review of the discussion about China's planning and market issues

I. Background and significance of China's discussion on planning and market issues

The discussions in China's economic circles on planning and market issues in the socialist economy mainly started after the Third Plenary Session of the 11th Central Committee of the CPC at the end of 1978. Although there are different views[1] on whether the wording like "planning and market", "planned economy and market economy", "planned economy and market regulation", "planning regulation and market regulation" and others are accurate, there had been continuous and very enthusiastic discussions on this issue for more than five years. It seems that the difference in wording or statement is unavoidable in any academic debate, but such lively discussions do reflect the profound background and significance of the problem itself. In this regard, it can be roughly summarized as follows:

A. It is the objective needs for invigorating the domestic economy and conducting economic system reform

Regardless of the divergent views of the comrades who participated in the discussions on the role of planning and market, they almost unanimously believed that this is a major economic problem that is closely linked to economic system reform. Some comrades said, "Correctly understanding and dealing with the relationship between planned economy and market regulation is a fundamental problem of China's economic reform."[2] Some of the comrades said, "All attempts to reform the socialist economic system revolve around how to overcome the shortcomings caused by the model of planned economy that is characterized by administrative command and complete exclusion of goods and market." Therefore, it is "an epoch-making economic problem". Solving this problem "will provide an objective scientific basis for the overall planning of China's economic system reform."[3] Some comrades discussed the importance of this issue from the perspective of the comparison and selection of different models of the socialist economic system, and they believed that "it is a very important issue related to the direction of the economic management system reform to compare gain and loss of various planning-market models and to choose or envision which model to establish."[4] Some other comrades believed that since "the relationship between planning and market is the core issue of institutional reform", we should "take the relationship between planning and market as the main symbol of dividing institutional models."[5]

B.   *It is an important reflection on the implementation of open policy*

During a long period before the Third Plenary Session of the 11th CPC Central Committee, the discussion of many issues in China's economic circles was carried out in a relatively closed environment, but following that important meeting, the discussions were carried out in the environment where China was opening up to the outside world. This change in the environment no doubt broadened the visions of the people in their discussions on planning and market issues. Some comrades said, "From the international perspective, the Soviet Union began to discuss the planning and market issues in the 1920s. Now the issue can be said to be a worldwide one."[6] Some comrades said that the issue "has been attracting the attention of theorists the world over since the birth of the socialist economy. The debate on this issue in the 1920s and 1930s was conducted in the western world."[7] In this sense, China's discussion of this issue is an integral part of world discussions. Although our discussion was carried out under the overriding theme of building socialism with Chinese characteristics, under the situation of increasing academic exchanges with foreign countries, our discussion naturally absorbed the useful results that had been achieved by the international community and were compatible with our national conditions. We not only absorbed some of the results of Eastern European economists, but absorbed some of the results of western economists. We had more communication with the outside world not only in the content of the discussions but also in the use of concept and terminology. This is also an important aspect of upgrading our knowledge. We also made our contribution to the international community with our own achievements.

C.   *It is the continuation and progress of the discussion on the issues of commodity production and law of value under the socialist system*

Since the founding of the People's Republic in 1949, China's economic circles have made long-term discussions on the issue of commodity production and law of value under the socialist system. More than five years of discussion on the issue of planning and market is both a new problem and not completely a new one. Some comrades said, "The discussion on the relationship between planning and market is sometimes carried out in the name of the relationship between planned economy and commodity economy, or the relationship between the law of planning and the law of value."[8] It is not new when seen from the perspective that it is the continuation of the discussion on the issue of commodity production and the law of value under the socialist system, but it is new considering the progress in both its content and expression. It seems that we can take the Third Plenary Session of the 11th Central Committee of the CPC as the dividing line; all the discussions before that mainly concerned commodity production and the law of value under the socialist system, while after that the discussions take the relationship of planning and market in the socialist economy as the main topic. However, this issue had been raised as early as 1956. For example, some comrades said that the proposition made by Chen Yun in 1956 that "the planned production is the main form of industrial and agricultural production, and the free production that changes in accordance with the market within the scope of national plan is a supplement to the planned production" is an important part of his thoughts about China's socialist economy.[9] Of course, after that, many discussions still surround the topic of how to develop commodity production and commodity exchange under the socialist planned economy.

Some comrades also discussed their significance from the important progress made in the study and discussion of planning and market issues in China's economic circles after the Third Plenary Session of the 11th Central Committee of the CCP. For example, first, the dominant view in the past looked at the following pairs of categories – planned economy and commodity economy, the law of planning and the law of value, planning regulation and market regulation – as being in opposition to each other and mutually exclusive, and now they are generally considered to be able to combine with each other. Second, the dominant view in the past held that the commodity relations in the socialist economy existed only between different forms of ownership, and that the commodity relationship existed only in name within the ownership by the whole people; the law of value only had an effect on the socialist production but did not play a regulatory role in it. Now it is generally believed that a commodity relationship exists throughout the ownership by the whole people, including the production and circulation of the means of production; the law of value, together with the law of planning, plays the role of regulating the socialist economy. Third, the former view that commodity relationship existed only in name within the ownership by the whole people derived from the "theory of the external origin", that is, attributing the existence of commodity relationship to external causes such as the existence of collective ownership; now the existence of commodity relationship is explained as inherent in the ownership by the whole people. Although the economic circles have a variety of explanations about this phenomenon – for example, some comrades' explanation focuses on the characteristics of the relationship between the nature of labor and material interests, and other comrades' explanation focuses on the immaturity of the socialist ownership by the whole people – they almost unanimously reject the "theory of the external origin". Fourth, in the past, it was believed that the socialist planned economy had only one model of highly centralized planning management system. Now, more and more people realize that as long as the socialist public ownership and the principle of "to each according to his work" are adhered to, and exploitation is strictly prohibited, we may have different models that combine planning with the market. Fifth, as for the way of combination of planning and market, in the past the view held that planned management should be conducted in the principal part of the national economy, and market regulation in the supplementary part. Now the view is that the part that falls under planned management should use the role of the law of value, and the part that falls under market regulation should be restricted by the national plan.[10]

D.   *It is a major question for discussion in the exploration of economic theories*

In the discussion, some comrades suggested that the importance of planning and market issues also rested with the fact that it was a major issue to be further studied in the political economy theory. "Up to now, no country has found a perfect solution to the relationship between planning and market." And,

> There seems to be a long discussion for this issue with the development of the socialist economy and its economic system. In respect of some more specific issues, we have no need to jump to conclusions which will restrain the later generations, but should continue to explore through practice, and find the answer that is appropriate for the conditions at the time.[11]

II.   How to understand the nature of the socialist economy from the relationship between planning and market

For more than five years, China's economic circles have discussed the basic characteristics of the socialist economy. Here, we would like to introduce some of the views on how to understand the nature of the socialist economy from the perspective of the relationship between planning and market or the relationship between planning and commodity. According to the differences in the estimated degree of planning and commodity in the socialist economy, it can be broadly divided into the following five views.

A.   *The socialist economy is a planned economy instead of a commodity economy*

People holding this view emphasize that the essential characteristics of the socialist economy can only be those of a planned economy. But there are still differences among them. Some people (such as Tao Dayong) deny the commodification of the socialist economy; others (such as Li Zhenzhong) do not deny the existence of commodity production in the socialist economy, but they do not consider this to be part of the basic characteristics of the socialist economy. Tao Dayong said,

> From the natural economy to the commodity economy and then to the planned economy, since it marks the three stages of human social and economic development, the socialist system is bound to replace the capitalist system, and the socialist planned economy will certainly replace the anarchic market economy or capitalistic commodity economy. This is the objective law of social history and economic development. Therefore, it is not appropriate to put the category of "socialist commodity economy" side by side with "socialist planned

economy" or mix them up. It is either commodity economy or planned economy. It must be one or the other. I think that the essential characteristics of the socialist economy can only be a planned economy.[12]

Some people said, "Socialism is but a planned economy, not a commodity economy."[13] Li Zhenzhong said,

> What is taken as the basic feature of the socialist economy should be planned economy instead of commodity economy. Planned economy can be one of the main features of socialist mode of production that differs from other modes of production, but the commodity economy cannot play this role.

Commodity economy can "neither be the basic characteristics of the capitalist economy", nor "can it serve as the basic characteristics of the socialist economy." Li Zhenzhong specifically pointed out,

> Denying the commodity economy as a special feature of the socialist economy does not deny the existence of commodity production under the socialist system, which are two entirely different things. That the socialist economy is a commodity economy and that there exists commodity production under socialist system are two different propositions.[14]

B. The socialist economy is a planned economy with commodity relationship or a planned economy with a market mechanism

People who hold this view attach importance to both the planning and commodification of the socialist economy, but they think that planning is the main attribute and commodification is a subsidiary attribute; thus they consider planned economy the foundation. They express this view from their own perspectives. Some people said,

> Commodity production and commodity exchange exist widely in socialism, so in this sense, it is all correct to say socialism is a commodity economy, but the most important feature of the socialist economy is not commodity economy, but the planned economy built on the basis of public ownership of the means of production.[15]

Other people made a more detailed exposition, stating that

> China's socialist economy at this stage is a planned economy based on the public ownership of the means of production which has an absolute advantage, and with a variety of economic components and the existence of a wide range of commodity production and commodity exchange.[16]

Still others said, "The essential feature of socialism is planning, and its auxiliary attribute is commodification."[17] Then there is the view that "The socialist economy is a planned economy with market mechanisms."[18]

C.   *The socialist economy is the unity of planned economy and commodity economy*

The people who hold this view emphasize the unity of planning and commodification (or marketability), rather than saying which feature is dominant. Some people said, "The combination of planning and marketability is the essential characteristic of the socialist economy."[19] Others said,

> We should not regard the socialist planned economy and the socialist commodity economy as conflicting opposites. The socialist commodity economy is one with planned development that [is] based on the public ownership. It is opposite to natural economy and product economy; while the socialist economy is the integration of planned economy and commodity economy. On the one hand it is the planned economy of commodity relationship, and on the other hand it is the commodity economy with a planned development.[20]

D.   *The socialist economy is a planned commodity economy*

People who hold this view do not deny the nature of planning of the socialist economy, but they emphasize the need to vigorously develop commodity production and commodity exchange under socialist conditions. Some of the comrades said,

> The socialist economy is a new commodity economy, which is based on public ownership, and the fundamental interests of commodity producers are consistent, so the production and circulation of commodities of the whole society is not blind or anarchic, but in a planned development.
>
> a planned commodity economy, like public ownership of the means of production and the principle of "to each according to his work", is an essential feature of the socialist economic system.[21]

Some people believe that the reason why we implemented a highly centralized, administrative management-based economic management system for a long term in the past

> is derived from our understanding of the nature of the socialist economy, specifically, because we did not take socialist economy as a planned commodity economy, but looked at it as a natural economy or semi-natural economy. Now we are carrying out economic reform, so we must have a correct understanding of the nature of our socialist economy.
>
> China's economy at this stage is a planned commodity economy.
>
> It is a big step forward theoretically to admit that the socialist economy is a planned commodity economy.[22]

E.   *The socialist economy is a commodity economy*

People who hold this view tend to raise questions from the perspective of looking at human socio-economic development in stages. Their views are somewhat different. Some of them (such as He Wei) divided human socio-economic development into three stages of natural economy, commodity economy and planned economy. Others (such as Liu Mingfu) divided it into three stages of natural economy, commodity economy and product economy (or three economic forms). Although they concur that China is currently in the stage of commodity economy, the former think that it has not yet entered the planned economy stage, while the latter believe that the planned economy should be built on the basis of commodity economy. He Wei said,

> Commodity economy is the product of human social development. If the economic development of human society can be divided into three stages of natural economy, commodity economy and planned economy, then the world is still in the stage of commodity economy. Natural economy has lagged behind and been out of date, the conditions are not yet right for the development of planned economy, which is especially true in some developing countries.[23]

Liu Mingfu said, "It is a great step forward in the history of mankind to transit from the form of natural economy to the one of commodity economy." He added,

> If different class relationships are not considered, and different economic forms are distinguished only by whether the relationship of division of labor is developed, or whether the exchange relations hold the essential position, so far in human history, there have been only two kinds of economies: natural economy and commodity economy.

He concluded, "Planned economy can only be established on the basis of commodity economy in modern China. This is an insurmountable historical process and an objective law that cannot be violated."[24]

Although these are all different views and expressions about the nature of the socialist economy, few people flatly deny that the socialist economy has the attribute of commodification or planning. As for the other diversified different views, some comrades suggested that an attitude of "seeking common ground while shelving differences" should be adopted, because "these views have a common point, that is, we should neither deny commodity production and commodity exchange because of the emphasis on the planned economy, nor should we deny the planned economy by emphasizing commodity production and commodity exchange."[25]

III. The specific relationship between planning and market in the socialist economy

If the previous discussion of the nature of the socialist economy is to help us better understand the relationship between planning and market in the socialist economy as a whole, the following is a more detailed discussion of the specific relationship between planning and market based on the aforementioned understanding.

First of all, we need to note that, given the understanding of the nature of the socialist economy, some people in the discussion hold that since the "socialist economy is only a planned economy, rather than a commodity economy", there is no market regulation at all in the socialist economy, and thus

> sayings like the adjustment with planning as priority supplemented by market regulation, the playing of the role of market regulation under the guidance of the national plan, combining planning regulation and market regulation rather than making them conflicting opposites and so on, are all wrong.[26]

Some people argued that planning regulation and market regulation "are contradictory and antagonistic to each other from the perspective of economic mechanism. The conditions on which they rely for their existence are totally different, and the effects they try to achieve are completely different."[27] However, most people believe that planning and market (or planned economy and market economy, planning regulation and market regulation, planned economy and market regulation, etc.) in the socialist economy can be combined.

A. *In what form can planning and market be combined?*

1. *Theory of plate combination*

This theory maintains that the national economy can be divided into several sections (plates), which are adjusted respectively by planning and market. For example, some people said,

> For products that are of great concern to the national interest and the people's livelihood, we must implement planning adjustment, that is, the state will make unified plan on their production, fix prices in a unified manner, and make unified distribution of the products.

In addition, "For other products, market regulation can be implemented."[28]

Some people disagree with this theory, saying that "the drawback of this view is the complete separation of the roles of planning regulation and market regulation."[29] If we follow this theory in practice, great harm will be done because

> in respect of the section falling under the so-called planning adjustment, the appropriateness of product parity is often ignored, so that the planned objectives will not be achieved properly; as for the section of the so-called market regulation, the guidance of the plan is often ignored, resulting in blind production and repetitive construction and other problems.[30]

Some people questioned this objection to the "theory of plate combination," saying that even if "the planning regulation cannot do without the role of the market, and market regulation cannot do without the guidance of planning", and that

> there is still the issue of which [is] playing the dominant role, planning or the market. Since there are things mainly regulated by planning and those mainly

regulated by market, it may as well be divided into two sections. Therefore, the division of the two parts is objective, rather than artificial.[31]

2.   *Theory of infiltration combination*

In view of the deficiencies of the theory of plate combination, many people put forward the "theory of infiltration combination", thinking that "the planning and marketability in the socialist economy are interpenetrative, and there is a bit of me in you and a bit of you in me";[32] or that

> planning regulation and market regulation are two forms of achieving the proportional development of socialist economy. They are originally closely integrated and interpenetrate each other. There is a bit of me in you and a bit of you in me, so it is not proper to separate them completely and even make them conflicting opposites.[33]

3.   *Theory of colloid combination*

This has developed from the theory of infiltration combination. It seems that the people who hold this view proposed the theory of colloid combination as a higher-level form of infiltration combination (and thus as a direction or objective of reform). They distinguish the interpenetrating relationship between planning and market into two cases,

> In the first case, the overall national economy is divided into two parts (two sections). One part falls under the planning regulation, and the other market regulation, while each part of regulation is infiltrated with the element of the other. In the second case, the entire national economy is no longer divided into two parts, the planning mechanism and the market mechanism are glued into one and under the guidance of a unified national plan, and they play the role of market mechanism.

And they think that from the point of view of development,

> with the narrowing of the scope of the mandatory plan and the expansion of the scope of the guiding plan and the regulation by using value leverage, a unity that takes full advantage of the market mechanism under the guidance of a unified national plan and tightly glue planning and market will eventually be formed.[34]

There have been some doubts about the theory of infiltration combination and the theory of colloid combination. For example, some people believe that both theories inappropriately extend the scope of market regulation under the guidance of non-mandatory national plans and include the production and circulation of all products, which fundamentally negates that the mandatory planning regulation is an integral part of the socialist economy. Developed in this way, it is difficult to link the socialist economy with the "conscious social regulation" of the advanced stage of communism.[35] Some others said, "The drawback of this view is that there is no primary and secondary differentiation between planning regulation and market regulation, and the scope of market regulation covers the entire social economy."[36]

4.   Theory of macro-MICRO combination

This, in fact, is the expression of the organic integration of planning and market infiltration from another perspective. Some people said that

> the fundamental point of the combination between planning regulation and market regulation is that in respect of macro-economy (mainly indicating the direction of development of the whole national economy), strict planning management must be implemented. With respect to the micro-economy (mainly referring to the economic activities of grass-roots enterprises), the role of market regulation must be given full play under the guidance of national plan.[37]

Other people said,

> in the field of micro-economic activities where market mechanism is thought to play a particularly significant role, it cannot, in fact, deviate from the track of planned development; in the field of macroeconomic activities where planning is considered to play a particularly significant role, it cannot, in fact, ignore the various preferences reflected in the market; as for the means of regulation that links macro-economic activities with micro-economic activities, it more clearly reflects the integration between planning guidance and market mechanism.[38]

During the discussion, some comrades expressed their disagreement to this point of view (see Section V).

5.   Theory of multi-level plate-infiltration combination

The focus of this view is on the analysis of the complex situation of the current and future combination of the two. For example, some people said,

> every part of the national economy uses the market mechanism under the guidance of the national plan, and the extent to which each of them is subject to planning control and market impact is very different. Calling this situation multilevel (similar to the plate) infiltration combination more or less accords with the actual present situation and the situation over a long period of time in future.[39]

Other people made a more specific analysis of this situation, saying,

> The combination of planning and market in the socialist economy is a complicated and interlaced combined system. It is not the combination of one

form, but the combination of several forms, in which larger combinations are interlinked with smaller ones. From an overall view, the first is the combination between the mandatory planning regulation and planned market regulation, which is a "plate type" combination. Look at the part of the market regulation under the guidance of planning, planning guidance and market regulation are combined in a infiltration mode, and the two are fused together; in the part of planning regulation, mandatory planning and the market regulation outside the guiding plan are combined in a "plate" mode, but it is not a "plate" in the absolute sense, because the regulation of the mandatory planning should also be accompanied by the role of economic leverage, and the market regulation outside the mandatory planning should also be guided by the national plan.[40]

B.   Which are the factors that determine the different degrees of integration of planning and market?

In discussing how planning and market are combined, some people raised the question of on what basis do we determine the degree of planning regulation and the degree of market regulation, or what factors need to be considered when deciding on the different levels of integration of planning and market. This is inextricably linked to the form of combination between planning and market, but there was not so much controversy as when the issue of form of combination was discussed.

Some people argued that since under the conditions of socialist public ownership, all products are subject to planning regulation and market regulation, then "the difference only lies in the degree and model of planning regulation of various products and the degree of market regulation and the way the various products enter the market." And that "the objective basis by which we determine the degree of planning regulation of different products" mainly includes the following five points: first, the degree of socialization of production; second, the status and role of the product in national economy; third, the supply and demand of the products; fourth, the ownership of the means of production; and fifth, key enterprises or non-key enterprises. "The factors that decide the degree of market regulation of various products and the way they enter market" mainly include the following four: first, nature of the ownership of the enterprise; second, the purpose of the product; third, size of the product (large or small), common use or exclusive use; and fourth, market supply and demand situation.[41]

Some people comprehensively analyzed the factors that determine the extent of planning effect and market effect and thought that in deciding the scope, extent and form of planning guidance and control, and in considering how to properly use the role of the market, the following factors should be taken into account:

First, the state of ownership of the means of production. Generally speaking, for economic sector under ownership by the whole people, the level of planning control and guidance is higher; for the collective ownership of the economy, it will be lower, and for the individual economy, it will be even lower.

Second, the degree of socialization of production. For the production and circulation of products that are sold nationwide, the degree of planning control and guidance is higher, and the degree of planning control and guidance for other products can be lower.

Third, the importance toward economic development. For the economic activities that have overall impact and the products closely linked to national economy and the people's livelihood, the degree of planning control and guidance will be higher, for other economic activities and products it can be lower; for materials with somewhat balanced supply and demand, it can be lower. Some oversupplied products must be strictly controlled through planning.[42]

C. Is there the issue that planned economy or planning regulation plays a major role while market economy or market regulation plays a subsidiary role?

There are two views: one is not advocating relying mainly on planned economy or planning regulation; the other is advocating relying mainly on planned economy or planning regulation while making market regulation subsidiary.

Among the people who hold the former view, there are all kinds of arguments. For example, some said that, "we must reform the existing planning management, let the law of value play a major role, to be supplemented by planning."[43] Some people do not agree with "relying mainly on planned economy supplemented by market economy," nor do they agree with "relying mainly on market economy supplemented by planned economy." They advocate that

planned economy plays the predominant role while market economy serves as the foundation, placing both in the same important position, giving full play to the role of planned economy and market economy, so that planned economy and market economy can be integrated, complementing and promoting each other.[44]

Some of the comrades said, "China's planned economy must be based on market economy."[45]

Among the people who hold the latter view, they have different understandings of the expression "planned economy playing a major role". There are mainly two understandings. One understanding is that the planned economy playing a major role means that mandatory plans are important. The reasons are:

The important enterprises related to the economic lifeline of the country are operated by the state, and the products related to national economy and the people's livelihood are controlled by the state. Implementation of the mandatory plan toward the production of these products that account for most of the total industrial and agricultural output value shows that our economy is basically a planned economy.[46]

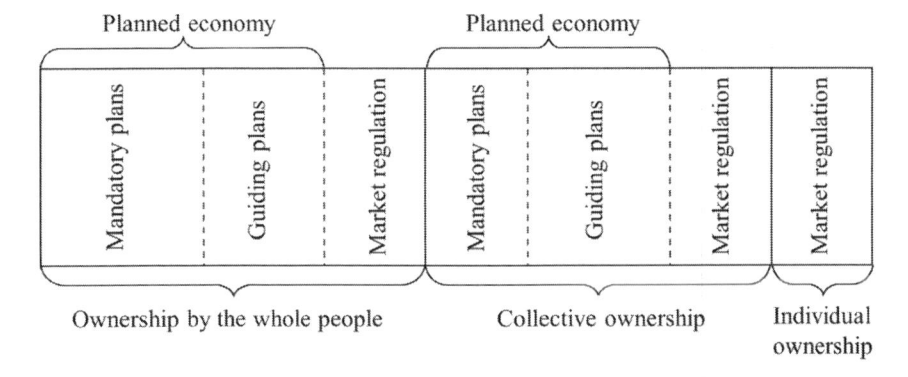

Figure 4.1 Planned Economy and Different Kinds of Ownership

Another understanding is that the planned economy playing a major role means that mandatory plans and guiding plans together play a major role in our economy.

Among them, mandatory plans and guiding plans belong to the category of planned economy, and they account for the vast majority of total industrial and agricultural output value, while the part of market regulation accounts for a relatively small proportion of total industrial and agricultural output value.[47]

This view was quite popular for some time, especially in the few years before and after 1982.[48]

D. How to understand the attributes of the three forms of management (mandatory planning, guidance planning and market regulation)?

In the discussion, it is generally believed that China's current economic management should take the three forms of mandatory planning, guidance planning and market regulation. However, there are different views on the attributes of these three forms of management, specifically, whether guidance planning and market regulation also belong in the category of planned economy, or whether they are a form of planned management.

1. How to look at guidance planning, or how to look at the planned use of economic leverage: there are generally the following three views

The first view: thinking that guidance planning is the regulation carried out by using price, tax, interest rates and other economic leverages. It should belong in the category of market regulation. But some of the people who hold this view changed their mind later, citing the reason that "this view believes that most of the planned regulation should be achieved through market regulation, which is not true."[49]

The second view: thinking that guidance planning is to use economic leverage to ensure the realization of national plans, so it should belong in the category of planned management. Some people argued that "it is true that guidance planning is a form of planning that is primarily achieved through the use of market mechanisms, but it is not market regulation" and that "Here, people consciously use the law of value to achieve their desired purpose rather than be manipulated spontaneously by the law of value. Therefore, it is unreasonable both logically and practically to regard guidance planning as market regulation."[50]

The third view: thinking that the planned use of economic leverage is both planning management and market regulation in "a dual role".

> From the perspective of the state, it is a means of guidance planning; and from the perspective of the enterprises, it is a tool which definitely embodies the economic interests of enterprises. Through the role of economic leverage, planning guidance and market regulation are fused, forming a unified body, that is, the market regulation under the guidance of planning.[51]

2.   How should we view market regulation?

Since there are differing views regarding the nature of market regulation or the nature of the role of the law of value and forms of combination of planning and market in the socialist economy among participants of the discussion, there are differing views on whether market regulation is part of planned economy or a form of planned management. There are two main kinds of views:

The first view: thinking that market regulation does not belong in the category of planned economy and that it is not a form of planned management. For example, some people said,

> We have three forms of economic management, namely, mandatory planning, guidance planning and market regulation. The first two belong in the category of planned management, and the last is a supplement to planned economy. We should not regard market regulation as a form of planned management.[52]

The second view: thinking that market regulation also belongs in the category of planned economy. For example, some people said,

> the part whose production is conducted in accordance with planning (including mandatory plans and guiding plans), of course, belongs in the category of planned economy, and it is the main part of planned economy. As for the part in which market regulation plays an auxiliary role, although it is not included in the national plan and it is spontaneous, it should also belong in the category of planned economy, because this part of the production should also be carried out within the scope of the permission of national plan, and it cannot deviate from the guidance of planning, completely free from control or restrictions.[53]

Some people further analyzed that

> the socialist planned economy is the planned socio-economic management based on the public ownership of the means of production and the requirements of socialized mass production, which includes both the part managed by mandatory planning and guidance planning, and the part of free production not included in the national plan. Free market is an integral part of the entire socialist unified market. The regulation of this part of the free market is subordinate and secondary, but it is still under the indirect control and influence of the unified national plan, and is subject to the management and scrutiny by the national industrial and commercial administration agencies, so it is not appropriate to completely exclude it from planned economy and make it into the category opposite to planned economy.[54]

IV.   How to evaluate the original economic system

As mentioned earlier, many people consider the issue of planning and market to be the essential issue in economic restructuring. When people link the discussion of this issue directly to the reform of the economic system, it is bound to involve the evaluation of the original economic system and the vision about the new economic system.

There is some consensus when it comes to the evaluation of the original economic system. For example: first, the original economic system is flawed, so it cannot remain unchanged; second, in the analysis of the shortcomings of the original economic system, problems that do not arise from the economic system itself should be put aside, in particular the factors of political turmoil should be put aside, so that economic system can be studied in its pure form; third, in the practice of economic life in the past, there are also periods of time when the economy runs normally or relatively smoothly, which is the case in the first Five-Year Plan period (1953–1957).

Of course, there are also divergent views in the evaluation of the original economic system.

A.   Why was China's economy running smoothly in some of the periods, especially in the first Five-Year Plan period?

The different views on this issue are revealed not in the lively debate on the issue itself, but when analyzing the reasons for the periods of better operation. Some people said,

> When China began to build a planned economy in the 1950s, it adopted the system of planned management borrowed from the Soviet Union. This system is characterized by a one-sided emphasis on mandatory planning, not using the law of value, and repelling the role of the market, so it has a lot of shortcomings. However, the defects of this kind of planned management system were not fully exposed in the first few years of the first five-year plan because the socialist transformation of our country's ownership of the means of production had not yet been basically completed, and there were five economic

components, so we could not completely take the Soviet Union's system of planned management. We only implemented direct planning toward some state-owned enterprises and large public-private joint ventures, while paying much attention to the use of price, tax, credit and other economic levers, and consciously taking advantage of the law of value and market mechanisms, and permitting self-production and free trade and letting the market play the role of regulation spontaneously in the places where state plans could not reach. In such circumstances, China's economic life was not as rigid as it was later, and its market was also prosperous. Coupled with sound economic policies, the economic development was healthy.[55]

Some people argued that, "The problem should not be simply blamed on centralization." The reason for this is:

During China's first five-year plan period, the speed of economic development was fast, the economic effect was good, and people's lives were significantly improved, the main reasons for the success were: correct guiding ideology, the plans we made were largely in line with the objective laws.

The fruitful economic adjustment in the 1960s once again shows the strength of the planned economy system. This shows that as long as we respect the objective laws, not only can we rely on the planned economic system to develop the economy quickly, but we can also rely on it to consciously correct the mistakes in economic work. In this regard, our socialist planned economy is much superior to capitalism, which relies on its spontaneous market regulation.[56]

From the two different analyses here we can find: as for the reasons for good economic performance during some periods of time of the Republic, especially in the first Five-Year Plan period, the first analysis mainly credits the good economic performance to the fact that the original economic system had not yet been fully established (during the first Five-Year Plan period); the second analysis credits the good economic performance to the fact that the original economic system could still operate relatively normally (during the first Five-Year Plan period and the early 1960s adjustment period). These two different conclusions reflect the different evaluations of the original economic system and also reflect the different views on the relationships between planning and market, between centralization and decentralization and so on.

B.   How to deal with the original economic system

The first view: emphasizing the transformation of the original system. Some people believe that what economic system reform is all about is

not only improve and supplement the imperfect and unreasonable details in the original system, but more importantly, transform the original economic model itself, that is, to remould the unreasonable basic framework and main operational principles of the original system. Of course, this transformation must be conducted under the premise of adhering to the socialist basic economic system.[57]

Some people said that a highly centralized planning management system

> will result in defects like simple pursuit of output and production value regardless of market and social needs, basing sales on production, separation between production and sales, blind increasing of production of surplus products, inefficiency in production of under supplied products and new products and others due to relying on administrative means to manage the economy, ignoring the role of market and the law of value and not paying attention to economic effect.

This planned management system has been unable to adapt to the requirements of the four modernizations, and it is time that it must be changed.

The second view: emphasizing the improvement of the original system. Some people said, "China's planning system established after 1949 is correct and is in line with the requirements of planned economy as far as its basic point is concerned." In addition, "The planning system should be improved, but it should not be smashed and replace it with something new." "The basic principles of planned economy must be adhered to, and the planning system must be improved." "We should not blame planned economic system for the mistakes in economic guiding ideology and the damage caused by political turmoil." And,

> Why do some people lose confidence in planned economy? An important reason is that there has been no thorough analysis of the main cause for the setbacks in our economic development in the past, and that the planning system was wrongly blamed for causing those setbacks. Planned economy is an invaluable pearl which is hidden under a layer of dust. When the dust is removed, planned economy will be bound to display its dazzling radiance.[58]

Also, some people said,

> We should, by no means blame the planned economic system for the shortcomings, errors and losses in our economic construction and economic work without analysis, on the contrary, planned economy has not only helped us make the achievements, but also helped us overcome and get through difficulties.[59]

V. How to look at mandatory planning – a focus in the debate for economic system reform

If the relationship between planning and market is a core issue in economic system reform, then how do we view mandatory planning as a core issue in the planning and market relations? That is why this question has become a focus of attention in the debate about what system or model we should follow in our reform.

Since 1979, a number of scholars have expressed the view in favor of gradually abolishing mandatory planning. For example, some people suggested that "mandatory planning should be gradually replaced by guidance planning."[60] Some people said,

> While we should admit that mandatory planning is necessary under some specific conditions and it is more timely and effective than other management methods, it has its limitations and drawbacks in the general circumstances. The experience of all countries that have adopted mandatory planning shows that it is very difficult for this type of planning management model to address the inherent shortcomings of the traditional centralized planning system like separation between production and demand, wasting of resources, poor quality and varieties, low micro-economic efficiency, etc.

Therefore, "we should gradually narrow the scope of mandatory planning and expand the scope of guidance planning." And, "Of the three forms of economic management, we should let guidance planning play a bigger role in future."[61]

The above point of view has sparked heated debate. This debate is largely about the following questions.

A.   Is mandatory planning the basic symbol of the socialist planned economy?

Some people said,

> There is nothing wrong with taking mandatory planning as the basic symbol of the socialist planned economy. The so-called planned economy refers to the national economy that is consciously managed by the society in accordance with prepared plans. In such an economy, means of production belongs to the whole society, and labor is the inevitable result and objective requirement of the joint labor of the whole society.

Also, "What will the situation be like if mandatory planning is abolished? As with the capitalist countries' planning, they will at most play some role of coordination toward the production and management of various enterprises."[62] Many people held similar views, such as: "it is correct to take mandatory planning as an important symbol which differentiate the socialist planned economy from the capitalist market economy";[63] "only by adhering to mandatory planning can we clarify the boundary between socialist planned economy and capitalist countries' state intervention in the economy";[64] "If the planning just serves as a guidance and reference rather than compulsory, then it is not a real planned economy";[65] and so on.

People who disagreed with these opinions argued that "completely equating planned economy with the implementation of mandatory planning" is a "deep-rooted bias" in the "traditional political economy theory that is adapted to the needs of the over-centralized planning system and formed under its influence."[66] Some people argued that the two views, "that where there are no instructions there is no planning" and "that exercising control through economic leverage obliterates the distinction between socialism and capitalism", are debatable. Because the issue about whether macroeconomic decision-making controls micro-economic activities through instructions or through economic leverage "is about what way is adopted to exercise the planning control, rather than whether planning is needed or not." And,

> Although these levers can be used by both capitalist economy and socialist economy, the major premises of using these levers are not the same: the socialist economy is based on the centralization of decision-making over macroeconomic activities, thus it ensures that the economy generally operates in accordance with plans. In the final analysis, it is promoting micro-efficiency improvement by using these levers under the premise of serving the common interests of society; but this premise does not exist in capitalist economy. In capitalist countries, these levers are used to coordinate the conflicting private interests between individual businesses. There is not the issue of serving the common interests of the whole society, and it is impossible to have planned economic development throughout the society.[67]

Some people cited examples to explain that "most of the production tasks of some companies are arranged in accordance with the needs of the market", and

> if a variety of indirect planning methods are adopted to make this part of production and operation of enterprises conform to the requirements of unified national planning, then even if it is not produced in accordance with the mandatory plans issued by the state, it is still planned economy.[68]

B. Is mandatory planning an important manifestation of the socialist ownership by the whole people?

Some people believed that "the implementation of mandatory planning" is not only "the basic symbol of the socialist planned economy", but also "an important manifestation of China's socialist ownership by the whole people in respect of the organization and management of production."[69] Some people argued that

> in the socialist system of ownership by the whole people, the abolition of mandatory planning . . . means that the socialist countries, possessor of the means of production, cannot directly control and use means of production as representatives of all the people. . . . And ownership by the whole people will not be financially realized. . . . Issuance of mandatory planning, despite its form of administrative orders, is not an 'administrative intervention' beyond economic relations and imposed on the economy, but are the internal requirements and manifestation of the economic relationship of socialist ownership by the whole people.[70]

Moreover,

> If the state abandons its right to use or control the means of production, that is, if it abolishes the mandatory planning, and the relationship between the state and the enterprises becomes a solely financial relationship, then it is not much different from the collective ownership.

Last, "With the passage of time . . . the socialist ownership by the whole people will become a collective ownership."[71]

Other people argued, "We must not, in a general sense, say that the realization of socialist ownership by the whole people in economy is manifested by the use of mandatory planning under all conditions." In addition:

> In the absence of a mandatory plan for an enterprise, as long as the state remains its macro decision-making power, as long as the state is still determining the rules of business behavior, and as long as the state can, through various means, ensure that corporate economic activities conform to the interests and requirements of the whole society, then we cannot say that the state has lost its right to control and to use.
>
> Since all the people can make proper arrangements for social production and achieve their own production purposes – meet the needs of society and its members – through the country's planning management and market regulation, how can we say that the ownership by the whole people cannot be achieved in economy?[72]

C.   Will macro decision-making become phantom if micro-economic activities are not controlled by mandatory planning?

Some people said,

> the view that the so-called macro economy (such as the determination of the proportion of accumulation and consumption in national income, the allocation of investment in the country's capital construction, the balance between social purchasing power and commodity supply volume, the control over gross payroll, etc.) be regulated by planning, while the economic activities of the enterprises (the so-called micro economy), including what to produce and how much to produce, be regulated by the market. As this separates what is "micro" completely from what is "macro", then the "macro" decision-making is very likely to become phantom.[73]

Other people argued,

> If enterprises are permitted to act in their own ways in terms of micro-economic activities, then the centralized decision-making within the scope of macro economy will only be a wishful thinking." And, "The result is likely to be that market regulation will replace planning regulation to become the

major player of the regulatory mechanism, thus causing blindness and anarchy in economic life, and affecting the stable development of socialist economy.[74]

People who held opposing opinions said, "It does not mean that we do not control the economic activities of the enterprises when we do not control the enterprises' economic activities through mandatory planning." In some models,

the control and regulation of micro-economic activities by macroeconomic decision-making are regarded as the focus of their own design, with planning regulation playing a leading role and market regulation restricted by planning regulation. For this reason, it seems that it is groundless to say that "there is complete separation between what is micro and what is macro" and that "macro decision-making has become phantom".[75]

Other people argued that

although the practice that the daily production-supply-marketing activities are decided by the enterprises themselves gives the enterprise a certain degree of freedom, this freedom is not infinite, because the central decision-making for macroeconomic activities delimits a general boundary within which enterprises conduct their activities.

Also, that "the state can also exert specific impact and control on these activities through a series of regulatory means." And,

The key to the orderly running of a social economic system lies not in making all kinds of mandatory rules for the minutiae of micro-economic activities, but in making sound strategic decisions at the macroeconomic level, and letting these decisions give guidance to micro-economic activities.[76]

D.   What are the variation trends of the management scope of mandatory planning?

Even those who advocate the abolition of mandatory planning are raising the issue from the perspective of the ultimate goals or directions of the reform, and they do not advocate the abolition of mandatory planning in all cases to achieve that goal immediately; that is, everyone agrees that there is the need to retain mandatory planning at the beginning of the reform. Therefore, the debate is about the trend of change in the management scope of mandatory planning. In this regard, there are generally two views.

The first view holds that the long-term trend is the scope will shrink. For example, some people said,

seeing from a long period of time, we should not take the expansion of the scope of mandatory planning as the direction of institutional reform. With the progress of economic adjustment, the gradual formation of a 'buyer's market', and with the rationalization of prices, we should gradually narrow the scope of mandatory planning and expand the scope of guidance planning.

Therefore, they think that "the more mandatory indicators there are, the stronger the planning will be, and with the improvement of planning management level, the scope of mandatory planning will become larger. This view needs to be studied."[77]

The second view holds that the long-term trend is the scope will expand. For example, some people said,

> As the scope in which we implemented mandatory planning in the past was so large that deviated from reality, therefore, for some time in the future, we should appropriately narrow the scope of mandatory planning, and correspondingly expand the field of guidance planning, and at the same time let market regulation play a better auxiliary role. However, after a long period of time, with the development of social productive forces, and with the enhancement of people's ability in management and the improvement of their planning work, we should, and also will be able, to expand the scope of mandatory planning gradually and appropriately in accordance with the needs of economic development. By that time, our socialist planned economy will have reached a new stage and a higher level.[78]

Some people said that "the opinion is debatable" to think that "the direction of reform is to gradually narrow the scope of mandatory planning and eventually cancel it."[79]

In addition, the economists have also discussed how to view the issue of the distribution or allocation of the means of production in kind. This is derived from how to look at the issue of mandatory planning. Because of limited space, the details are omitted.

VI.   What is the essence of the debate?

A.   *Is it a debate about two directions (socialism or capitalism) and two principles (planned economy or market economy)?*

Some people emphasized that

> whether the discussion of the "feature" or that of "regulation", is related to a substantive problem. That is, is China's economic management system reform based on the principle of socialist planned economy, or in accordance with the principles of market economy?

In addition,

> Some people may say that no one has proposed to reform the economic management in accordance with the principles of market economy. Yes, no

one has put forward a complete and systematic idea in this regard. However, if some of the views put forward by different people from different perspective are summed up, they, in fact, are in favor of the principle of market economy.

For example:

> there is a view that is in favor of turning state-owned enterprises into completely independently accounting economic entities who are responsible for their own profits and losses, and some saying more clearly that the state-owned enterprises should be changed into ones of corporate ownership, or of collective ownership (this does not refer to those economic units that should not have been nationalized but have prematurely taken the ownership by the whole people).

Some people are "advocating that the economic relationships of the society are commodity-money relationships. The only form of social and economic ties is commodity exchange"; "advocating that the law of value is the basic economic law, and that market regulation is the only economic regulator"; "advocating that competition is the driving force of economic development"; "advocating that the nature of the role of planning is predictive and indicative. It is not binding, or mandatory." And, "This set of propositions is, in fact, the principle of market economy."[80]

Some people also said,

> There is such a view: . . . to give up mandatory planning regulation and establish the management system that makes full use of market can ensure proportional and coordinated development of national economy. According to this, the capitalist economy will guarantee a proportional and coordinated development, because there is no regulation by mandatory planning there, where market plays the role to the fullest.[81]

However, many people did not agree to the view that simply the existence or not of mandatory planning will decide whether it is a planned economy or a market economy, or whether it is socialism or capitalism. In this vein, some people said,

> Over a long period of time, people think that the implementation of planned economy must be accompanied by issuance of mandatory plans. Some even take whether there is mandatory planning as a symbol that differentiates the socialist planned economy from capitalist market economy, and that whether a country adheres to the socialist direction or implements revisionism and restores capitalism, which is a misunderstanding.
>
> Neither Marx nor Engels said that in the socialist economy, all economic activities of every economic unit must follow the instructions from above.
>
> Lenin did not say that mandatory planning indicators should be issued to enterprises either.[82]

Some people argued that

> since we acknowledge that the socialist planned economy has different models, we should also admit that the issuance of directives is merely a feature of one model (or several models) of the socialist planned economy rather than the feature of all models.[83]

It seems that the people who held this opinion tended to resolve the discussion about different degrees of combinations between planning and market in the socialist economy, especially the argument of whether there should be mandatory planning, into the issue of the comparison and selection of different models of socialist economy. Other people pointed out that:

> since we have affirmed that socialist economy has two regulatory means in planning and the market, we need to further study the relationship between the two. Many of the recent discussion on the choice of models of socialist economic theory focus on the issue of how to deal with the relationship between the two means of regulation.[84]

B. How to view certain out-of-control and out-of-balance phenomena that appear in the process of economic restructuring?

Some people attributed these to the attempts that try to "get rid of planned economy" and "deviate from the socialist direction". For example:

Some people listed some of the out-of-control and out-of-balance phenomena that appeared in the economic life:

> in agriculture, some local authorities reduce state purchase quotas, and expand the scope of raised and negotiated prices for excessive purchases; in industry, some companies do not accept the state's reasonable production and appropriation plans, wantonly raise prices for means of production and enlarge the scope of negotiated prices; in capital construction, some areas, departments and enterprises go beyond investment plans arbitrarily, with unplanned projects taking quotas of the planned ones; in foreign trade, some units engage in blind competition with other Chinese enterprises in sales toward foreign countries, giving economic benefits to foreigners.

And they thought that this "is a tendency to weaken and break away from the planned economy", that "it does not comply with the principle of giving priority to planned economy and taking market regulation as an auxiliary measure. If it is allowed to develop unchecked . . . will cause economic disorder and deviation from the socialist direction."[85] Some people said that this phenomenon showed that "the scope of economic activities that should fall under strict planned management of the state has been improperly reduced, and some are out of control."[86]

What some people emphasized are issues like methods and steps, such as "synchronization is not fully considered" in respect of reform measures, not being good at "using various indirect planning means" and others. For example, some people said that the shortcomings of China's economic reform work

> are not too much market regulation that has been carried out, rather, it is the fact that neither planning regulation nor market regulation has been well developed and therefore incapable of playing their role properly, and the two could not work in coordination to form a unified regulation system for the national economy. All this resulted as the steps taken in economic reform fall short of the requirements of adjustment and rectification and also because we did not give full consideration to the integrity of the economic management system and the synchronization of the reform measures.[87]

Others said, "we have seen some out-of-control phenomena in our economic life, but this is not because the indirect planning means does not work, but we failed to use a variety of indirect means to guide economic activities consciously and systematically." The out-of-control phenomena like too fast growth of consumer funds, too much production of products with high prices and profits, unwillingness on the part of enterprises to make products of low prices and profits are all related with the fact that we are not good at using tax, price and other means.[88] Some people said:

> some of the decentralization measures we have taken over the past few years in respect of the relations between central and local authorities, and between state and enterprises are not wrong in direction, but in steps, that is, in that the quantitative limit of decentralization measures has exceeded the limits that our economy can now bear.
>
> From the long-term goal of invigorating the economy, giving more power to enterprises is still at the beginning stage, and the autonomous rights that have already been given to enterprises, such as planning rights, material rights, rights for human resources and others, are not enough.[89]

VII.   A few views

The preceding is a brief overview of the discussion on the relationship between planning and the market in the socialist economy by China's economic circles between the Third Plenary Session of the 11th CPC Central Committee and the Third Plenary Session of the 12th CPC Central Committee. Due to the limitations of materials and knowledge, careless omissions are inevitable. In the following paragraphs, I would like to present my personal opinions on the following issues involved in the discussion.

A.   *The issue of operational mechanism*

For a long time, the studies of China's economic circles on some of the basic theoretical issues of the socialist political economy are fairly closely related to the ideological struggle, and there is deeper analysis of the essence of the issues; with the shifting of CPC's focus on work, more efforts are devoted to the link between economic theory research and socialist economic construction, and the study of the operation of socialist economy is also strengthened. Such a good trend is undoubtedly reflected in the discussion of the relationship between planning and market, and the debate on many of the issues involves the operation of socialist economy, and people have offered a lot of useful insights. However, from the perspective of future development, the study on the issue of operation is insufficient.

For example, although the debate on how to view mandatory planning involved the issue of operation, some of the debates still remain on the ideological issues, and the ideological judgments are not obtained naturally through the specific analysis of the operational mechanism. This shows that the study of the operational mechanism remains to be deepened and specialized.

For another example, as far as the question of operation is concerned, our discussion still remains on the question of "whether or not it is controllable", rather than closely linking the question of "whether it is controllable" to the question of "whether it is effective"; in other words, we need to go further in our studies about the issue of operational efficiency. Whether or not an economic system is sound cannot be judged only by whether it is controllable in operation; more importantly, it should be judged by the results of the control – the efficiency of operation. The comparison between different degrees of integration of planning and market, and the comparison between different models of socialist economy, in the final analysis are about their operational efficiency. If discussions on how to view mandatory planning can be carried out more around the issues of how to improve the efficiency (including micro-efficiency and macro-efficiency), perhaps it will be more conducive to the depth of the discussion.

In the case of coexistence of mandatory and non-mandatory parts, how can we solve the contradictions brought about by the "dual systems", so that the loss can be reduced to a minimum? Should we gradually change the "dual systems" themselves? If so, how should it be achieved? These issues involve not only the objectives of reform but also the steps of reform, but obviously these questions have not been discussed and researched adequately so far.

B. *The issue of methodology*

There were also some methodological issues involved in the discussions. In order to improve the level and efficiency of the discussions, it seems necessary to clarify the boundaries between some issues, such as: the boundary between conceptual dispute and substantive issues; the boundary between long-term strategic objectives and current tactical measures; the boundary between inherent defects of a system and errors caused by external interference; and so on. From the previous discussions, many people have realized that they should make clear the aforementioned boundaries, but it has proved not to be easy in practice.

For example, the conceptual disputes and the disputes about substantive issues are often intertwined. Although the participants generally hope that they can enter into discussions of substantive issues with the help of certain concepts and means of expression, it is sometimes difficult to do so. When discussing the nature of the socialist economy, some people advocated "a planned commodity economy", and others advocated "a planned economy of commodities", but what the actual difference is between their understandings of the nature of the socialist economy by people using different wordings cannot be simply judged by their expressions. In order to grasp the essence of the problem, some people pointed out that these two expressions are mutually complementary propositions, while others suggested that we should seek common ground while reserving differences, which both seem quite inspiring.

For another example, the debates over how to view mandatory planning, planned purchase and marketing by the state, supply on ration, etc., have caused some unnecessary controversies because the boundaries between strategic targets and tactical measures and those between general circumstances and special circumstances had not been clearly defined. Obviously, the instructions given in normal circumstances are not the same as those in special circumstances; supply on ration in normal circumstances is not the same as that in special circumstances. Of course, we need to have a clear definition of what are normal circumstances and what are special circumstances. Wartime constitutes a special circumstance, which is not controversial; what about demand exceeding supply or commodity shortage? Is it a general phenomenon or a special phenomenon? Views are not necessarily consistent. Perhaps it is appropriate to say for the traditional socialist economic model with centralized planning, commodity shortage is a general phenomenon, but for the target model that our reform is to achieve, commodity shortage is definitely not a general phenomenon. Therefore, in our vision about the target model, we should not take commodity shortage as a general phenomenon to be investigated; it should be given up as a special phenomenon. Otherwise, we will not be able to present the defining nature of our target model and its operational mechanism.

It is not so easy to distinguish, in practice, the boundary between the inherent defects of a system and the errors as a result of external disturbances. For example, although some people suggest that we exclude the factors of political turmoil when analyzing the economic system, in the specific investigation, they attribute the setbacks in China's economic performance during the "Great Leap Forward" and Cultural Revolution to the decentralization of the economic system. It seems that how to really separate the two different problems of political stability and chaos and concentration and decentralization in economic system remains a problem to be solved.

C. The issue of style of study

Looking back at over five years of discussions, we think the atmosphere is good in general. Obviously, in terms of breadth, depth and degree of freedom, the discussions about the issue of planning and market during this period are much better than any previous discussions about commodity production and the law of value before the Third Plenary Session of the 11th Central Committee of the CPC after the founding of the People's Republic of China. Of course, there is still room for improvement in our style of study.

For example, in some cases, the atmosphere of exploration and discussion was lacking, and the atmosphere of quickly jumping to conclusions reigned. In my opinion, the atmosphere of exploration and discussion not only is a general requirement of any academic discussion, but should be specially valued in the discussion of issues such as planning and market. This is because, first, this problem is of special complexity. The issue has been discussed for at least 70 years since the October Revolution of the Soviet Union, but so far, a satisfactory conclusion has not yet been found. It is not a solemn attitude for anyone to make conclusions easily. Second, in the case of our country, in a long period, the study of this issue was ignored and completely stopped. Many of the scholars participating in the discussion found they lacked the knowledge or their knowledge was out of date, so they need to re-learn in the process of exploration. In the theoretical teams of socialist political economy in China, more than one generation grew up under the influence of the traditional concept represented by Stalin, and it is impossible not to re-learn if we are to reform the traditional model established in accordance with Stalin's traditional ideas. Obviously, it is rash, to say the least, to jump to conclusions and final verdicts simply by virtue of the old knowledge and experience.

Another problem worth mentioning in terms of style of study is the problem of information quality. The extensive breadth of discussion is undoubtedly a good thing, but it has created another problem – too many repetitions in the discussion. In the era of "information explosion", it is not an economical practice when many people write articles talking about more or less the same thing or when the same author repeats himself/herself again and again in a number of articles, in terms of the author's and the reader's time and energy, or in terms of publishing, printing and distribution. Of course, this is not only a problem found in this special discussion, and not even the only problem found in the economic community, but should the economic community take the lead to overcome this uneconomical phenomenon or not?

(Published originally in *Economic Research Information*, total issue 7–8, April 10, 1985.)

Notes

1 Sun Yefang. (April 13, 1982). 坚持以计划经济为主市场调节为辅 [Insists on Planned Economy Supplemented by Market Regulation]. *China Finance News*.
2 Fang Sheng. (1982). 认识相互联系的三个层次 – 对"以计划经济为主，市场调节为辅"方针的一点理解 [Getting to Know The Interrelated Three Levels: My Understanding of the Policy of 'Insists on Planned Economy Supplemented by Market Regulation']. *Economic Research Journal*, 7.
3 Shu Dong. (1982). 基本特征与调节机制 [Basic Characteristics and Adjustment Mechanism]. *SHE HUI KE XUE DONG TAI*, 14.
4 Liu Guoguang & Zhao Renwei. (1979). 计划和市场关系的几个问题 [Several Issues on Planning and Market Relations]. *Hong Qi*, 9.

5 Zhang Guofu & Shi Qingqi. (1982). 首都经济理论界座谈计划经济和市场调节问题 [A Symposium of the Capital Economic Theory Circle on the Issue of Planned Economy and Market Regulation]. *Economic Perspectives*, 2.

6 Liu Guoguang. (1982). 关于研究和讨论计划与市场问题的一点想法 [Some Thought on the Study and Discussion of Planning and Market]. *Finance & Trade Economics*, 2.

7 Su Xing. (August 15, 1982). 我对计划经济和市场的理解 [My Understanding of Planned Economy And Market]. *Guangming Daily*.

8 Liu Guoguang. (1982). 关于研究和讨论计划和市场问题的一点想法 [Some Thought on The Study and Discussion of Planning and Market]. *Finance & Trade Economics*, 2.

9 Deng Liqun. (February 22, 1982). 正确处理计划经济和市场调节之间的关系 [Correct Handling of the Relationship between Planned Economy and Market Regulation]. *Jing Ji Xue Zhou Bao*.

10 Zhang Guofu & Shi Qingqi. (1982). 首都经济理论界座谈计划经济和市场调节问题 [A Symposium of the Capital Economic Theory Circle on the Issue of Planned Economy and Market Regulation]. *Economic Perspectives*, 2.

11 Liu Guoguang. (1982). 关于研究和讨论计划与市场问题的一点想法 [Some Thought on the Study and Discussion of Planning and Market]. *Finance & Trade Economics*, 2.

12 Tao Dayong. (June 26, 1982). 是计划经济，还是商品经济？ [Is It a Planned Economy or a Commodity Economy?]. *Guangming Daily*.

13 Wen Tong & Rui Pu. (October 16, 1981). 全国党校政治经济学教学座谈会 [A Teaching Symposium on Political Economics for Party Schools Nationwide]. *People's Daily*.

14 Li Zhenzhong. (December 26, 1981). 也谈计划和市场问题 [Also on Planning and Market Issues]. *Guangming Daily*.

15 Xue Muqiao. (June 21, 1982). 计划经济和市场调节 [Planned Economy and Market Regulation]. *World Economic Herald*.

16 Gong Xuelin. (1982). 关于计划经济和市场调节的几点看法 [Some Views on Planned Economy and Market Regulation]. *Journal of Social Sciences*, 9.

17 He Jianzhang. (1982). 坚持计划经济为主，市场调节为辅 [Insists on Planned Economy Supplemented by Market Regulation]. Speech Made at the Symposium. *Finance & Trade Economics*, 4.

18 Zhao Renwei. (1980). 社会主义经济是含有市场机制的计划经济 [Socialist Economy Is a Planned Economy with Market Mechanisms]. *Finance & Trade Economics*, 4.

19 Sun Shangqing, Chen Jiyuan & Zhang Zhuoyuan. (1980). 再论社会主义经济的计划性与市场性相结合 [Also on the Integration of Planning and Marketability of Socialist Economy]. In *The Relationship between Planning and Market in Socialist Economy of China*. Beijing: China Social Sciences Press.

20 Wang Jue. (1982). 计划经济与市场调节 [Planned Economy and Market Regulation]. *Finance & Trade Economics*, 5.

21 Wang Jue & Wu Zhenkun. (February 28, 1981). 社会主义经济是有计划的商品经济 [Socialist Economy Is a Planned Commodity Economy]. *Guangming Daily*.

22 Ma Hong. (1981). 关于经济管理体制改革的几个问题 [Some Questions about the Reform of Economic Management System]. *Economic Research Journal*, 7.

23 He Wei. (1979). 论社会主义制度下的商品经济兼论企业的独立性问题 [On the Commodity Economy Under the Socialist System and the Independence of Enterprises]. *Economic Perspectives*, 3.

24 Liu Mingfu. (1979). 社会主义经济的经济形式问题 [Issues about Economic Forms of Socialist Economy]. *Economic Research Journal*, 4.

25 He Jianzhang. (1982). 坚持计划经济为主，市场调节为辅 [Insists on Planned Economy Supplemented by Market Regulation]. Speech Made at the Symposium. *Finance & Trade Economics*, 4.

26 Wen Tong & Rui Pu. (October 16, 1981). 全国党校政治经济学教学座谈会 [A Teaching Symposium on Political Economics for Party Schools Nationwide]. *People's Daily*.

27 Ma Liwen. (1981). 对计划调节与市场调节的一种看法 [An Opinion about Planning Regulation and Market Regulation]. *Finance & Trade Economics*, 3.

28 Thirteen Colleges and Universities in North China. (1979). 政治经济学（社会主义部分）[Political Economics (Section on Socialism)] (p. 321). Xi'an: Shaanxi People's Publishing House.
29 Gong Xuelin. (1982). 关于计划经济和市场调节的几点看法 [Some Views on Planned Economy and Market Regulation]. *Journal of Social Sciences*, 9.
30 Huang Zhenqi. (1981). 对计划调节与市场调节的几点看法 [Some Views on Planning Regulation and Market Regulation]. *Finance & Trade Economics*, 4.
31 You Lin. (1981). 计划生产是主体自由生产是补充 [Planned Production Is the Principal Part and Free Production Is the Supplement]. *Economic Research Journal*, 9.
32 Sun Shangqing, Chen Jiyuan & Zhang Zhuoyuan. (1980). 社会主义经济的计划性与市场性相结合的几个理论问题 [Several Theoretical Issues on the Integration of Planning and Marketability of Socialist Economy]. In 社会主义经济中计划与市场的关系 [The Relationship between Planning and Market in Socialist Economy] (p. 106). China Social Sciences Publishing House.
33 He Jianzhang, Wang Jiye & Wu Kaitai. (1980). 关于计划调节和市场调节相结合问题 [On the Combination of Planning Regulation and Market Regulation]. *Economic Research Journal*, 5.
34 Liu Guoguang. (1980). 略论计划调节和市场调节的几个问题 [A Brief View about Several Issues on Planning Regulation and Market Regulation]. *Economic Research Journal*, 10.
35 Gu Shutang & Chang Xiuze. (1981). 论社会主义经济的计划与市场的结合 [On Combination of Planning and Market in Socialist Economy]. In *A Collection of Economic Research: National Economy Regulation and Reform of the Economic System* (p. 13). Jinan: Shandong People's Publishing House.
36 Gong Xuelin. (1982). 关于计划经济和市场调节的几点看法 [Some Views on Planned Economy and Market Regulation]. *Journal of Social Sciences*, 9.
37 Xu Dixin. (1981). 在国家计划指导下充分发挥市场调节的辅助作用 [Giving Full Play to the Auxiliary Role of Market Regulation under the Guidance of National Plan]. *Shi Jie Jing Ji Zeng Kan*, 4.
38 Dong Fureng. (1981). 社会主义经济制度及其优越性 [Socialist Economic System and Its Strengths] (p. 200). Beijing: Beijing Publishing House.
39 Gui Shiyong & Zhou Shulian. (June 11, 1981). 加强计划指导，正确利用市场的作用 [Strengthening the Guidance of Planning and Correctly Using the Role of Market]. *People's Daily*.
40 Gu Shutang & Chang Xiuze. (1981). 论社会主义经济的计划与市场的结合 [On Combination of Planning and Market in Socialist Economy]. In 国民经济调整与经济体制改革 [National Economy Regulation and Reform of the Economic System]. *A Collection of Economic Research* (pp. 20–21). Jinan: Shandong People's Publishing House.
41 Huang Zhenqi. (1981). 对计划调节与市场调节的几点看法 [Several Opinions about Planning Regulation and Market Regulation]. *Finance& Trade Economics*, 4.
42 Gui Shiyong & Zhou Shulian. (June 12, 1981). 加强计划指导，正确利用市场的作用 [Strengthening the Guidance of Planning and Correctly Using the Role of Market]. *People's Daily*.
43 He Wei. (1979). 论社会主义制度下的商品经济兼论企业的独立性问题 [On the Commodity Economy under the Socialist System and the Independence of Enterprises]. *Economic Perspectives*, 3.
44 Wang Zhanghu & Dai Erde. (1979). 把计划经济建立在市场经济的基础上 [Building Planned Economy on the Bases of Market Economy]. *Cai Jing Yan Jiu Tong Xun*, 1.
45 Shen Haishan. (1979). 市场经济是计划经济的历史前提和现实基础 [Market Economy Is the Historical Premise and the Realistic Foundation of Planned Economy]. *Journal of Nanjing University* (Edition of Philosophy and Social Sciences), 3.
46 Deng Liqun. (February 22, 1982). 正确处理计划经济和市场调节之间的关系 [Correct Handling of the Relationship between Planned Economy and Market Regulation]. *Jing Ji Xue Zhou Bao*.

47 Li Zhenzhong & Hu Naiwu. (1983). 关于"计划经济为主、市场调节为辅"的几个理论问题 [Several Theoretical Issues about "Insists on Planned Economy Supplemented by Market Regulation"]. *Economic Theory and Business Management*, 4.

48 Wang Renzhi & Gui Shiyong. (1983). 坚持和改进指令性计划制度 [Sticking to and Improving Mandatory Plan System]. In *Collected Works of Planned Economy and Market Regulation* (Vol. 1, pp. 283–289). Beijing: Red Flag Press.

49 Xue Muqiao. (May 19, 1982). 关于经济管理体制改革理论问题的讨论 [A Discussion on the Theoretical Issues of Structural Reform of Economic Management System]. *Guangming Daily*.

50 Lin Zili. (1982). 论计划与市场 [On Planning and Market]. *Economic Theory and Business Management*, 5.

51 Gu Shutang & Chang Xiuze. (1981). 论社会主义经济的计划与市场的结合 [On Combination of Planning and Market in Socialist Economy]. 国民经济调整与经济体制改革 [National Economy Regulation and Reform of the Economic System]. *A Collection of Economic Research* (p. 18). Jinan: Shandong People's Publishing House.

52 Gui Shiyong. (1984). 关于正确认识计划经济为主市场调节为辅的几个问题 [Several Issues on Correct Understanding of "Insists on Planned Economy Supplemented by Market Regulation"]. *Economic Research Journal*, 5. See Jing Ping. (1982). 计划经济和市场调节问题讨论述评 [A Review of the Discussion of the Issues about Planned Economy and Market Regulation]. *Hong Qi*, 22.

53 Fang Sheng. (1982). 认清相互联系的三个层次－对"以计划经济为主、市场调节为辅"方针的一点理解 [Getting to Know the Interrelated Three Levels: My Understanding of the Policy of "Insists on Planned Economy Supplemented by Market Regulation"]. *Economic Research Journal*, 7.

54 Liu Guoguang. (September 6, 1982). 坚持经济体制改革的基本方向 [Sticking to the Fundamental Direction of the Reform of Economic System]. *People's Daily*.

55 Liao Jili. (June 8, 1982). 谈谈计划经济和市场 [On Planned Economy and Market]. *China Financial and Economic News*.

56 Gong Shiqi & Xu Yi. (1983). 坚持计划经济为主市场调节为辅 [Insists on Planned Economy Supplemented by Market Regulation]. *Economic Research Journal*, 6.

57 Liu Guoguang. (1984). 关于经济体制模式问题 [Issues on Models of Economic System]. In Jilin Federation of Economic Organizations (Ed.), *Theoretical Problems on Reform of the Economic System* (pp. 4–5).

58 He Jianzhang. (1979). 我国全民所有制经济计划管理体制存在的问题和改革方向 [Problems Existing in and Reform Direction of the System of Planned Management of China's Economy under Ownership by the Whole People]. *Economic Research Journal*, 5.

59 Fang Weizhong. (1982). 一条不可动摇的基本原则－对坚持计划经济为主，市场调节为辅的几点认识 [An Unshakable Basic Principle: Some Thoughts on Adhering to "Insists on Planned Economy Supplemented by Market Regulation"]. *Hong Qi*, 9.

60 Ye Junzhe. (1982). 必须坚持以计划经济为主 [We Must Insists on Planned Economy]. *Hubei Cai Jing Xue Yuan Xue Bao*, 2.

61 Liu Guoguang. (September 6, 1982). 坚持经济体制改革的基本方向 [Sticking to the Fundamental Direction of the Reform of Economic System]. *People's Daily*.

62 Deng Liqun. (February 22, 1982). 正确处理计划经济和市场调节之间的关系 [Correct Handling of the Relationship between Planned Economy and Market Regulation]. *Jing Ji Xue Zhou Bao*.

63 Xue Shen & Ma Biao. (May 9, 1982). 坚持社会主义道路必须实行计划经济 [Planned Economy Must Be Implemented to Adhere to the Socialist Road]. *Guangming Daily*; Also see Xu Jing'an. (June 20, 1982). 怎样实行以计划经济为主的体制 [How to Implement the System That Gives First Place to Planned Economy]. *Guangming Daily*.

64 Lü Lüping & Zheng Xinli. (April 20, 1982). 试论指令性计划 [On Mandatory Planning]. *China Financial and Economic News*.

65 Gong Shiqi & Xu Yi. (1982). 坚持计划经济为主，市场调节为辅 [Insists on Planned Economy Supplemented by Market Regulation]. *Economic Research Journal*, 6.

66 Wu Jinglian & Zhou Shulian. (1983). 试论社会主义计划经济的调节方式 [On the Regulation Models of Socialist Planned Economy]. *Social Science Journal*, 5.
67 Zhao Renwei & Rong Jingben. (1982). 我国应该选择什么经济模式？ [What Economic Models Should China Choose?]. *Economic Perspectives*, 3.
68 Sun Xiaoliang. (1982). 坚持计划经济与发挥市场调节的辅助作用 [Adhering to the Planned Economy and Leveraging the Supporting Role of Market Regulation]. *Economic Research Journal*, 6.
69 Jing Ping. (1982). 计划经济和市场调节问题讨论述评 [A Review of the Discussions on the Issue of Planned Economy and Market Regulation]. *Hong Qi*, 22.
70 Wang Renzhi & Gui Shiyong. (1983). 坚持和改进指令性计划制度 [Sticking to and Improving Mandatory Plan System]. In *Collected Works of Planned Economy and Market Regulation* (Vol. 1, pp. 283, 284, 289). Red Flag Press.
71 Lü Lüping & Zheng Xinli. (April 20, 1982). 试论指令性计划 [On Mandatory Planning]. *China Financial and Economic News*.
72 Wu Jinglian & Zhou Shulian. (1983). 试论社会主义计划经济的调节方式 [On the Regulation Models of Socialist Planned Economy]. *Social Science Journal*, 5.
73 You Lin. (1981). 计划经济是主体自由生产是补充 [Planned Economy Is the Principal Part and Free Production Is the Supplement]. *Economic Research Journal*, 9.
74 Wu Shuqing. (1981). 理论上阐述社会主义经济优越性的有益探索 – 评<社会主义经济制度及其优越性> [A Theoretical Interpretation of the Useful Exploration for Advantages of the Socialist Economy: On Socialist Economic System and Its Superiority]. *Economic Research Journal*, 12.
75 Wu Jinglian & Zhou Shulian. (1983). 试论社会主义计划经济的调节方式 [On the Regulation Models of Socialist Planned Economy]. *Social Science Journal*, 5.
76 Dong Fureng. (1981). 社会主义经济制度及其优越性 [Socialist Economic System and Its Superiority] (p. 196). Beijing: Beijing Publishing House.
77 Liu Guoguang. (September 6, 1982). 坚持经济体制改革的基本方向 [Sticking to the Fundamental Direction of the Reform of Economic System]. *People's Daily*.
78 Wang Renzhi, & Gui Shiyong. (1983). 坚持和改进指令性计划制度 [Sticking to and Improving Mandatory Plan System]. In *Collected Works of Planned Economy and Market Regulation* (Vol. 1). Beijing: Red Flag Press. However, in a later article, Gui Shiyong only mentioned that "from now to the near future, the scope of mandatory planning should be gradually narrowed, the scope of guidance planning should be appropriately expanded, while market regulation should be carried out in a certain range"; but he did not mention the long-term trends. (See Gui Shiyong. (1984). 关于正确认识计划经济为主市场调节为辅的几个问题 [Several Issues on Correct Understanding of "Insists on Planned Economy Supplemented by Market Regulation"]. *Economic Research Journal*, 5).
79 Wu Shuqing. (April 22, 1984). 计划体制与社会主义商品生产 [Planning System and Socialist Commodity Production]. *Guangming Daily*.
80 Li Zhenzhong. (December 26, 1981). 也谈计划和市场问题 [Also on Planning and Market Issues]. *Guangming Daily*.
81 You Lin. (1981). 计划生产是主体，自由生产是补充 [Planned Economy Is the Principal Part and Free Production Is the Supplement]. *Economic Research Journal*, 9.
82 He Jianzhang. (1979). 我国全民所有制经济计划管理体制存在的问题和改革的方向 [Problems Existing in and Reform Direction of the System of Planned Management of China's Economy under Ownership by the Whole People]. *Economic Research Journal*, 5.
83 Zhao Renwei & Rong Jingben. (1982). 我国应该选择什么经济模式？ [What Economic Models Should China Choose?] *Economics Perspectives*, 3.
84 Wu Jinglian & Zhou Shulian. (1983). 试论社会主义计划经济的调节方式 [On the Regulation Models of Socialist Planned Economy]. *Social Science Journal*, 5.
85 Li Guang'an. (November 25, 1981). 为什么必须坚持"计划调节为主、市场为辅"的原则 [Why Must We Adhere to the Principle of 'Giving First Place to Planned Economy and Taking Market Regulation as Auxiliary Measure']. *Economic Daily*.

86 Wang Renzhi. (1982). 必须坚持社会主义计划经济 [We Must Stick to Socialist Planned Economy]. *Finance & Trade Economics*, 7.

87 Wu Jinglia. (1982). 坚持计划经济为主、市场调节为辅 [Insists on Planned Economy Supplemented by Market Regulation]. Speech Made at the Symposium. *Finance & Trade Economics*, 4.

88 Sun Xiaoliang. (1982). 坚持计划经济与发挥市场调节辅助作用 [Adhering to the Planned Economy and Leveraging the Supporting Role of Market Regulation]. *Economic Research Journal*, 6.

89 Liu Guoguang. (September 6, 1982). 坚持经济体制改革的基本方向 [Sticking to the Fundamental Direction of the Reform of Economic System]. *People's Daily*.

5 Several difficulties encountered in China's market-oriented reform

I. Introduction: the goal of China's economic system reform is market-oriented

China's economic system reform started in circumstances where it was not well prepared theoretically and lacked practical experience, and it has been ten years since the reform began. Although people have different understandings of the goal of reform, as expressed by such phrases as "planned commodity economy", "national regulatory market, and market-oriented enterprises", and so on, the overall objective of the reform in these ten years is to realize the marketization of economic activities under the premise of ensuring macro control. As far as economic performance is concerned, we have indeed taken an important step forward in the path of market-oriented reform. In the production of agricultural products, the mandatory plan has been canceled, and in the circulation of agricultural products, the task of unified and fixed state purchase was canceled in 1985, replaced by the contracted ordering and free purchase and sale. Although the role of the market mechanism in contracted ordering is still relatively insignificant, as a whole, the production and circulation of agricultural products has been largely influenced by the market price signal.

There are also significant changes in industry. For example, the number of varieties of products under the mandatory plan of the State Planning Commission fell from 123 before 1984 to 20 in 1987, and the proportion of their output value in the country's total industrial output value fell from about 40% to about 17%. The number of materials in the means of production under the unified allocation of the state was reduced from 256 before 1980 to 23 in 1987. The share of some important materials under the unified allocation of the state in the total national output also fell significantly. From 1980 to 1987, the share of rolled steel dropped from 74.3% to 47.1%, timber from 80.9% to 27.6%, cement from 35% to 15.6% and coal from 57.9% to 47.2%. By the end of 1987, among the raw materials bought by the industrial sector, about two-thirds were bought on the market, and about one-third were allocated by the state. The proportion of investment directly arranged by national budgets in capital construction in companies with ownership by the whole people decreased from 62.4% in 1978 to 22.6% in 1986.

In terms of the reform of business management mechanism, the State Council has issued 13 documents and 97 provisions to expand the decision-making power of enterprises since the reform. Now enterprises can make their own decisions regarding production plan, product purchase and sales, use of funds, labor and personnel, wages and bonuses and other aspects, a big step forward on the road of turning enterprises into relatively independent commodity producers and operators, and initially changing the status of enterprises as subsidiaries to administrative organs.

Therefore, in the past ten years, the dominant trend of China's economic operation was to move toward marketization.

II. The first difficulty: coexistence of dual systems in the process of economic system transformation

In the process of transition from the old system to the new system, there was the coexistence of dual systems for a fairly long period. Since implementation of the State Council's "Interim Provisions on Further Expanding the Decision-Making Power of State-Owned Industrial Enterprises" (The 10 Articles) in May 1984 and "Decision of the CPC Central Committee on Economic System Reform" in October of the same year, the coexistence of dual systems has become obvious and legitimized. The enterprises that used to produce in accordance with the mandatory plan now divide their production into two parts: production within the state plan and production outside the state plan. The supplies needed by the enterprises are also divided into two sources: the part allocated by the state, and the part procured freely on the market. In line with this new situation, pricing of the products within the state plan was regulated by administrative approaches of the state, while products outside the state plan can be sold at higher prices that reflect the law of the market to varying degrees (floating price, negotiated price, free price). Here, the dual production system, the dual material circulation system and the dual price system are a trinity. The dual production system (which determines how to produce) is the basis of the dual economic system, the dual material circulation system (which determines how to invest) is the guarantee of the dual production system and the dual price system is the manifestation of the entire dual economic system.

Over the years, much analysis has been made on the pros and cons of the dual system. People in favor of the dual system think that its positive role can be summarized as follows. First, it is conducive to adjusting the economic interests between people step by step, reducing the turmoil in and resistance to the reform, defusing the risks of reform, and turning major shocks to minor ones. Second, higher market prices for some of the products are conducive to increasing their supply and easing the contradiction between supply and demand. Third, it partly changes the situation in which prices of resources (energy, raw materials, etc.) are on the low side, which is conducive to saving resources and urging economic management personnel to familiarize themselves with the discipline of market operation so as to improve the level of management.

However, the coexistence of the dual economic system has brought a series of contradictions and frictions to economic life: first, it results in the dual behavior of enterprises. As production and sales units, enterprises always strive to lower the mandatory planning indicators so as to use their excessive production capacity for the production of products outside the state plan; as buyers and users of raw materials, enterprises strive to have more quotas in the unified allocation of materials. In the process of implementation of the plan, the materials flow, through various channels, from inside the plan to outside the plan, so that the contract fulfillment rate between enterprises declines, affecting the realization of the plan. Second, it is difficult to form a unified market mechanism and competition mechanism, so that it is hard for enterprises to carry out equal competition in equal price conditions, and the standards for assessment of an enterprise's management competence are also in a mess, whether output, sales or profits and other standards are distorted. Third, the huge difference between the dual prices provides a breeding ground for speculation and illegal profiteering activities, corrupting social values and government officials. Fourth, the high price of products outside the state plan stimulates increased production of certain commodities in short supply and is therefore conducive to the rationalization of interdepartmental structure; yet at the same time it stimulates the high-cost production of some inefficient small-scale enterprises, resulting in unreasonable use of limited resources, and leading to the decline in economic efficiency and irrational industrial structure within the sector.

The contradictions and frictions of the dual system also extend to the areas of personal income distribution. Economic activities within the state plan, or economic activities within the range controlled by the state, normally generate low incomes; for economic activities outside the state plan or those where direct control of the state cannot reach and where indirect control system has yet to be established and operate effectively, the income of some people and economic activities is rather too high. For example, the income of workers in the ownership by the whole people, including workers in state-owned enterprises, staff of government institutions and school teachers, is low, while the income of the workers in private companies and self-employed people is high, and the income of a small number of people in certain industry such as taxi drivers is significantly higher.

How to deal with the contradictions and friction brought about by the dual system? People can come up with a variety of solutions. Summed up, there are four possibilities: (1) adopt centralization again and return to the original system; (2) maintain the dual system and even regard the dual system as our objective, taking only some remedial measures to alleviate the frictions between each other; (3) put an end immediately to the dual system and rapidly transit to the system of indirect control; (4) regard the dual system as a transitional stage from the old system to the new one, and strive to embark on the operating track of the new system as soon as possible. I am in favor of the last solution.

III.   The second difficulty: materialization tendency in the process of market-oriented reform

In the process of market-oriented reform, the process of monetization and commercialization of the whole economic life is not as smooth as expected, and it often suffers repression from some anti-market factors. This opposing force or repressive factor is the materialization tendency that we are talking about. Since 1984, due to overheating of the economy, imbalance in supply and demand has become more serious, commodity shortages have exacerbated, the inflation rate is higher, and the materialization tendency becomes more obvious.

The materialization tendencies are shown in the following:

1 The return of rationing coupons. Since the reform, the number of commodities that was rationed to urban residents, such as food, clothing and daily necessities, was greatly reduced, but in recent years, the rationing coupons have made a comeback. Not only the system of rationed supply of basic foodstuffs such as grain and oil remained unchanged, this also extended to other non-staple food like eggs, meat and bean vermicelli, and even soaps and matches were rationed; In addition, only "a limited number of coupons" were available for people who wanted to buy a color TV, refrigerator or other similar household appliances.

2 The expansion of welfare spending. Since the reform, with the growth of residents' income, the total household budget expenditure has also increased. However, of the daily expenses of the urban residents, a number of very important expenditure items have remained stable or even declined. One of the most prominent is that the proportion of per capita annual rental expenditure in per capita annual living expenses shows a downward trend, declining from 2.32% in 1957 to 1.52% in 1983 and 0.87% in 1987. This shows that since the reform, the welfare degree and materialization tendency of urban residents' housing consumption has somewhat expanded. Other expenses, such as public transport, utilities and so on, showed a similar trend to rents.

> If the subject of study is the leadership, especially the senior leadership of Party and government organs, the high welfare and non-monetization characteristics of their consumption will be more obvious. They were provided with private cars, telephones, spacious homes, advanced free medical care, domestic service staff at public expenses and other special supply and material benefits, and these costs greatly exceeded their salaries. This kind of special supply system is virtually against marketization.
>
> Over the past decade, we have made no substantive progress in the reform of the monetary salary system but have made a lot of effort in providing a variety of physical benefits to government officials at different levels. More specific stipulations than ever have been made regarding benefits to officials at department, bureau and ministerial levels. Leaders even have the power to approve the extension of the scope or level of their benefit enjoyment. According to statistics, there are 90,000 officials at deputy bureau level nationwide, but 210,000 officials have been approved to enjoy the benefits of this level.

3 The rationing within the "unit". In the reform of "delegate powers to lower levels and surrender part of the profits", many work units make up all kinds of excuses to distribute goods among their employees. The materialization

degree of "unit" rationing is higher than that of the government rationing, because the former is often "giving for free", and the employees do not have to or rarely pay for the goods.

4   The physical exchange. In the current economic life of our country, especially in the economic field with a high degree of shortages, the physical exchange is popular in various forms. The following are the most popular forms of physical exchange: (a) exchange of one commodity for another, such as bartering steel for cars, fertilizer for food, and so on; (b) exchange rationing coupons for goods, using food coupons to exchange for eggs, for example; and (c) exchange power for things, such as using the power you have to help other people, and then receive free gifts from them.

5   Extraordinary subsidies. According to estimates, China's current supply consumption of urban workers (including subsidies for housing, transportation and public health care) is equivalent to about 80% of the average wage income of workers; for every square meter of house that workers live in, the government subsidizes more than 2 yuan per month, for every kg of food that urban residents consume, the state subsidizes at least 0.34 yuan, and for every kg of peanut oil, the state subsidizes 1.6 yuan. At present, the per capita annual living allowances enjoyed by Beijing residents are 550 yuan.

The causes of the materialization tendency are multifaceted. There are causes not only in respect to political system, economic system and social organization structure, but also ones in respect to level of development; there are causes both in the traditional concepts and habits, but also ones in decision-making mistakes. These factors constitute the power to resist the market-oriented reform process. The study of the causes of these "anti-market" factors and of how to weaken their role becomes a major task of deepening the reform.

IV.   The third difficulty: constraints by low level of development

It is natural that China's market-oriented economic reform suffers the restriction of the country's low degree of development. Ten years of experience has shown that in a country with low levels of development, the problem of low degree of market development posed a big challenge to accomplishing the market-oriented reform. China is a developing socialist country. For a long time, modern industry, relatively backward industries and traditional farming and handicrafts coexisted. The degrees of socialization and commercialization of production are relatively low. As some economists have pointed out, China is still in a developmental stage of semi-self-sufficiency and semi-monetary economy. China still does not have an efficient market system. The scope of the commodity market is limited and has been made inefficient because of regional development imbalance and outdated traffic and communication tools; the development degree of the factor market (capital, labor, etc.) is even lower. However, the regulation of the economic parameters in the indirect control system depends largely on the degree of development of the market. When the market is immature, enterprises and individuals cannot make a sensitive response to prices, interest rates, tax rates, wages and other market signals, so that these economic parameters cannot play a positive guiding role in the allocation of resources. Obviously it is impossible to establish an indirect control system that encompasses the whole society in a short time at the present stage of China's economic development. Of course, this is not to say that it is impossible to establish such a system within a certain range that features relatively higher levels of socialization and commercialization. In the strict sense, at the present stage of China's economic development, whether it is to establish a direct control system or an indirect control system, the result will surely be watered down. Even at the peak of China's direct control system, the coverage rate of products under the central unified plan is much lower than that of the Soviet Union and Eastern European countries.[1] Some foreign economists have analyzed that since China's socialist economy is an economy of a low-income developing country, although China's original economic system can be defined as a system of centralized management with planned physical resource allocation, because of the influence of low-income conditions the actuating range of the system is limited to part of the national economy. While conducting the reform of the economic system (i.e. taking advantage of market mechanisms), China must give full consideration to such constraints as "low income and low productivity". "As long as the Chinese economy remains in the low-income" stage, "development of the effective part of the market economy will be limited to certain areas."[2] Therefore, it is reasonable to say that in the near future, we can expect only to establish preliminarily an indirect control system which has limited breadth and depth and which uses market parameters as its signal. Only with the further increase of the degree of commercialization and marketization can the system be gradually spread and stretched, and run more effectively.

In addition to the three difficulties mentioned here, there are many other difficulties. For example, the problem of how the market-oriented reform is combined with ownership reform has always been one of the focuses of debate in the economics circle. The reform of ownership refers not only to the realization of transformation of ownership relations from a single form to diversified forms – that is, the coexistence of various economic components – but also to the deepening of reform into public ownership, especially into national ownership, fundamentally solving the problem that everyone is the owner of the property, but no one is responsible for the property. Some economists have emphasized that the role of market mechanisms should be played within the framework of public ownership without breaking through the pattern proposed by O. Lange in the 1930s, but other economists seem to favor the realization of market-oriented reforms because of private ownership. This is a controversial issue in both theory and practice.

V. Conclusions

From the challenges that China's market-oriented reform encounters, it seems that we can draw the following conclusions:

1 We must be fully aware that implementing market-oriented economic system reform in China is an arduous, long-term task that can be accomplished only

step by step. Past experience shows clearly that all the ideas and practices of a quick victory in the reform of the economic system are not realistic. With no successful experience in similar reforms in other countries serving as reference, and given that we ourselves lack theoretical preparation and practical experience, we should not expect to accomplish the task of reforming the economic system in one go even though we have the pioneering spirit.

2   Whether in the choice of development strategy or the choice of reform strategy, we should overcome and prevent the shortcomings of overheating. The aggravation of the aforementioned materialization tendency is directly linked to the degree of imbalance between supply and demand and to worsening of shortages. However, the increase in the degree of shortages leads to overheating in the choice of development strategies and the rush for quick results (a kind of overheating) in the choice of development strategies. Therefore, overheating in the choice of the two strategies will produce the adverse effect of "more haste and less speed", impeding the process of market-oriented reform.

3   In the short-term adjustment and tightening process, we should avoid the abuse of administrative methods and should use the market means as much as possible. Under circumstances when there is an intensified shortage, we are accustomed to the implementation of the traditional approach of rationing by issuing coupons. By using this approach, it is easy to achieve administrative balance of economic performance, but in the long run it will hinder the development of the market. Therefore, when using certain administrative measures to adjust the economy, we must not forget that our goal is not to maintain a balance in the supply of goods, but to achieve a market price balance – this is a fundamental difference between the adjustment of China's current stage and that of the early 1960s.

(This is an article submitted to the International Symposium on Development Strategy for Third World Countries held in April 1989 in Beijing.)

Notes

1 Hua Sheng and others. (1986). 经济运行模式的转换 [Transformation of Economic Operation Mode]. *Economic Research Journal*, 2.
2 Shigero Ishikawa. (1986). 社会主义经济和中国的经验—对经济改革的展望 [Socialist Economy and China's Experience: The Expectations for Economic Reform]. *Science and Technology Review*, 2.

Part 2

Transformations of economic system and development

6 Target model of China's economic system reform

I. Purposes and preconditions of studying the reform model of China's economic system

A. Merits of studying the reform model of China's economic system

Since the mission of economic reform was raised in the third Plenary Session of the 11th CPC Central Committee, the economics professions in China have been studying and exploring the ideal model of China's economic reform, which have quite a few merits listed as follows.

Firstly, studies and explorations in terms of the economic reform model may help avoid blind attempts. The concept of economic reform was raised shortly after 1976, which means the theoretical and practical experience for the reform is insufficient. The economic system is huge; thus it is an enormous project to cast reform upon it. Consequently, studies on the goal and direction of economic reform are particularly important. These studies would be able to guide the practice of reform and avoid taking reform steps blindly. Of course, the process of reform will not be smooth all the time; it is more like a curve to a straight line. A general target or an ideal model is nonetheless needed to guide the process. Twists and turns during the reform are inevitable, and so are the prices to be paid for them. Trial-and-error,[1] as well as "cross the river by feeling for the stones" addressed by Deng Xiaoping, are strategic approaches to reaching the final goal rather than the goal itself. Blind practice would be made if the approach and the goal are confused or an approach is overstated as a final target. An economist once criticized that

> the theoretic foundation for China's economic reform is insufficient. The ideology of ignoring theoretic importance from former agrarian society remains widely influential in modern Chinese society. For quite a long time, the idea remained dominant that a framework for the reform is impossible and unnecessary, and that a framework could be designed along the reform process.[2]

This idea, regardless of its possible benefits, is definitely harmful for reform practice. Admittedly, studies for the final target of reform take some time. For many years, although many economists emphasized the importance of a target model and raised their own doctrines, there is no ideal one by far. Another economist commented:

> As known to all, a general reform framework is needed. But there is no enforceable plan to it. We all realize a systematic framework is required to deploy different reform actions, the fact is, however, reform policies were made temporarily and released by chance, which resulted in the imbalance of economic system as a whole.[3]

This criticism is somewhat poignant to the ear, but it points out the necessity of further studies in target model of economic reform.

Secondly, the studies could reaffirm our determination in reform. Reform of the economic system refers to the transformation of economic pattern within the fundamental system of the socialist economy. The reform is not simply amending and changing details in the former economic system, but casting transformation on the impropriate framework and main operation principles. This train of thought is based on the theory that the socialist economic system could include more than one economic pattern.

As early as in the 1930s, the Lange Model was put forward, changing the idea that socialist system allows only one economic system (as in the former Soviet Union). Countries in Eastern Europe (with Yugoslavia being the first) started reforms on economy, breaking out from the rigid economic pattern in the former Soviet Union. In China, however, the idea that socialism has more than one pattern has been widely spread until the 6th Plenary Session of the 11th CPC Central Committee. From many years' experience of reform, however, the transformation of pattern has been interfered with many times. For instance, some comrades believe we are "improving" the economic system or "amending" planned economy instead of transforming the economy pattern. Others may take the reform as a "recovery", which is aimed at changing our economy system back to that of 1956 or 1965.[4] This doctrine, which takes reform as "recovery", was once particularly popular during the beginning and hard times of the reform. In conclusion, we need to further studies on the target model of reform and make prudent choices.

Thirdly, studies help us to probe essential problems occurring in the reform process. An economic pattern doesn't equal to the actual economic system of a country, but more of a conclusion to its basic principles. This kind of theoretical conclusion reflects essential parts of an economy.[5] For example, Friedman's model is a conclusion to the productive relations of pre-monopoly capitalism. When we are studying different models under the socialist economy, we also use the method of concluding and abstracting to reveal basic characteristics of the pattern, which has helped us from being interfered by minor factors. When there is no target model for whole reform, different departments have developed independent plans for their own sake, which were too detailed yet quite inclusive. These plans were barely linked together, causing troubles for cooperation and coordination for different departments. This situation also accounts for the urging for more studies and explorations on reform theory and a general reform framework.

B. Principles of establishing target model

After clarifying the purposes of studying the target reform model, we also need to determine the model's guiding principles.

First of all, we need to consider the range and time span of the framework. In terms of range, the economic reform must follow the socialism orientation and insist principles as public ownership, distribution on the basis of labor, etc. Specific margins will be elaborated later. Various designs have been raised up in terms of the time span: five-year plan, two-decade-plan or of even longer time. It seems rather hard to determine the time span for a reform framework. All in all, the time span should be tightly linked to the stages of China's socialism development. Now at its primary socialism stage, China is challenged with a task to develop its established but yet immature socialist economic system. The development takes two steps: the first is to enforce systematic reforms on the economic system, politics, culture, education, science and technology, with economic reform being the center. Hopefully the reforms would remove all systematic problems that are not suitable for the primary socialist stage. On the basis of the first step, China needs to comprehensively promote commercialization and socialization of production and continue to adjust elements that are not beneficial for production. A conclusion can be drawn that transformation of economic pattern is not an endless process, but the first task in the primary socialism stage. However, the transformation will continue throughout the primary phase of socialist development.

Secondly, setting up the framework is a significant, strategic move, instead of a temporary policy as the reform proceeds. Unfortunately, some arguments confused strategic framework and temporary policy. For example, although command economic plans cannot be cancelled immediately, this does not mean that command plans remain dominant in the new economic framework, nor that economic commands will remain exactly the same in form in the future. Other instances would be the coexistence of the planned economy and market economy and labor market. Our target economy is an effective combination of plan and market, but this does not suggest that the two types of economy can't coexist in an independent way during a certain period. For the time being, we will continue to control the population and labor flows, but we may need a labor market in the future economy.[6] Thus, temporary policies and restrictions, if taken as long-time and fixed plans, would lower the expectations of reform.

Thirdly, the choice of target framework should be realistic. As addressed before, an economic pattern is a theoretical conclusion of the economic system it is from. It should always be closely related to reality and show insights and characteristics of the economy in an abstract and profound way (for both empirical and normative studies, as long as the conclusion is drawn scientifically). Thus, a good or appropriate economic model can't include all advantages of other models while excluding all disadvantages. We need to balance out in our target model by weighing advantages and disadvantages.

C. China's national conditions are an important basis for the target economic model

The exploration of the socialist economic system with Chinese characteristics includes two interrelated aspects. The first one is to explore the framework of a more efficient socialist economy, while the second is to apply the theoretical framework to Chinese society. The framework should coordinate with national conditions and keep developing as reform proceeds. When discussing the models in the former Soviet Union, Yugoslavia and Hungary, their economic patterns have been related to national conditions in these countries. These patterns show not only general disciplines and orders of the economy, but characteristics of the aforementioned countries. Strictly speaking, categorizing economic pattern by country is not scientific, as the economic systems keep changing as the nation develops.

It is well accepted that the target economic system must be deeply rooted in the national conditions in China. But it remains problematic to enforce. It doesn't help much to make a long list of national conditions, and neither does linking only one condition to one economic system. A good example here would be studying how slow economic development has influenced our economic system. A theory is popular in international economic professions that a centralized economic system is suitable for a country with low production and an "extensive" economy, while a decentralized system is better for a country with high production and an "intensive" economy. Admittedly, the level of economic development is related to the economic system, but this does not suggest that every development phase of a country requires a different economic system. The truth is, multiple economic systems could coexist in a certain development phase. If we use the theory of extensive and intensive development to proof the centralization and decentralization of economic system directly, the necessity of transforming overcentralized economic mechanism will be denied.

However, as a country with a vast territory, economic dualism and imbalanced regional economic developments, our practice should have idiosyncrasies. Taking policy-making as an example, at the beginning of reform, the phenomenon of ignoring enterprise autonomy was criticized, as the decentralization reached only the administrative level of central and local authorities. The criticizing was undoubtedly correct. But considering actual conditions in China, decentralizing administrative power is nonetheless important. How to take advantage of local authorities, especially those in underdeveloped provinces, remains an inevitable problem when building up a target economic model. This is a perfect example of how meso-economic decisions play in a decision-making mechanism.

The economic system is also subject to social and cultural factors. The design of the economic reform target should consider these factors in the first place, and guide society and culture towards a reasonable direction in return. An economist said the reform on economy is "a definite reform for culture as well".[7] People hold different ideas of how traditional Chinese culture has influenced China's economic system. Some believe China is deeply influenced by concepts of natural economy, and that establishing a planned commodity economy means demolishing the theory of natural economy.[8] Others think that traditional Chinese culture includes not only natural economy theories, but traditional concepts of monetary economy, including values and merits of independence, confidence, honesty and a sense of honor, which are enormously beneficial for developing a commercial culture. Thus, rejuvenation of traditional culture is a crucial part in economic reform.[9] Despite different opinions on traditional culture, the reform on economic system should always be based on China's reality, and reviving and cultivating commercial culture should be carried out. After the third Plenary Session of the 11th CPC Central Committee, the idea of "all businessmen are dishonest" has been gradually abandoned and replaced by the idea of "businessmen bring vigor and opportunities". Thus, the process of economic reform is also a process of selecting the essence and discarding the gross of traditional Chinese culture.

II.   The target model of economic system reform by comparison

A.   Elements and categorizing standard for the economic system

In documents and chapters of comparative economics, many economics scholars analyzed the characteristics of an economic system based on elements of the economy. Structural differences of these elements (like the centralization degree of decision-making authority) were used as a standard to categorize economies into different patterns. Egon Neuberger and William J. Duffy believed that any economic system consists of three interrelated parts: Decision-making authority, information authority and enforcement authority. Differences of economies resulted from differences of these three authorities.[10] Lindbeck established his theory from eight aspects: (1) the economic decision-making is centralized or decentralized; (2) information, resource allocation and coordination mechanism are dominated by market or administration; (3) property relations are public-owned or private; (4 and 5) the individual and company are driven by economic stimulus or orders from government; (6 and 7) the relationship of individual and company is competitive or non-competitive; and (8) the economy is open and international or closed and subsistent.[11]

When studying different models of the socialist economic system, some economists categorize these patterns with one characteristic for analysis. Bruse and Kornai are two representative economists with this kind of achievement. Bruse categorized socialist economic systems by how economic decisions are made. He divided these decisions into three types: (a) fundamental and major macroeconomic decisions; (b) ordinary and daily micro-economic decisions; and (c) individual or household decision in labor allocation and consumption. Four patterns are raised in which (a), (b) and (c) are centralized or decentralized. The first pattern is named the "military communism" pattern, as (a), (b) and (c) are all centralized; the second pattern, called the centralized pattern, occurs when (a) and (b) are centralized, while (c) is decentralized in principle. The third one is a pattern combining market and government plan. In this pattern, only (a) is centralized. The last one is when three types of economic decisions are all decentralized.[12] Kornai focused more on the coordination mechanism. He pointed out two kinds of coordination mechanisms: Administrative (I) and Market (II). Each mechanism had two sub-divisions: Direct Administrative Coordination (IA), Indirect Administrative Coordination (IB), Market Coordination with Macro Control (IIA) and Market Coordination without Macro Control (IIB).

Admittedly, different standards result in various categories, each with a characteristic. Categorizing with various standards indicate multiple features of economy, while that with a single standard is highly brief and concise. Some economists in China have developed a well-rounded system to analyze patterns and characteristics of the socialist economic system from five dimensions: ownership system, decision target, structure of adjustment, interest and structure of enforcement.[13] Different standards of an economy are interrelated; emphasis on one standard is not necessarily ignorant of another, but made for the need of clarifying problems. For instance, categorization by decision-making mechanism or by coordination system usually overlaps. The centralization of decision-making matches with administrative coordination, while decentralization of decision-making is related to coordination on the market side. As addressed beforehand, the studies of economic patterns should be rooted from practical examples. Different standards are mostly for the purpose of theoretical studies. Kornai's categorization is closely related to the IB (Indirect Administrative Coordination) pattern Hungary has been in since its 1968 reform. Bruse's theory of four economic patterns was first raised in the autumn of 1980, when he wrote a chapter on China's economy for the World Bank. This theory was also influenced by his conclusion that China's pre-reform economic system had characteristics of military communism.

B.   Spectrum of socialist economic systems

Despite different standards, patterns of the socialist economic system are like a spectrum, with each pattern in its own position. By summarizing the experience of many countries since the October Revolution, socialist economic systems could be categorized into the following six patterns.

1.   Supply system of military communism

All economic activities, including macroeconomic activities, daily economic activities of a company, and household economic activities (like choice of profession, choice of labor and rest, choice of consumption) are centralized by national authority. All economic activities are state-owned except for agriculture. The use of commercial currency and the market mechanism are completely denied; economic information flows vertically. The whole society is deemed as a large factory, instead of being divided into production units. Economic accounting is made on the basis of the whole society; revenue and expenditure are monopolized by the state. Material supplies are dominating the economy in both production and allocation.

This kind of economy is an emergent model executed during war or economic blockade. It has advantages in emergent mobilization and collecting manpower, materials and money when a country is faced with war and economic challenges. But it will hinder people's willingness for work and efficiency. Generally speaking, this pattern has been history. It was, on the other hand, product of the tendency to eliminate currency. In addition, those with this tendency usually take this pattern as the ultimate target. As a result, it had more profound influence than a temporary measure.

2. Planned economic pattern

This pattern includes two types of public ownership: ownership by the whole people, and collective ownership. Both are dominated by the country, just slightly different in controlling level. Macroeconomic activities and company economic activities are controlled by country, while individual and household economic activities are independent. Individual or household has the freedom in consumption and choosing professions. There is, as a result, a market of commodities and labor. In this economic pattern, the country's control is realized by indirect measures. But corporations remain subordinate to the country; the production, supplies and sales of the company should follow the directive orders of the government. Economic decisions are made and enforced by administrative policies from higher- to lower-level administrations. Information of economy is passed down from higher- to lower-level administrations or collected from lower- to higher-level administrations. Economic accounting is made on the basis of the whole society; revenue and expenditure are monopolized by the state. There is no commercial relationship between state-owned companies, as "commodity" is not the real commercial goods, and "currency" is used only for accounting and allocation, instead of forming the basis of choice. Both the buyer and the seller can't decide how many goods to buy and how much to pay for them, but follow the orders of resource allocation. In this case, the flow of currency subjects to the flow of goods.

In the second pattern, labor, resources and fortune are highly centralized and can be deployed to industries and regions that have a higher priority level in development. With this pattern, an underdeveloped socialist country could realize fast economic growth in a short period of time and facilitate industrialization. This pattern has its immanent conflicts and disadvantages. A dilemma often occurs that "people who with information have no right to make decisions, while decision makers have no enough economic information". Although products flow horizontally between corporations, the decision/information of how products move flows vertically between central authorities and each corporation. This imbalanced mechanism often leads to disjoint of production, supply and sales, as well as bureaucracy of decision-making authorities. From the point of interest, corporations, which are subsidiaries of different levels of governments, are only enforced by compulsory administrative orders. The government simply uses planning targets to measure the operation of companies, which may lead to a ratchet effect. Under this system, corporations are prone to report less actual output and require more input. Bargains between higher and lower levels are common in this mechanism, which lacks an automatic regulatory mechanism led by market. If the first one is known as "war-time" economy, this economic pattern should be named a "pre-wartime" economy.

3.   Adapted planned economic pattern

This pattern keeps most characteristics of the planned economy, but corporations reserve autonomy in a small part of daily economic activities. For example, they are allowed to sell the rest of their products after fulfilling the production target, or part of the interest could be kept for future development or bonus for employees. State-owned corporations are still directed by target and orders, but the proportion of the target is lowered in total production. Appraisal indexes are changed, too. Index of total output value is replaced by sales, which is then replaced again by fixed net productivity. By loosening the control over collectively owned entities (although still with different levels of control), this pattern allows private entity and expands the scope for market adjustment. However, the influence of the market remains supplementary. This type of economy also attaches greater importance to economic levers like price, interest, salary and credit. Directive orders and planned target are kept, and administrative measures remain dominant.

In this economy, conflicts mentioned in the second pattern have been mitigated, which, to a certain degree, has facilitated economic development and improved efficiency. With just a few modifications to the second model, this pattern is not able to tackle immanent disadvantages of the system. These modifications, being disconnected to the original framework, cause new conflicts. For instance, the assessment index has been transformed from a physical index (total output or types of product) to a value index (net output or interest) to stimulate a corporation's production, but the pricing system remains unchanged, making it meaningless for corporations to pursue interest. Worse still, pursue of interest conflicts with fulfilling social needs and even harms the right of consumers. The change of evaluation index fails to settle the drastic mismatch of production and supply. This is why countries with this economic pattern repeatedly linger around increasing and decreasing directive orders and frequently change the central target.

4.   Pattern with indirect administrative regulation

In this pattern, direct administrative orders that control a company's production, supply and sales are abolished. However, the system to regulate corporations via market and economic measures hasn't been established yet. This pattern is a conclusion to the economy in post-reform Hungary. This pattern approves the hypothesis that a socialist country could run its economy normally after abolishing directive economic orders. This pattern also suggests that abolishment of directive orders is not equal to the establishment of a regulatory system led by the market;

there is one more pattern in between, which is indirect administrative regulation. In this kind of economic pattern, corporations enjoy greater autonomy in economic activities, including supply, sales, investment, sharing of interest, negotiation on price and employee's salary. However, a corporation needs to watch both market and authority at the same time. This is because: (1) the leader of the corporation is still deployed by higher-level authorities; (2) the establishment and closing of a company is decided by authorities instead of the market; (3) the profit of a corporation is decided by bargaining with high-level authorities instead of management and operation; and (4) abuse of subsidy and tax weakens the stimulus on interest and stiffens the budget restraints in corporation revenue. In addition, without a well-established pricing system, too much administrative interference during the pricing process results in a corporation's weak response to price variations.

Both the third and fourth patterns make modifications to the traditional directive economy, while remaining more or less characteristic of the administrative regulatory system. Compared to other patterns, these two are volatile (not stable) patterns during the transformation period.

5.   *Effective combination of plan and market*

In this pattern, macroeconomic activity is centralized. Strategic decisions on the national economy are made by the country; while corporations have autonomy in daily economic activities, households and individuals are in charge of economic decisions. The country uses economic parameters or measures to guide and control corporation's economic activities, so that corporations can make decisions according market signals while meeting the country's plans and targets. This mechanism is an integrated combination of administrative plans and market regulation. Corporations, with higher independence, are driven by interest-related inner impetus and external pressure of competition on the market. Horizontal economic connections between producers and consumers have been largely expanded, and an information network of national economy is established, linking authorities, corporations and consumers. Corporations break free from chains and restraints of many levels of administrations, and administrative management is gradually replaced by economic management. Meanwhile, an interlaced economic system is established, with corporation and administrative organization being separated.

Under this pattern, the inherited problems of traditional collectively planned economy have been largely overcome. A hierarchical decision-making structure improves the reliability of decisions. A system of indirect orders boosts the vigor of the corporation and effectively prevents the macro-economy from going out of control, thus improving economic efficiency at both macro and micro levels. This model has its conflicts and problems, though. For example, do we need a certain limit to a buyer's market, and how do we realize it? Are economic activities of corporations, based on their own interests, beneficial for the whole society? All these problems require further exploration. Another problem would occur as the reform on economic mechanism deepens. Corporations, playing the roles of producer and operator, are responsible for their profits and losses. It will also need to tackle soft budget constraints, and managers and employees of corporation need to be highly responsible. This means that the system of ownership also requires a reform to match an economy where plan and market regulation are effectively combined.

6. Socialist market economy

In this pattern, public ownership consists of individual autonomy operated collectively. Development of private economy and individual economy is widely allowed. Decisions of macro, micro-economy and household are decentralized and led by the market. Thus, the framework built by centralized decisions of macro-economy does not exist, the responsibility of expanded reproduction is almost entirely shifted from authority to corporation itself, and so is the allocation of income. The market is dominating the national economy. This economic pattern has inevitable disadvantages of the market economy, which includes galloping inflation, high unemployment rate and periodic fluctuation of the economy. Thus, success gained in the micro-economy might be offset by loss from the macro-economy.

C. Starting point and target of China's economic reform

On the basis of comparing different patterns of socialist economy, we need to figure out what was China's economic pattern and which pattern we are targeting.

There are debates on what is the origin of China's former economic pattern. One popular belief is it originated from the former Soviet Union in the 1950s, so it belongs to the traditional planned economy. Another idea, however, thinks the planned economy of former Soviet Union never really occurred in China, despite its casting a huge influence on the Chinese economy. In fact, these two ideas are supplementary to a large degree. Discussion of this topic actually demonstrates the adaptions and variations of the traditional planned economy in China. Studies of variations in planned economy help us understand where we are now. Variations as such can be analyzed in terms of scope and sequence.

From the perspective of scope, we can find how much influence planned economy had on China. The fact is, even when its influence peaked (as in 1956), planned economy didn't have wide coverage.[14] According to an economist, in a broad sense, China's economic system can be defined as "a planned allocation system where material resources are managed collectively". Limited by conditions like low-income level, this allocation system was confined to a part of the national economy, while the rest were taken in charge by the market economy and the customary economy.[15] Consequently, it would be fair to say only the majority of our former economy was based on planned economy. Our laborers enjoyed much greater freedom in consumption and employment than in a planned economy even back in the 1950s.

Basically established in 1956, former economic system of China had experienced various changes during 20 eventful years until 1976. In principle, the direction of economic reform is towards either decentralization or centralization. Our economy moved towards both directions from time to time in past two decades. Taking the relationship of central and local government as an example, devolutions of power occurred many times, particularly in 1958 and 1970. Decentralization also happened between authority and corporation. The depreciation fund of the corporation, which had been completely collected for national revenue, was then allowed to be partly allocated by the corporation.

During this period, policies had been large interfered by the "left", causing obvious changes in the following aspects:

1   Ownership and decision-making were further centralized. Devolution of power was confined to the area of central and local administration; there was no expansion of corporation's power to make decisions. Collective ownership in rural areas was often forced into transition to socialist state ownership or even communist entities, regardless of poverty conditions. In the urban area, some collective entities like handicraft cooperative were forced to transform as well, so they become state-owned in nature. As for individual economies, the situation is even worse; they were simply wiped out as "remnants of capitalism". Decision-making power for laborers continued to shrink as more products were included into the allocation system and movement of labor was further restrained.

2   Market influence was further excluded. In the aforementioned 20 years, waves that denied socialist commodity production occurred many times (especially in 1958 and 1975), resulting in materialization of economic relations every single time. Based on administrative orders, the accounting system, where currency had minor influence, still suffered from shocks or even was replaced by a plan-and-supply system many times.

3   Equalitarianism expanded influence in allocation. Similar to commodity production, distribution according to labor was widely criticized, and the piecework system was largely denied. Equalitarianism caused the phenomenon that people receive the same allocation no matter how hard they worked, or if they didn't work at all, inevitably hindering the improvement of productivity. Low productivity and economic difficulties intensified egalitarian distributions in return. Consequently, salaries for senior employees weren't able to change according to how much they work, while salaries for new employees were dramatically influenced by equalitarianism.

4   Mobilization is widely used in organizing economic activities. Decreased commodity relation and distribution according to labor means material interest was unclear. Thus, the method of army mobilization was applied to organize economic activities, particularly in the distribution of labor resources. Actually, egalitarian practice and mobilization were two sides of one problem: on one hand, mobilization was necessary to maintain the practice of equalitarianism; on the other hand, when people worked as mobilized by the country, what they got in return was of course egalitarian reward. These phenomena showed unclear interest relations and material responsibility between state, corporation and individual.

In summary, our economy before reform (or the majority of it) generally belonged to the planned economy with supply factor of military communism. Using Kornai's theory to explain, traditional planned economic pattern is IA, and China's economy before reform is partly IA, as addressed by an economist.[16]

By this analysis, we can find that our country's reform stated with more unfavorable conditions than the former Soviet Union and countries in Eastern Europe. These unfavorable parts were partly caused by policy mistakes and partly due to long-term factors like development level and traditional cultures. Practical analysis on the starting point does not mean lowering the reform target, but it helps us understand what is needed to realize the final target.

To choose the target model of economic reform, we need to narrow down the range of choices first. As discussed previously, the first and second patterns are rather rigid and inefficient with excessive centralization and lack of market regulation. These two patterns are where we started, instead of our target. Studies on the first and second patterns are necessary, too, as they provide us resolution to reform and prevent us from falling back to rigid patterns. The sixth model is similar to Kornai's IIA (without macro regulation) in form, which is an economy completely regulated by the market. This pattern, however, does not exist in today's world. Some socialist countries had tested an incomplete IIA model, but complete market regulation brings with it inevitable and immanent disadvantages, so this pattern is not a choice. As for the third and the fourth, characteristics of these will appear as our reform proceeds, as will unsolvable conflicts and problems of these. In this train of thought, the third and fourth patterns will be transitional patterns for our economy. In other words, they are not our final goal. The fifth, namely, the effective combination of plan and market, is our best choice.

Specific conclusions and expressions of the target model could be diversified as long as the basic direction, mechanism and inner logic of the model remain unchanged. An economist concludes our target model as "our country takes charge of market, while market guides corporations".[17] Another economist describes our target model as "an indirect management model of state-market-corporation".[18] Similar conclusions and expressions are conducive not only to brainstorming, but also to exploring the target of economic reform in the same direction.

In this section, the basic direction of China's economic reform has been clarified by comparing the different economic patterns. In the next section, analysis on framework of target economic model will be elaborated because of the basic direction.

III.   Framework of the target model of China's economic system reform

Based on the basic reform direction discussed in the last section, we will analyze the target model in this section from five dimensions: ownership, decision-making, interest, regulation and economic organization. Since these five dimensions will be elaborated in independent chapters, this section will involve only brief descriptions of these dimensions, then emphasize their interrelations, particularly some complex problems by cross-section study.

We need to establish a system based on public ownership, dominated by state ownership and that allows the existence of various ownerships. The new system should have the following characteristics:

a   More than one type of ownership. Not only state and collective ownerships, but individual ownership, state capitalist ownership (foreign capital or Sino-foreign joint ventures) and private capitalist economy should also be included.

b   Different ownerships are open to each other. Production factors flow freely between different ownerships, improving the efficiency of operation and resource allocation. In our reform process, cross-ownership joint ventures and corporation groups have been established, and corporation and penetration between ownerships have occurred, proving this emerging trend.

c   Adhering to the ownership structure dominated by public ownership, in an effort to ensure the socialist direction in economic reform. Domination of public ownership refers not only to proportion, but that the lifeline of the national economy is controlled by public ownership.

d   Reform should penetrate into public ownership, particularly state ownership. Only in this way can we solve the problem that "everyone is an owner but no one is responsible". A small state-owned company could bear its own profit and loss by contracting, renting or selling to a collectivity or individual. Large and medium-sized state-owned companies are much more difficult to reform. They are small in number but share large proportions of national assets and production. We need to explore different forms of reform on them by separating ownership and operation right. The state-owned company should become an independent producer and operator, instead of a subsidiary of different levels of governments. Under the premises of public ownership, explorations on management responsibility system and stock system are beneficial.

A multi-layer system of decision-making should be established, including levels of national (including central and local administration), corporation and individual. Since the socialist economy is a huge system based on socialized production, economic activities include multiple levels. Thus, the decision-making structure should also be a multi-layered one to enhance harmonious development of the national economy. An economist raised an idea that fundamental decisions should be made by the state, including aspects of growth speed of the national economy, national income allocation of saving and consumption, industrial structure transformation, scale, major direction of investment, significant investment project, necessary price control, proportions of public consumption and individual consumption, etc. Micro-economic decisions, including production, supply, sales, employment, revenue, materials, updating of equipment and use of its own fund, will be handled by corporations.[19] Another economic scholar believes that socialist government should control three types of production (army supply, basic food and infrastructure) and three types of price (basic food, salary and exchange rate). According to actual needs, the government may also control the proportions of investment and consumption, allocate more resources to underdeveloped regions and take charge of housing supply in urban area.[20] Economic professions both at home and abroad have explored the minimum control of government. Specific boundaries and controller target require more study, but there is no dispute that government should minimize its control. The biggest difficulty here lies in how to divide the decision-making power of investment. A scholar believes corporations should be responsible for for-profit investment (productive project), while for-service investment (infrastructure, national defense, scientific research, culture and education) should be taken care of by central and local governments. The profit and risk of investment should be tied together to establish a self-adjusting mechanism for corporations.[21] Another economist thinks that national investment should sufficiently influence future productivity.[22] These are all insightful ideas. As for the decentralization of individual economic activities in the target model, laborers should enjoy the freedom of consumption, as well as choosing profession and working sites by then, while labor is allowed to flow in only a "limited way" and in a "certain range" for the time being.[23]

There should be an indirect adjusting system between the micro- and macro-economy, or a market regulatory system with plan and macro control. In broad sense, economic regulation includes regulation of the micro-economy and that on the macroeconomy. If we take regulation of the macroeconomy into the scope of planned decisions, economic regulation, in this sense, only refers to that on micro-economic activities. With the premises that the macroeconomy is planned and controlled, the debates are centered on how to turn macroeconomic decisions into micro ones and how to ensure micro decisions meet the common goal of the entire economy. Different regulation systems are often fundamental indicators to distinguish economic patterns. Directive or guiding order, direct or indirect control are all consequences of the regulation system. In our target model of economic reform, an indirect regulatory system is between the micro-economy and macroeconomy. In principle, the country will no longer send directive orders to corporations, which no longer need to acquire production materials from the material department. The country guides corporation and adjusts resource flows by economic parameters like price, tax, interest rate, salary, etc. How well a corporation is run is no longer measured by fulfilling its target or plan, but by how much profit it gains. Corporation is not able to manipulate these parameters; it needs to adjust its activities to adapt.

After clarifying the interest boundaries of different economic entities, we need to establish an interest balancing system where interests of state (society), collectivity (corporation) and individual, long-term and short-term interests, interest restraint and interest incentive are taken into consideration.

Corporations with different operation levels should be allowed to differentiate in terms of income and distribution; differential income caused by objective causes (resources, fertility of soil, location, equipment) should be submitted to national revenue. Corporations should be responsible for both benefit and loss. Individual income should be linked to individual contribution, as influence equalitarianism should be avoided. To prevent huge income gaps, especially the income gap caused by non-labor income, higher tax rates should be applied to regulate. All laborers should be provided with a level playground to compete and work to avoid the income gap caused by unequal opportunities. In addition, we need to overcome the restraint on individual consumption and avoid inflated consumption via an interest-balancing mechanism in corporation and state plans on saving and consumption.

As required by socialized production, we need an interlaced economic organization system that separates corporation and administration. The fundamental task of economic reform is to change the position of corporation as subsidiary of the government, so that the corporation could break free from restraints of levels of authorities. Central and local governments should pledge their duties on managing the economy following the principle of separating corporation and administration. Firstly, industrial organizations should increase their influence after separating corporation and administration. Meanwhile, we should prevent new restraints from being formed between industrial organizations and cities. Secondly, corporations become professional and united to gradually optimize their organization structures. There could be various forms of cooperation and professionalization, as long as united corporation is an economic entity that bears its own profit and loss and has an independent accounting system. We need to protect positive competitions and prevent monopoly during this process.

We have discussed five parts of the framework separately; now we are going to look into their interrelations and a few comprehensive problems, for the purpose of cross-section study on target framework.

A. Two fundamental clues of reform from the perspective of interrelations

The five dimensions elaborated in the previous section are not separated from each other; they and their interrelations as a whole constitute an integrated economy, just like a human being consists of interrelated systems (skeletal system, nervous system, respiratory system, circulatory system, digestive system, etc.). The decision-making and regulatory systems involve the resource allocation in economy, and the interest system as the impetus (as decision-makers of all levels are driven by economic interests). Regulatory systems, directed by country or guided by market, are all driven by the force of interest. Economic organizations are the carrier of economic systems; any activity in the economy, just like any activity of a cell in one's body, is realized by the platform of economic organizations. In a word, a coordinate economic system requires intrinsic unity of these five dimensions; the decision-maker, driven by interest, makes certain decisions. The regulatory system adjusts the decision for coordination, which is then realized by economic organization.

These five elements form economic operation system from different aspects, while ownership makes up another important part of an economy. Many economic reform theorists in Eastern Europe focused their research on the operation system of the economy, while socialist ownership was taken for granted. From our reform practice, we also emphasized operation system as the reform started; very few scholars paid attention to the necessity of reforming ownerships.[24] As the reform deepens, however, we have come to the knowledge that reform on operation mechanisms is inevitably interlaced with the reform on ownership. Our economic reform, as found in practice, follows two essential clues of re-forging micro-foundation and transformation of operation mechanism. An economist said: "Economic system is consisted of two parts: economic operation mechanism and ownership. The substance of reform is the transition of operation system and re-shaping of micro ownership."[25] Another scholar wrote: "There are now two directions for our reform. The first is to change operation mechanism, the second to change the relations of laborer and production materials. The correct direction, however, is to combine both."[26]

In recent years, there has been an ongoing debate on key of reform. One side holds the idea that "ownership is the crucial part of economic reform",[27] while the other side believes "adapting unreasonable pricing system is the key to reform".[28] Price reform is the most comprehensive part of operation system reform; thus, the essence of this dispute is the relation of ownership reform and operation system reform. We think reforms on these two sections are interrelated and mutually encouraging. With twisted prices, a company can't bear its own profit and loss, even if the stock system is not enough to harden the budget constraint. In other words, if there is no ownership reform to make a company a self-run entity that bears its profit and loss, its budget constraint will remain soft. Even with reasonable economic parameters, reasonable price in particular, the company is not able to make correct and swift response to market signals, especially price signals. Only when the two clues are combined properly can we lay a solid micro foundation for indirect economic control and thus creating a healthy market for corporations.

B.　Two clues of decentralization: economic decentralization and administrative decentralization

Economic decentralization refers to releasing the corporation from the control of authorities. When independent from levels of government organizations, corporations become economic entities that bear their own loss and gain, or relatively independent producers and operators. When the importance of such devolution became aware to us, another question – the decentralization of administrative power (between central and local governments) was raised. Considering the fact that China is a developing socialist country, an economist came up with a model "combining highly centralized government and commodity economy".[29] Another scholar regards our reform target as "dual expansion", which is shrinking local government's power while expanding the power of the central government and corporation.[30] This is indeed a complex problem involving multiple aspects of decision-making, interest, regulation and organization.

It seems we need to define two kinds of administrative devolution herein: one refers to the control over the corporation being transferred from the central government to local government, another refers to the situation that when the corporation become relatively independent, power on economic management is partly passed down from central government to local government. In conclusion, in the first type, administrative decentralization excludes economic decentralization, while the second embraces both. In our exploration of the target model of reform, other than pointing out disadvantages and infeasibility of the first kind of decentralization, we need more studies on the second type, especially when we are looking for a target model for ongoing economic reform.

As a country with vast territories, with the premise that corporation and government are separated, it is a significant topic for us to give full play to local governments (provincial and municipality mostly) in terms of economic management. This is where our economic reform differs from those in Eastern European countries. As addressed by Reynolds: "Which decisions should be made by central government and which by local government? This is a question always there for a huge country. And it becomes more important as the economic activities get more important."[31]

Under special circumstances, it is possible for a local government to have too much power in decision-making and too large a share in interest. Adjustment for such a case is entirely necessary. Simply taking "dual expansion" as a target is impropriate, as it makes no distinction between economic and administrative decentralizations and oversimplifies the functions of national economy. "Dual expansion" is not an ideal solution for large countries like China. In fact, the economic function of local government should be a component of the country's economic function, as well as an extension of the central government's economic power. Local government should connect central administration and corporation in terms of making local plans, applying economic regulation, enforcing management on industries, reinforcing infrastructure and supervising economic activities.

Attaching importance to local government does not equate to bragging about it. If local government is able to play the roles of decision-maker, interest entity and regulator, we believe it will have greater influence in decision-making and interest than regulation. While applying various measures on the economy, local government should be aware that these measures could neither hinder the development of a united market nor form a local economic blockade. Some countries realized rapid economic growth by combining highly centralized government control and market regulation; they provide experience for our reform and development, but we cannot simply copy the formula, because there were cases where powerful local government achieved a high growth rate.[32] It is more clear to address in this way: we need to combine economic decentralization and administrative decentralization (the second type), instead of the combination of economic decentralization and administrative centralization.

C.   Integrated combination of plan and market under indirect control

Direct control is an important characteristic of the planned economic system, while indirect control is an indicator of the new economic system. In other words, the change from direct control to indirect control marks the successful transformation of the economic system. To further explore how to combine plan and market regulation, we are going to analyze differences of direct and indirect controls from several aspects.

Major differences of two types of control are summarized into six points as follows:

1 The premise of direct control is administration and corporation being unseparated, while indirect control is based on the separation of administration and corporation.
2 Direct control is applied to a highly centralized decision-making structure, while indirect control is based on the complex decision-making structure of different levels.
3 Direct control is a measure to realize directive order, while indirect control is a form to realize guiding plans.
4 Direct control works on material first, while currency is passive in this process; indirect control usually works currency first, which then influences material.
5 Direct control takes form of administrative order, while indirect control uses economic parameters.
6 Direct control denies or ignore the interest of the controller target, while indirect control admits independent interest of controller target and takes it as impetus.[33]

From these differences, we can find when direct control is replaced by indirect control, not only has the controlling system been transformed, but the economic system as a whole has been transformed.

In our target model where indirect control is dominant, what is the relationship between plan and market? Is it simply combining different proportions of directive order, guiding plan and market regulation?

When discussing the relationship of plan and market before, people tended to argue about different combinations of directive order, guiding plan and market regulation, as if the design of the target model is confined to stitching three parts in different ways. An economist thinks, to keep the socialist nature in our economy, we need to ensure that directive production makes a larger proportion, or at least ensure that production under directive order and guiding plan makes a larger proportion.[34] Admittedly, our economy has been going on with three types of regulations, but this thought is oversimplified for the target model. National economy is a complex system; the relationship of plan and market is set in a three-dimension space even if we do not consider dynamic factors. Directive order may exist in the target model, but it no longer plays as an indispensable part of the economy. Guiding plans, together with market regulation, will become two hands in the economy. With a strategy of state guides market and market regulates corporations, a stereo regulation system will be built up in the target model. On the basis of this idea, we agree that "in the long run, directive orders could be cancelled completely, replaced by guiding plan, which is the only form of economic plan in our country".[35]

> Guiding plans are not compulsory. The state translates policies into economic signals, and takes these signals as lever to regulate corporation's activity to meet the requirement of national plans. In essence, this system is an integrated combination of market and plan regulation.[36]

However, we should also be aware of the importance of economic plans, which are a major accordance of management on macro economy. Plan still plays a significant part in setting social and economic development strategies in various aspects, including direction of economic development, economic growth rate, industrial structure, allocation of productive forces, territorial development, environment protection, education, etc. In addition, national plans balance the macroeconomy and its major structures via the distribution of national income. Specifically, the plans decide the proportions of saving and consumption, of social and individual consumption, and strike a balance between major production sections. In the meantime, national plans remain crucial in the scale and direction of investment, as well as in key projects. In summary, the transformation from direct to indirect control does not equate to giving up general plans and management on the national economy. The transformation is aimed at removing direct control over micro-economic activities.

D. From a seller's market to a limited buyer's market

Recent years have witnessed quite a lot debates on the seller's and buyer's markets, or on the relationship of total social demand and total social supply. Most of the debates have centered on the ideal environment for reform, which is also an important topic for the target model of reform.

It is quite clear that when the reform can be accomplished in one action, a buyer's market in which supply slightly exceeds demand should be both the goal and the environment of reform. However, our reform will be pushed forward in several phases, which means the equilibrium of market keeps changing as the reform proceeds. Those changes, if denied, will obscure boundary of our target and the actual conditions we are in.[37]

No matter how differently we think on the environment of system reform, we should be clear that target market equilibrium (a limited buyer's market) is not simply an environment of economy. It is a necessary and integrated component of the new economic system. Thus, without a condition that total demand and supply are in balance, the market will not be able to play normally, and our target model will be in vain. Bruse believes decentralized decision-making of a corporation's production, supply and sales is incompatible to an intensified economy that fails to reach equilibrium. When an obvious seller's market occurs, it is almost impossible to take market regulation as a measure of economic plan. Administrative approach and material allocation are therefore needed.[38]

The condition that demand grows faster than production and supply exceeds demand should not be taken as a constant phenomenon of the socialist economy, or even taken as an advantage of the socialist economic system. On the contrary, shortage economy and a seller's market are results of the traditional socialist economic system (including traditional development strategy) in a certain phase, instead of nature or accompanying of a socialist economy. If a socialist fails to tackle shortage or even denies the necessity to solve it, why would we spend so much effort on economic reform in the first place?

It takes a process to transit form seller market to buyer market, during which reform and the forming of the buyer market promote each other. Taking buyer market as the premise of reform is not appropriate enough; neither is taking the formation of buyer market as a natural result of reform. From our experience, it is not impossible to have a buyer market for certain products during certain phases of the reform.[39] By increasing supply or cutting demand, the severe shortage of supply can be eased to a certain degree. It is hard to imagine the entire reform will be enforced in a shortage and seller market all the way through, while the buyer market appears overnight when reform is accomplished.

When the market reaches equilibrium, we pursue a condition that supply slightly exceeds demand. This is our exploration for a new economic system to give play to the superiority of the socialist economic system. Such a market condition increases the competition among producers (sellers) and encourages producers to improve their technologies and optimize their service, as they never worried about sales in the traditional economic system (a seller market), just like "the daughter of an emperor does not worry about finding a husband". By saying that supply should exceed demand slightly, we are emphasizing that there should be a limit to the buyer market, which is how our system differs from a capitalist economic system. When the total supply continues to increase, problems like overproduction and underutilization of equipment may occur, decreasing efficiency in resource application and reproduction. Therefore, equilibrium in our target model is neither disequilibrium in the planned socialist economy ("resource-restrained system") nor disequilibrium in the capitalist economy ("demand-restrained system").[40]

IV. Conclusion of the target model and further explorations

The target model of China's economic reform is such a difficult research topic. Designs of framework and direction of the target model mentioned in this essay are achievements in a stage; more efforts are needed on unsolved problems and doubts. In this section, a few questions, together with their brief commentary, will be raised as the conclusion of this essay and an introduction for more problems.

A. Scope and boundary of reform

We are researching the reform of the socialist economic system, regardless of the reform needed in society and culture; we still need to study how to enforce the reform while following a socialist direction. In other words, we need to explore the scope and limit of our reform. Firstly, the boundary is always insisting public ownership as the majority. We need to prevent the situation that private ownership or privatization of property becomes dominant in our society. In the traditional socialist economy, public ownership failed to give full play to the superiority of the socialist economic system. However, our practice has indicated exploration of economic system does not need the domination of private ownership. Since the Ranger model appeared in the 1930s, socialists have been working on how to combine public ownership and market mechanism. Undoubtedly, we will continue explorations in this aspect. Complete public ownership oversimplifies the situation; so is the idea that only the domination of private ownership activates market regulation and laborer. On the basis of public ownership, it has been proved that public-owned enterprises can be set in and regulated by the market, when ownership and operating right are separated.

Secondly, our reform is designed to change the exclusion of the market in the traditional economic pattern, but the reform should not move towards a market without restrictions even from the perspective of economic efficiency. In reality, "market failure" is an objective fact even in a capitalist economy. The market is not always reliable in general and long-term investment, as well as in external cost-effective analysis. From the two clues of reform, we can draw a conclusion: the goal of ownership reform is not completely privatization, and the regulation system should not be based on the market completely. The boundary of the reform should be a moderate combination of plan and market under the premises that public ownership is dominating in our economy.

B. Certainties and uncertainties of the reform target

The merits of studying target model of reform were discussed at the beginning of this essay, pointing out it is wrong to think the reform cannot and need not be designed. Some foreign economists, however, believe China's decision on reform provides too rough a sketch. Despite various target models being put forward, the future economic system remains uncertain. Therefore, China's economic reform is an "open-ended reform".[41] This has raised for us a topic of certainty and uncertainty of reform target, as well as their interrelations. We believe the reform consists of certainties and uncertainties. Its certainties lie in the general direction, framework, range and boundaries. The reform started without abundant theoretical support and practice; thus hypothesis about it may prove wrong in later practice. Therefore, our reform target should not be a rigid one. Boundaries, plans and policies should be corrected, amended and supplemented as the reform goes on. From this perspective, there are quite some uncertainties in the plans and policies of reform. Only when we handle both certainties and uncertainties well can we make clear the direction of reform while leaving space for further exploration.

C. Measurement of completion degree of the target model

Professor Gao Hongye believed it was unrealistic to build a set of concrete targets for China's economic reform and that infusing vigor to the economy was a rather a loose concept. To define "infusing vigor into the economy", we need to choose a comprehensive index to represent the level of labor productivity, and use this index to measure how "vigorous" our economy is and how much we have achieved against the target model.[42] Gao designer a graph (see Figure 6.1) to illustrate this. The horizontal axis shows the degree of market regulation from 0% (completely regulated by government) to 100% (completely regulated by market). Points between 0% and 100% mean combination of government and market regulation to different ratio. The vertical axis shows the productivity level. Curve AC indicates that as the market regulation continues to grow, productivity level will keep rising and peak at point B, where centralized plans and market regulation play a half-and-half role. Productivity level will start to decrease after point B. The turning point where productivity peaks is the ultimate goal for system reform (as shown in Figure 6.1). Thus, Professor Gao believed we could use productivity level to measure if we've achieved our target.

Using productivity to measure an economic system is correct to the essence, as the fundamental purpose of reform is looking for a more efficient economic pattern. Simply taking the variation of productivity as an index for the reform target is somewhat unrealistic. Many factors in and out of the economic system may affect productivity, which are usually closely related to each other. External factors may lead to confusion that we have achieved the target. Moreover, market and plan are not two separated modules. The proportion of market regulation, which is even more unclear than the proportion of centralized plan, is hard to define and quantify. In this train of thought, we believe Professor Gao's study is influential in theory but lacks practical value.

D.   Is our target model for reform naive?

Kornai believed targets raised by Eastern European reformers, which influenced the 1968 Reform Documents of Hungary and now Chinese reform documents,

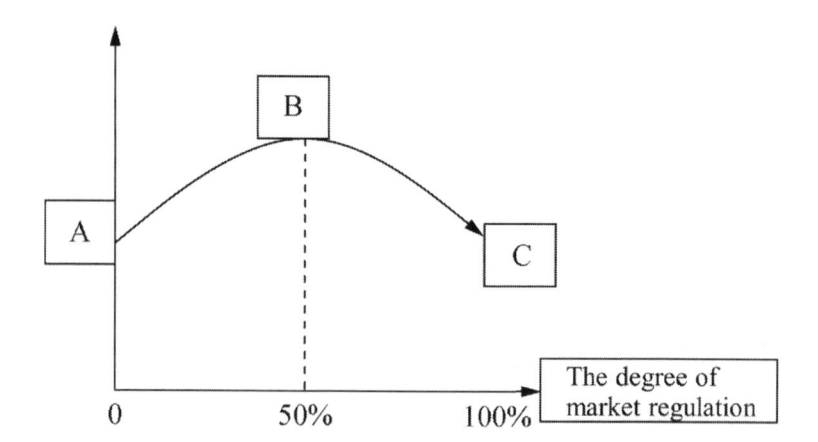

Figure 6.1 The Relationship between the Productivity Level and the Degree of Market Regulation

were naive. He mainly had two arguments. Firstly, these targets failed to prospect complex situations, which have already hindered the reform from its set goal. Secondly, all these targets tried to strike a balance between plan and market (or administration and market) where they regulated each other, or the targets tried to divide the responsible range for administration or market. These were impossible in reality.[43]

It is fair to say our target model is immature. But we cannot deny a reasonable framework simply because of complexities ahead. Even Kornai admitted it was natural for a model to leave out irrelevant, complex details in reality. It was easy to criticize a model according to reality, but also unfair. Unfortunately, Kornai failed to hold on to this idea throughout his studies. In his point of view, targets of enterprise autonomy, correct price signal, interest stimulus, use of market and transition to a buyer's market became rather naive when faced with complexities and obstacles as the reform proceeded. None of the socialist countries has realized its set targets by far, and all of them have been hindered with various difficulties and obstacles. But this should not be a reason to deny the necessity of reform target. Kornai criticized the theory that simple reproduction should be regulated by market and extended reproduction should be regulated by plan; we consider his criticism reasonable to a certain degree. Regarding any efforts in an attempt to combine plan and market regulation as an act of naiveté is rather unfair and biased.

The reason why we have raised the questions in this essay is to arouse wider thought and further explorations as well as address our attitude: confronted with such a difficult problem of economic reform, no one reserves the ultimate right to verity. As economic theorists devoted to socialism, we are entitled to everlasting explorations and improvements.

(Composed from late 1986 to early 1987, this essay was firstly published as the first chapter of *Studies on the Model of China's Economic Reform*, China Social Sciences Press, 1988. A few changes were made when the book was published. The essay was the original version when included in this collection.)

Notes

1 The process of experimenting with various methods of doing something until one finds the most successful. *Oxford Advanced Learner's Dictionary* (1980).
2 Wu Jinglian. (1987). 关于改革战略选择的若干思考 [Thoughts on Strategic Choices of Reform]. *Economic Research Journal*, 2.
3 Sun Xiaoliang. (Saturday, January 3, 1987). 论经济改革面临的抉择 [Choices Confronted by Economic Reform]. *Guangming Daily*.
4 Editorial Department of Economic Research Journal (Ed.). (1985). 建国以来社会主义经济理论问题争鸣 [Discussions and Debates on Socialist Economic Theories Since the Founding of People's Republic of China] (p. 488). Beijing: China Financial & Economic Publishing House.
5 Bruse (1984) held that the term "model" showed the operation pattern of economy, which set aside complex details and outlined abstract, main principles of economy. (Virlyn W. Bruse. (1984). 社会主义经济的运行问题 [Operation Problems of Socialist Economies] (p. 2). Beijing: China Social Sciences Press) Morris Bernstein (1986) believed economic pattern was the abstraction of system, which indicated main

characteristics in the structure and operation process of different economies. 比较经济
制度综述 [General Introduction to Comparative Economics]. In *Collection of Modern
Foreign Economic Papers* (Vol. 9, p. 42). Beijing: The Commercial Press.

6 A report of the World Bank (1997) pointed out that the fundamental problem China
confronted in economic reform was the deploying of labor and restriction on population immigration. Policy as such carried important political and social reasons, and any
change submitted to a step-by-step process. However, either on the account of economic
efficiency or justice, this policy seemed hardly reasonable. (See the World Bank's investigation report on Chinese Economy, *World Development Report: Government in a
Changing World*).

7 John C. H. Fei & Bruce Reynolds. (1986). 中国经济体制改革合理顺序的探讨 [Dis-
cussion on Reasonable Sequences of China's Economic Reform]. *Comparative Economic & Social Systems*, 6.

8 Among all economists that supported economic reform, Sun Yefang developed the most
systematic criticizing theories on natural economy while taking natural economic theories as a basis to criticize traditional economy. He emphasized in a series of works that
overcoming the influence of natural economy is necessary for economic reform. (Sun
Yefang. (1984). 孙冶方选集 [Selected Works of Sun Zhifang] (pp. 237, 252–253).
Taiyuan: Shanxi People's Publishing House). In recent years, we have further widened
our horizon on reform, as we began to relate economic reform to revolution in traditional cultures and values. An economist thought China has been deeply influenced
by kinship and monarch-subject relation for several thousand years: "Despite the fact
that large-scale commodity exchange and regional market occurred in Chinese history,
China lacked social regulations that related to commodity economy. As a result, the
commodity economy failed to come into final formation." (伟大的实践需要伟大的理
论–社会主义初级阶段学说 [Great Practice Requires Great Theories: The Theory of
Primary stage of socialism]).

9 John C. H. Fei & Bruce Reynolds. (1986). 中国经济体制改革合理顺序的探讨 [Dis-
cussion on Reasonable Sequences of China's Economic Reform]. *Comparative Economic & Social Systems*, 6.

10 Egon Neuberger & William J. Duffy. (1984). 比较经济体制 [Comparative Economic
Systems] (pp. 17–18). Beijing: The Commercial Press.

11 Assar Lindbeck. (1981). 新右派政治经济学 [The Political Economy of the New Left]
(pp. 130–132). Beijing: The Commercial Press.

12 Virlyn W. Bruse. (1983). 社会主义经济的各种体制 – 历史的经验和理论的构想
[Socialist Economic Systems: Experience and Models]. In *Selected Works on Socialist
Economic Patterns* (pp. 69–70). Beijing: People's Publishing House.

13 Research Group on Comparative Economic System. (1984). Institute of Economics, Chinese Academy of Social Sciences. 关于我国经济体制改革的目标模式问
题 [Issues of Target Model of China's Economic System Reform]. *Social Sciences in
China*, 5.

14 Hua Sheng. (1986). 经济运行模式的转换 [Transformation of Economic Pattern]. *Economic Research Journal*, 2.

15 Shigeru Ishikawa. (1986). 社会主义经济和中国的经验–对经济改革的展望 [Social-
ist Economy and China's Experience: Outlook to Economic Reform]. *Science & Technology Review*, 2. He wrote in this essay that custom economy bound everyone to
economic activities they were used to. Rule as such aimed at the welfare for every social
member; it regulated everyone's rights and duties. The allocation of resource was the
result of it. The term custom economy was first used by John Hicks. It took a typical
form of village community in rural areas. It also occurred in urban areas, especially
in commercial organizations and the labor market where individual relationship and
lifetime employment were popular.

16 Liu Guoguang et al. (1985). 经济体制改革与宏观经济管理 – "宏观经济管理国际
讨论会"评述 [Economic Reform and Macro Economy Management: Comments on
Macro Economy Management Conference]. *Economic Research Journal*, 12.

17 Li Chengrui. (1986). 关于宏观经济管理的若干问题 [Questions on the Management of Macro Economy]. *Finance & Trade Economics*, 11.

18 Li Youpeng. (1985). 关于宏观经济管理的若干问题 [Discussion on Establishing Planning Management System with Chinese Characteristics]. In *Thoughts on Economic Take-Off* (p. 135). Shenyang: Liaoning People's Publishing House.

19 First raised by Research Group on Comparative Economic System, Institute of Economics, Chinese Academy of Social Science. (1984). 关于我国经济体制改革的目标模式问题 [Issues of Target Model of China's Economic System Reform]. *Social Sciences in China*, 5.

20 Lloyd Reynolds. (1986). 比较经济制度 [Comparative Economic System]. In *Collection Modern Foreign Economic Papers* (Vol. 9, p. 24). Beijing: The Commercial Press.

21 See Interview of Lin Senmu (Tuesday February 24, 1987). *Economic Daily*.

22 Virlyn W. Bruse. (1985). 共产主义经济制度的演变 – 范围和限度 [Change of Socialist Economy: Range and Scope]. *From an International Conference at University of California*.

23 Lanrui R. Feng, & Gu Z. Liuzhen. (Friday, January 2, 1987). 劳动力流动及其调节机制 [Labor Flow and Its Regulatory Mechanism]. *People's Daily*.

24 Dong Fureng. (1979). 关于我国社会主义所有制形式的问题 [Problems about the Form of Chinese Socialism Ownership]. *Economic Research Journal*, 1.

25 Bian Yongzhuang. (Monday, February 9, 1987). 经济体绘改革的两条主线 [Two Principal Lines of Economic System Reform]. *Beijing Daily*.

26 Sun Xiaoliang. (Saturday, January 3, 1987). 论经济改革面临的抉择 [Choices Confronted by Economic Reform]. *Guangming Daily*.

27 Li Yining. (Monday, June 9, 1986). 关于经济体制改革的基本思路 [Basic Ideas of Economic System Reform]. *World Economic Herald*.

28 Xue Muqiao. (Thursday, March 5, 1987). 建设有中国特色的社会主义的必由之路 [A Destined Road to Building a Socialism with Chinese Characteristics]. *Economic Daily*.

29 Wu Jinglian. (1987). 关于改革战略选择的若干思考 [Thoughts on Strategic Choices of Reform]. *Economic Research Journal*, 2.

30 Zhao Renwei. (1987). *作为改革的方向和目标应是经济性分权和行政性分权的结合* [Reform Target Should Be a Combination of Economic and Administrative Decentralization]. *Economic Research Journal*, 4.

31 Lloyd Reynolds. (1986). 比较经济制度 [Comparative Economic System]. In *Collection of Modern Foreign Economic Papers* (Vol. 9, p. 25). Beijing: The Commercial Press.

32 Yang Peixin. (Monday, January 5, 1987). 论我国投资体制改革方向 – 从联邦德国的联邦、州、地方分权的投资体制说起 [A Study of Chinese Investment System and Reform Orientation: Speaking from Federal Germany's Investment System Separated by Federations, States and Local Government]. *World Economic Herald*.

33 Shen Liren. (1986). 经济体制改革的新课题 [New Subjects on Economic System Reform]. *Economic Research Information*, 4. (in different summaries).

34 计划经济与市场调节文集 [Collections of Planned Economy and Market Regulation] (Vol. 1). (1983). Beijing: Hongqi Publishing Press; 建国以来社会主义经济理论问题争鸣 [Discussion of Socialist Economic Theories since the Founding of PRC] (pp. 484–485). (1985). China Financial & Economic Publishing House.

35 Li Yining. (Monday, June 9, 1986). 关于经济体制改革的基本思路 [Basic Ideas of Economic System Reform]. *World Economic Herald*.

36 Li Youpeng. (1985). 试论建立具有中国特色的计划管理体制 [Discussion on Establishing Planning Management System with Chinese Characteristics]. In *Thoughts on Economic Take-Off* (p. 137). Shenyang: Liaoning People's Publishing House.

37 Liu Guoguang & Zhao Renwei. (1985). 当前中国经济体制改革遇到的几个难题 [Current Difficulties Confronted by the Economic Reform of China]. *Economics Digest*, 1. Also see *Economics Weekly* (Sunday, September 22, 1985).

38 Virlyn W. Bruse. (1981). *社会主义的政治与经济* [Politics and Economy of Socialism] (p. 16). Beijing: China Social Sciences Press.

39 Xue, M. Q. said: "Buyer's market occurred for many products in 1983, which created good conditions for price adjustment." See Xue Muqiao. (Thursday, March 5, 1987). 建设有中国特色的社会主义的必由之路 [A Destined Road to Building a Socialism with Chinese Characteristics]. *Economic Daily*. Liu Guoguang pointed out, buyer's market was not impossible. It occurred once at the beginning of the 6th Five-year-plan. See Liu Guoguang. (1986). 关于发展社会主义商品经济问题 [Questions on Developing Socialist Commodity Economy]. *Social Science in China*, 6.

40 János Kornai. (1986). 短缺经济学 [Economics of Shortage] (Vol. 1, p. 34). Beijing: Economic Science Press.

41 Lin Zhiren of Oxford University first raised this idea in an international conference. Cross referenced from Dong Fureng. 中国经济体制改革及其若干社会后果 [Economic Reform in China and Its Implications].

42 Gao Hongye. (1987). 关于建立我国体制改革的目标模式的困难和避免困难的方法 [Difficulties to Establish Target Model for China's Reform and Solutions]. In *Discussion on China's Macro Economy Management*. Beijing: China Economic Publishing House.

43 J. Kornai. (1986). 经济改革的设想和和现实的对照 [Comparison of Economic Reform Target and Reality]. *Comparative Economic & Social Systems*, 6. All references of Kornai in this section were quoted from this essay.

7 Dual systems during economic reform in China

I. Dual systems are produced during the system transformation in China

Economic system reform refers to the transformation of operational mode. Before China launches all-around economic system reform and leads to obvious dual systems, many economists in economic reform research field advise that the transformation of the economic system should carefully avoid creating dual systems, because every single economic system has its unique operational mechanism and internal logic and the mix of two different economic systems will surely cause conflicts and chaos.[1]

In accordance with the reform theory mentioned earlier, many economists, especially those in Eastern Europe, think that economic reform should take a package plan so that the reform can work in relevant fields. They hold this view for the following reasons: (1) A piecemeal reform is hard to rebuild original organizations and completely transform original management principles and methods. Once the new system faces some problems, the old one will soon replace it again. (2) A piecemeal reform is hard to fully carry out new operational principles. Those enterprises adopting the new system will have more autonomous right with no constraint from mandatory plans. But when these enterprises need to purchase materials from other enterprises, the latter might reject their demands because they get no command from the government. In this case, it is impossible to establish a new production-supply-marketing relationship and implement new operational principles.[2] In their view, a progressive reform will lead to dual systems, just like the dual traffic rule in which some drivers should drive left while others should drive right, which will surely cause chaos.

During the economic reform practice, there have been no successful precedents of realizing the transformation from an old system to a new system through dual systems. Though during the reform of some socialist countries in the 1960s, there was a short period when two systems existed, they were soon centralized; namely, the mandatory plans were restored and the dual systems were replaced due to all kinds of conflicts and contradictions.[3]

Though China's economic reform in its early stage has encountered the theories and experience mentioned earlier, seven years of reform practice has proven that

China has failed to avoid the appearance of dual systems. In particular, after the implementation of comprehensive economic system reform centering on urban reform, China has obviously embarked on dual systems. The situation is far more complex than what the economists in Eastern Europe expected. The dual systems mentioned by economists in Eastern Europe originally mean that some enterprises adopt the new system while others adopt the old system. But the dual systems in China have penetrated into large and medium state-owned enterprises where some production-supply-marketing activities are conducted according to the new system while the rest are conducted according to the old system.

Since the implementation of The Interim Provisions to Further Expand the Autonomy of State-Owned Industrial Enterprises (Clause 10) in May 1984 and The Central Committee of the Communist Party of China about the Decision of the Economic System Reform in October 1984, the coexistence of dual systems is further clarified and legitimized. Those enterprises that used to follow mandatory plans now have divided their production into two parts, namely, production within the plan and out of the plan ("plan" here specifically means mandatory plans). They also have two sources of materials supply, that is, unified distribution from the state and free procurement. In such cases, the products within the plan will be priced according to the state's regulations, while those out of the plan will be sold at relatively higher prices that can reflect the market law (floating price, negotiated price and free price).[4] In this situation, the dual planning system, dual material circulation system and dual price system are correlated as a trinity. The dual planning system (determines the output) is the foundation of the dual economic system, the dual material circulation system (determines the input) is the guarantee for the dual planning system and the dual price system is the concentrated expression of the whole dual economic system, also the focus of conflict and contradiction for the dual systems. Under dual systems, the behaviors of enterprises and the state's macro regulation will also be dual. With certain autonomous rights, enterprises are still restrained by administrative commands. They have to follow both the market law and administrative decisions. In the meantime, the state controls enterprises by combining direct administrative approaches and indirect parameter methods.

At present, during the production and circulation of some important products, there is no precise statistical data for respective percentage of the dual systems. Besides, the mandatory plans of central government will vary after they are given to provincial and municipal governments. So the percentage of dual systems may not be the same for central government, local government and enterprises. According to the materials provided by the national materials conference convened in early 1986, the categories of materials distributed by the State Development Planning Commission and State Commodities Bureau have reduced from the previous 256 to 23 in 1985. The percentage of coal, steel, wood and cement distributed by the state have been respectively reduced to 50%, 56.9%, 30.7% and 19.4% of total output. In 1985, the steel, wood and cement that local enterprises acquired from the market respectively took up 38%, 46% and 61% of total consumption.[5]

China's dual systems exist not only in the production and circulation of industrial products, but also in that of agricultural products. Since 1953, China has been adopting the policy of unified purchasing according to state fixed price of important agricultural products such as cereal, cotton and oil. In 1979, after the state increased the purchasing price for agricultural products, the dual systems began to take shape. That is, the agricultural products within unified purchase quota will still be purchased according to the unified purchasing price, while those exceeding the quota will be purchased according to the above-quota purchasing price (50% higher than the unified purchasing price) and the negotiated price. Taking cereal as an example, the state purchased about 40 million tons of cereal at the unified purchasing price in 1984, about 40 million tons at the above-quota purchasing price and about 45 million tons at the negotiated price.

The reason for dual systems in China's economic reform is generally because China can take only progressive methods instead of a package approach to transform its economic system. Why are only progressive methods feasible? This paper will analyze this question from the following aspects:

1   In terms of the reform background in China, the productivity is relatively low, the division of labor and commodity relations are not developed enough, there exists a dual economic structure, the gap between urban and rural areas are still large, regional development is extremely imbalanced, there exist dual economic growth types (intension and extension), the culture is relatively underdeveloped, the management experience for talents is not enough, etc., all of which has made it difficult for China to transform all old systems into new ones at the same time.

2   In terms of reform starting point and goal, from the initial establishment of China's economic system in 1956 to the proposal for reform during the Third Plenary Session of the 11th Central Committee of the Chinese Communist Party in 1978, due to the erroneous "left" thinking of leadership, the supply system of military communism has been strengthened, which has resulted in the situation in which China's economic system was more centralized, materialized, isolated and egalitarian than that of Eastern European countries at the beginning of the reform. Yet the reform goal should not be compromised. Through years of exploration, China has clarified the goal of transforming the focus of economic system from direct control to indirect control, which means that it will take a longer time for the reform.

3   In terms of reform process, as nothing great comes into being all at once, the reform can only be carried out progressively. For example, it requires a progressive process to push the reform from rural areas to urban areas, from circulation field to production field, from few pilot enterprises and cities to more enterprises and cities or even the whole country, from coastal areas to inland areas.

4   In terms of reform prospect, it requires a process to transform the economic development mode, improve the development level, govern the economic environment (realize the balance between total supply and total demand), rationalize the economic structure, change the behaviors of economic subjects and transform state regulation and control functions.

II.   Advantages and disadvantages of dual systems

Dual systems can bring new vitality to economic activities by breaking the deadlock of the original system. Hence, compared to the original system, dual systems have its advantages, as specified in the following:

A.   *Adjust the economic interest relationship and reduce fluctuations and resistance during the reform step by step*

Economic system reform will surely involve adjustment of the economic interest relationship. Any major reform measures will definitely change the economic interest relationship between the state, groups and individuals, different enterprises and different communities. Too drastic changes may cause social instability and add resistance to the reform. The dual systems can buffer these changes. For example, the old system features relatively low prices for agricultural products, but it involves adjusting the economic interest relationship between the state, farmers and employees to increase the purchasing price for agricultural products. The price cannot be increased without considering employees' salary and the state's fiscal capacity. Therefore, since 1979, China had to take various measures, such as unified purchase, mark-up purchase (later, unified purchase and mark-up purchase were merged into purchase by order), purchase at negotiated price and multiple prices to break the original unified purchase situation while ensuring that the economic interest relationship does not vary too much. According to the experiments in some areas in recent years, it is impossible to even up the prices for purchase by order and negotiated prices because too high prices will put stress on the state and employees while too low prices will reduce the positivity of farmers. Only by maintaining dual price systems within a certain period can the government properly handle the economic interest relationship.

In addition, the dual systems play a similar role in the production and circulation of industrial products. As the original system cannot be eliminated all at once, the state retains some mandatory plans so as to maintain normal production and circulation of some products and keeps the original economic interest structure through planned price. Meanwhile, the state also includes the production and circulation of those products out of mandatory plan into the regulated market operation, and partially adjusts the economic interest relationship through prices that reflect the market law. For example, the state-adjusted unreasonable price structure in the original system, where prices of mineral products are relatively low but prices of processed industrial products are relatively high, have turned around some money-losing enterprises and partially adjusted unreasonable economic interest structure. The dual systems can effectively spread risks for the reform.

B.   *Increase production and supply and ease contradiction between supply and demand*

Those enterprises that used to produce and sell products completely according to mandatory plans now are given the right to produce and market products out of plan all by themselves, which have greatly improved their positivity in production. In this case, price has partially become a parameter capable of adjusting enterprises' production, supply and marketing activities or even investment activities. At the same time, enterprises can also positively answer to some price signals. Many enterprises make every endeavor to raise funds, innovate technologies and expand production capacity to add production and supply of products that used to be in short supply, which have effectively relieved the shortage problems. With eased contradiction between supply and demand, the prices for some products out of plan gradually decrease. The progressive adjustment of purchasing prices for agricultural products has effectively promoted agricultural production development, and enabled China to be self-sufficient in production of cereal and cotton, which once needed to be imported. The dual systems also partially changed the situation of "produce according to plans" in the old system, which makes for better circulation of commodities and strengthens the connection of supply and demand. Moreover, the materials supply departments are also transforming their distribution mode from unified distribution to operation and service type.

C. Save resources and improve managerial level of administrative staff

Under the old system, the production tasks for mandatory plans are based on the low-price materials provided by the state, so enterprises don't have enough internal motivation to save resources. While China's high consumption rate of raw materials and fuel results mainly from low industrial technology level, low cost also fosters waste to some extent. Under dual systems, in addition to unified distribution of materials by the state, enterprises can acquire more materials through two channels: (1) products sold by state-owned enterprises; and (2) products produced by township enterprises. As these products are purchased according to negotiated prices, enterprises have to carefully calculate and strictly control the cost by making efforts to save raw materials and energy or searching alternative products. It is a good opportunity for administrative staffs who are used to the traditional operational mechanism to gradually understand the market law and improve their managerial capacity.

However, it seems that people mostly discuss the disadvantages or negative effects of the dual systems. The coexistence of two systems will cause dual micro decision-making behaviors and macro control behaviors, which will bring a series of contradiction and conflicts for economy development.

Firstly, during the alternating process from old system to new system, there might be a vacuum state between two systems where the indirect control methods are not taken correspondingly after some direct control methods are eliminated, thus resulting in economic disorder or chaos. In the fourth quarter of 1984, the uncontrolled fiscal expenditure, credit expenditure and issuance of paper money, investment inflation and consumption inflation were largely caused by the disconnection of new and old systems.

Secondly, under the dual systems, the signal system, especially the price signal system, may lose order. Several prices for the same commodity will impair the function of currency as a universal equivalent, causing dual measure values and obeying the principle of price identity. This kind of disorder will bring a series of conflicts to economic activities. For example, the products within the plan have relatively lower prices while those out of the plan have relatively higher prices, resulting in more products out of the plan. As a result, enterprises' contract fulfillment rate will decrease, impairing the realization of mandatory plans. According to the statistics, compared with 1984, the contract fulfillment rate of 12 categories of products such as steel has decreased in 1985. Under dual systems, as production and marketing units, enterprises try to abate the mandatory plan indexes so as to spare more productivity in producing products out of the plan; as the purchaser and user of raw materials, enterprises try hard to get more indexes for materials through unified distribution. Therefore, under the dual systems, it is difficult to form a unified socialist market mechanism and competition mechanism so that enterprises can compete fairly with the same price conditions. Besides, the criteria to evaluate different enterprises' management will also be disordered, as will the standards for output value, sales volume and profit. Moreover, the difference between list price and market price also provides fertile grounds for speculative profiteers, causing many profits acquired by lawbreakers and adding unreasonable intermediate links.

Thirdly, the dual systems have pros and cons for the allocation and utilization of resources. While high prices for products out of the plan will stimulate the production of some products in short supply, making for a more reasonable industrial structure, it will also encourage some low-efficiency enterprises to produce these products with high costs, causing improper utilization of limited resources, which will in turn lead to an unreasonable industrial structure. In recent years, the rapid development of some township enterprises has played a supplementary role in social economic development, such as increasing production and expanding employment opportunities. But it also resulted in some problems. For example, some small enterprises contend for raw materials and energy with large enterprises, which has reduced social economic interest. The dual price systems also encouraged uneconomical long-distance transportation.

III.   Analysis of possible solutions

Regarding the problems mentioned earlier in this paper, economists have suggested an array of solutions. To sum up, there are mainly four kinds of solutions: (1) restore the old system and enforce centralization; (2) maintain the dual systems, or even take the dual systems as target mode with only some repair measures taken to reduce the conflicts; (3) rapidly transit to the system with indirect control as the focus and end the dual systems; and (4) treat the dual systems as a transition stage for the transformation from old system to new system, gradually transforming to new system completely. This paper will analyze these four possible solutions one by one.

In principle, it is not impossible to restore the old system, but it is dangerous to the road of retrogression. In terms of the difficulty for macro control, direct control under traditional system is the simplest way, indirect control under target system is much more difficult, and macro control under dual systems is the most difficult and complex. "The conflicts and problems caused by weakened direct control and incomplete market regulation will put us in a dilemma."[6] People hold different views towards the disorder and inflation in the fourth quarter of 1984 and the deflation policies taken in 1985. Some think that the main problem is too much inflation in 1984 while others think that the main problem is too much deflation in 1985. Regardless of these different views, it is an objective fact that it is dangerous to take the road back. Some people hold the view that

> the macro deflation policy at present mainly includes four aspects: in terms of investment scale, local and department leader responsibility system is implemented for index control; in terms of credit scale, the bank imposes uniformity in all cases for quota control; in terms of consumption fund, special management accounts for the wage fund are adopted for fund control; in terms of short-handed energy and raw materials, unified distribution is adopted for planned control. These four deflation measures can be summarized as old administrative management methods.

They also think that these measures serve to "stealthily regress"[7] "in [the] name of strengthening macro control". This paper will put aside whether these comments on the deflation measures taken since 1985 are comprehensive at the moment, but it is undeniable that it is possible and dangerous for the reform to regress. It can be seen that in some special situations (such as the disorder mentioned earlier), it is necessary to strengthen some administrative methods. But it is important to note that, first, the functions of direct control should be controlled within a limited range. It is not advisable to apply it casually or abuse it. Second, proper utilization of direct control can provide favorable conditions for the transformation into indirect control, but special attention should be paid to avoid restoring the old system.

Only a few people have ever clearly expressed and systematically proved the opinion of maintaining the dual systems, or even taking the dual systems as a target mode. With insufficient theoretical preparations, China's economic system reform gradually adopts the dual systems. In fact, the opinion of regarding the dual systems as the target mode was once popular in China. Around 1982, during the discussions on the relationship of plan and market, the prevailing opinion at that time treated the combination of mandatory plans, guiding plans and market regulation as the target of China's economic system reform, and most people held that the majority of total output value should follow mandatory plans. Though the term "dual systems" was not used at that time, the coexistence of mandatory plans and parameter plans (refer to guiding plans) was actually the same with dual systems. The author thinks that the opinion of treating the combination of plan and market as the reform target is basically treating dual systems as the reform target (more details will be explained later). In recent years, similar opinions can be seen in some economic literature. Some think that

> in the entire planned system, mandatory plans have been reduced, but they are still important as the foundation and core of the entire planned system. Just as

an old saying goes, the sliding weight of a steelyard, though small in volume, may hold down a thousand catties.

According to these people, "The old system has many deficiencies, but it is still socialist. Both the old and new systems are socialist, so why not keep them both."[8] However, others think that the dual price system for means of production will live or die with the regulation method combining plan and market. According to this view, as long as the regulation method combining plan and market exist, so will the dual systems. This view has obviously rigidified the transitional measures, which will actually impair the reform target. In the long run, it has disobeyed the internal logic of economic system. As a result, the conflicts between two systems will impair the reform process and cause long-standing maladies.

Considering possible disorder, regression and economic fluctuations that might be caused by dual systems, some people suggest rapid transition. To be specific, some people think that "dual systems have more disadvantages than advantages, so we should transit to new system rapidly."[9] "The most fundamental countermeasure is to cancel the macro and micro reform measures as soon as possible so as to establish [a] relatively complete commodity economy system. The history does not leave us much time. We must hold on and get out of trouble as soon as possible."[10] Some people think that "the fundamental source for economic fluctuations in recent years is the coexistence of dual systems." "The fundamental solution is to break the dual systems and keep new economic system in dominant position."[11] Let's just call these views rapid transition theory and the opinion in the following gradual transition theory. This paper will differ the balanced state of dual systems from the coexistence of dual systems. The former means that the old system and new system are at a stalemate. The latter means that during the transformation from old system to new system, one system occupies the dominant position while the other system is an important subordinate; that is, neither of the dual systems governs all. Based on this differentiation, the rapid transition theory mentioned earlier can be divided into two types: one aims to realize the new system where indirect control takes a dominant position by rapidly ending the dual systems; the other aims to make the new economic system play a leading role by breaking the deadlock between two systems but not ending the coexistence of dual systems all at once. The latter theory is actually similar to gradual transition theory. It is understandable that the former theory aims to get rid of the problems brought by dual systems, but it seems that it has underestimated the consequences.

Considering the complexity and difficulty of China's reform, some people think that though it is important to shorten the coexistence period of dual systems, it should be decided according to objective conditions instead of subjective expectations. When the conditions are insufficient for establishing comprehensive indirect control system, haste does not bring success and it will even cause worse situations than the dual systems. The author agrees with this view. As is known by all, China faces complex national conditions. The reform in Hungary, the country with much less complex conditions than China, hasn't reached the reform target since 1968. According to Kornai, though Hungary's reform has gotten out of the traditional direct control system (IA), it has not yet realized the macro control market regulation system (IIB) and it is still implementing the transitional system of indirect control (IB). The IB system in Hungary is different from China's dual systems. Hungary has cancelled mandatory plans since 1968, but due to many indirect administrative interventions, the state-owned enterprises rely heavily on both higher authorities and the market, especially on the former. In this respect, considering the dual behaviors of enterprises, the IB system can also be called as dual systems in a broad sense. This is not to manually extend the transition period, but realistically estimate the necessity for the transition period. Kornai said,

> I'm not sure whether there should be a transition from I A to II B before realizing II B for Hungary. History cannot be played back for experiment. If the old system has entered a stage where the I B system plays a dominant role, it should be pointed out that this is only a transitional stage. If the reformers have long-term perspective and strategic thinking, they will realize that the transitional stage mentioned above is necessary to realize long-term target of economic system reform.[12]

Hence, instead of being frustrated by the transitional stage, we should understand it with strategic thinking. People hold different views on how long the transitional stage will take. Some think that "the macro balance between total supply and total demand should firstly be solved in order to get through the transitional stage. Otherwise, the dual-track system in planned system, material circulation system and price system will be impossible to disappear." Moreover, "[a]s the macro balance problem mentioned above cannot be solved completely at once, it is difficult to shorten the period of transforming the dual systems into [a] single new system and dual price systems into single-track new price system. This transition may probably exist during the whole process of China's economic system reform."[13]

The author is not sure whether the dual systems will exist during the whole process of China's economic system reform. While it takes a long time to fundamentally end the dual systems, it is feasible to improve the stalemate of dual systems in shorter time.

IV. Macro management under dual systems

If the dual systems are going to exist for a long period, it is crucial to figure out how to conduct macroeconomic management in complicated conflicts and contradiction. This paper proposes the following measures.

A. Gradual decrease of direct control and gradual increase of indirect control should be dovetailed, namely, while loosening restrictions for micro-economic activities; the state should also take corresponding macro indirect control measures

To be specific, firstly, because the state weakens its direct control on enterprises does not mean leaving economic activities under the control of the "invisible hand", the management thinking and habit that either strictly restrain economic activities through administrative methods or let things drift and try to adopt indirect control through economic parameters such as price, interest, tax rate and salary. Secondly, the decrease of direct control depends on the capacity of indirect control instead of subjective feelings. In other words, the decrease of direct control should be based on the formation of corresponding indirect control methods. In the future, while designing major steps for the reform, the government should take cautious measures to properly handle the relationship between old and new systems. Some scholars have analyzed the relationship between the economic fluctuation since the fourth quarter of 1984 and dual systems, which were quite inspiring.[14] But the author thinks that before analyzing the relationship between dual systems and economic fluctuations, it is necessary to specifically differ those fluctuations that are hard to avoid from those caused by disconnection of two systems during the transformation process (and the deflation measure taken in this case). In this way, the dual systems' advantages and disadvantages can be analyzed appropriately, which can effectively mitigate or even avoid economic fluctuations caused by disconnection of two systems during the transformation process. In other words, if the state can better handle the dual systems, especially the alternation process, the economic fluctuations like those that have happened in the most recent two years can be possibly avoided.

B. *While the operational mechanism of original system cannot be completely eliminated at once, the state should continue to use administrative commands to maintain the effectiveness and seriousness of original operational mechanism*[15]

That is, regarding the penetration and conflicts between two systems, corresponding measures should be taken to mitigate possible conflicts. For example, for the production and marketing of products produced according to mandatory plans and low prices, the state should supply relatively low-price materials, adhere to the principle of "buying low and selling low; buying high and selling high" and avoid the materials within the plan being used in production out of the plan. Legal means should be taken to ensure that enterprises perform supply contracts based on mandatory plans and punish those who fail to supply goods according to mandatory plans. It is explicitly stipulated in the 7th Five-Year Plan for National Economic and Social Development of the People's Republic of China (1986–1990),

> strengthen management of means of production directly owned by the state. For those enterprises who refuse to supply products according to the state's planned allocation or fail to deliver products according to the state's order, administrative accountability should be traced and those enterprises' self-marketing right should be cancelled.[16]

These measures are taken to enable enterprises to create a relatively fair competition environment in an environment lacking fair competition. Some people query these measures by pointing out that they will cause the materials within the plan to be used in production out of the plan and encourage speculation and profiteering. It is impossible to completely separate the old and new systems, but the measures mentioned here can effectively avoid the problem that the materials within the plan are used in production out of the plan.

Based on these two measures, the paper designs the following five diagrams in simplified form (see Figure 7.1). The circle represents central control or management authorities, the square represents enterprises, the solid line represents the direct administrative control method, and the dotted line represents indirect parameter control methods. The square representing enterprises is divided into two parts, indicating dual enterprise behaviors under the dual systems. In order to focus on analyzing the relationship between the state and enterprise, the diagrams have left out the relationship among different enterprises.

The first diagram shows direct administrative control under the traditional system; the fifth diagram shows indirect parameter control under the target system; the third diagram shows mixed control under dual systems; the fourth diagram shows that indirect control methods are overused because necessary administrative control is abandoned or the objective conditions for indirect control are not mature enough after the appearance of dual systems, resulting in disordered macro control. The paper will hereafter refer to it as forward deviation; the second diagram shows overused direct administrative control methods under dual systems. The paper will hereafter refer to it as backward deviation. As the lines in the second diagram and fourth diagram are simplified, they can only indicate the trend or tendency of

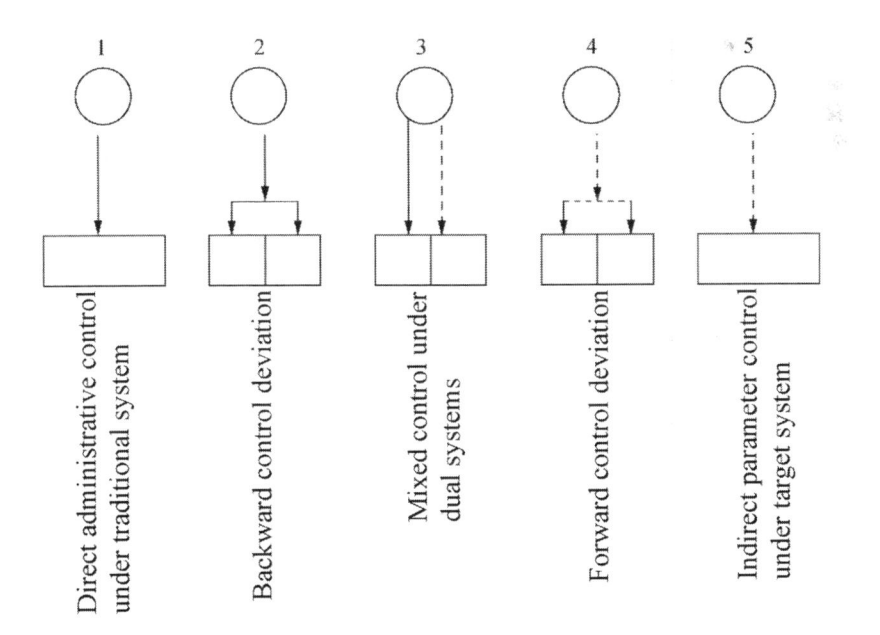

Figure 7.1 Relations between Country and Enterprises

deviation. In this way, the fourth diagram has reflected the tendency of disordered macro control in the fourth quarter of 1984 to some extent; the second diagram has reflected the tendency of strengthening direct administrative control through deflation measures in 1985 to some extent. These two deviation tendencies are the price we have to pay in learning how to realize reform targets through the dual systems. The third diagram shows a good state of "maintaining order in chaos (natural chaos in dual systems)". The diagrams are still, but the reform process is dynamic. Therefore, the mixed control and transformation of dual systems should be understood from dynamic perspectives.

C.   *While the dual systems cannot be fundamentally changed, the state should take some measures to mitigate the conflicts*

Taking Shijiazhuang as an example, it implemented unified prices for some important production materials. Since 1985, Shijiazhuang has initiated market prices for steel and wood regardless of the fact whether they are within or out of the plan and enterprises can directly buy steel and wood in the market. As for the money that enterprises paid for steel and wood supplied to all units according to mandatory plans, the material supply department should refund the amount overpaid. This approach has effectively expanded enterprises' autonomous right to choose their preferred raw materials, reduced intermediate links during material circulation, reduced demands for building warehouses and saved costs. Besides, it also helped material enterprises transform from an administrative management type to an operation and service type, which can effectively reduce those problems such as exploiting relations, corruption, speculation and profiteering. Meanwhile, while implementing this approach, the state also had to solve many problems such as price difference, timely refund and capital occupying.[17] In addition, this approach was designed only to solve the problem of several prices for the same commodity in the market; it cannot fundamentally solve the supply problem of means of production according to mandatory plans. Yet it has played a positive role in mitigating the conflicts of dual systems, proving to be an effective experiment. With further development of the reform, the author believes that more effective approaches will be created.

D.   *Promote the wane and wax of old and new systems through combination of delegating power and strengthening regulation*

The transition from direct control system to indirect control system is realized through the wane of the old system and wax of the new system. To be specific, it is realized through two correlated processes of gradually reducing the proportion of some products within the plan in production and circulation and expanding the proportion of some products out of the plan ("delegating power") and gradually increasing planned price in order to narrow the gap between planned price and market price ("strengthening regulation"). The approach of combining delegating power and strengthening regulation has achieved some successful results during the procurement of agricultural products, especially cereal products.

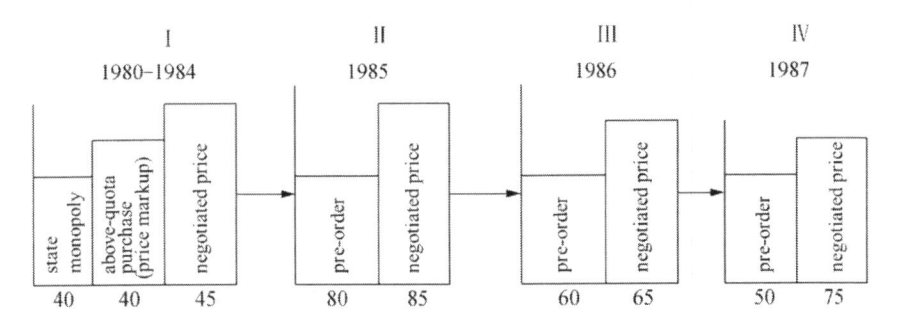

Figure 7.2 The Evolution of Dual Systems in the Procurement of Cereal Products since
    1980

Figure 7.2 shows an analysis of the evolution of dual systems in the procurement of cereal products since 1980. The horizontal axis represents the procurement
volume of cereal, and the vertical axis represents price level. In order to focus on
the influence of delegating power and strengthening regulation, the paper assumes
that the procurement of cereal and money issued to purchase cereal (supply and
demand) are fixed, the numbers under the horizontal axis are calculated based
on approximate procurement volume of cereal in 1984 (unit: million tons). From
1980 to 1984 (as is shown in part I of Figure 7.2), the procurement of cereal was
divided into three parts, including unified purchase, above-quota purchase (50%
markup) and purchase by negotiated price. In 1985 (as is shown in part II), unified purchase was cancelled and unified purchase and above-quota purchase were
merged into purchase by order. The price for purchase by order was made up of
30% of the original unified purchase price and 70% of the original above-quota
purchase price. This year, the proportion of purchase by negotiated price stayed
the same. However, compared to the difference between unified purchase price and
negotiated price, the difference between price for purchase by order and negotiated
price has been narrowed. In 1986 (as is shown in part III), the price for purchase
by order was the same, but the proportion has decreased, and the proportion of
purchase by negotiated price has increased correspondingly. Without considering
other factors, corresponding to decreased negotiated price, the difference between
price for purchase by order and negotiated price will also decrease. It was estimated that in 1987 (as is shown in part IV), the proportion of purchase by order
will decrease, and the purchase by negotiated price will further expand. Without
considering other factors, the difference between the prices will also be narrowed.

From the outlined evolution of dual systems, it can be concluded that: with cancellation of unified purchase, increase of purchase by order (compared to unified
purchase price) and decreased proportion of purchase by order, the administrative
plans will also decrease, while market factors gradually increase with the expansion of proportion of purchase by negotiated price. And the difference between
these prices tends to narrow. Obviously, the experience of dual system evolution
in procurement of cereal can also provide reference for that in urban economic

system reform. The production and circulation of industrial materials in urban areas will surely be transited to the new system through combination of delegating power and strengthening regulation. But the progress will depend on social bearing ability.

E. Avoid demand inflation and endeavor to create an economic environment with balanced total demand and total supply to reduce the conflicts between two systems

The degree of conflicts of dual systems mainly depends on the difference of prices. The larger the price difference, the more serious the conflicts. The price difference is also positively correlated with the degree of imbalance between supply and demand. The more the demand exceeds the supply, the larger the price difference. Hence, the state should take macro measures to balance supply and demand so as to reduce conflicts of dual systems. Based on previous experience since the comprehensive implementation of urban economic system reform, the state should mainly focus on preventing and overcoming demand inflation, including investment and consumption inflation. Of course, a limited buyer's market where total supply slightly exceeds total demand cannot be realized in a short time, but the state should move towards this target by controlling demand and adding supply. So to speak, the wane of the old system and wax of the new system, and the process of reducing the conflicts of dual systems, can also be understood as the process of gradually forming a limited buyer's market.

V. Theoretical inspirations from dual systems

The progressive reform and dual systems have made people reflect on many theoretical problems. The author will analyze two of them in this part.

A. The relationship between reform duration and development level

The reform duration and speed are influenced by many objective factors. Only by analyzing these objective factors in a practical and realistic manner can the state make positive and reliable arrangements for the progress and steps of the reform. Putting aside political, social and psychological factors, the paper will focus on economic factors. The author thinks that there are mainly four economic factors influencing the reform duration.

First is the system's starting level, i.e., the situation of original system. If the reform is started from a good foundation, the duration will be shorter; conversely, if the reform is started from a poor foundation, the duration will be longer. As far as the author is concerned, China's reform starts from a relatively poor foundation, so the influence of starting level on China's reform should be considered carefully.[18]

Second is the selection of the target mode. With a high target where the reform aims to transform into the new system that realizes indirect control through the market regulation mechanism, namely, various economic parameters, the reform will last longer. With a lower target where the reform only aims to adjust the quantity of mandatory plans without changing the direct control nature of the entire economic system, the reform will last for a shorter time.

Third is the transformation of the economic development strategic mode. Many economists think that economic system mode is a function of the economic development strategic mode, which means that the economic system mode should correspond to the economic development strategic mode. In case of successful process of transforming the target and main approach of the development strategic mode from rapid growth and extensional development into satisfying consumption and intensional development, the reform will take a shorter period of time. On the contrary, if the transformation of the economic development strategic mode is not clarified or even repetitive and wavering, the reform will take a longer amount of time.

Fourth is the development degree. The development degree here refers to productivity level, particularly the socialization and commercialization level. With a high development degree, the reform takes shorter time; on the contrary, the reform has to proceed with the development process, which will take a longer amount of time.

Previous economics literature has had some discussions on the influences of the first three of these factors on the economic reform process, but only a few discussions on the last factor. For example, in terms of the relationship between development and reform, most of the previous studies focused on the relationship between development strategies and reform instead of development degree and reform. But it is important to study the relationship between development degree and reform, especially the influence of the former on the latter. China is still a developing socialist country where modern industry, relatively lagging industry and traditional agricultural and handicraft industry have coexisted for a long time, so the socialization and commercialization level of production is still low. Just as some economists said, China is still a developing country featuring half self-sufficient and half monetary economy. At present, China has not formed an efficient market system due to a limited commodity market, imbalanced regional development, lagging transportation and communication tools and an underdeveloped factor market (capital, labor and so on). The regulative functions of various economic parameters in the indirect control system mostly depend on the market development level. In an immature market, enterprises and individuals cannot make sensitive reactions to market signals such as price, interest, tax rate and salary, so these economic parameters will fail to play a guiding role in resource allocation. In this case, it is impossible to establish an indirect control system covering the whole society in a short time under the current economic development situation. But it does not mean that it is impossible to establish such a system within a certain range in a society with advanced socialization and commercialization level. Strictly speaking, China's current economic development level makes it difficult to establish a direct control system as well as an indirect control system. Even during the heyday of the direct control system, the coverage of planned products was much lower than that in the Soviet Union and the Eastern European countries.[19] Some foreign economists analyzed that as China's socialist economy featured low-income developing countries, the original economic system can only work on part of its entire national economy though it can be defined as a centralized system with planned resource allocation. Therefore, while conducting economic system reform through the market mechanism, China should take into account the constraint conditions such as "low income and low productivity". "China's low-income economy will constantly restrain the development of effective parts of market economy in some areas."[20] Hence, it can be concluded that it is feasible to establish an indirect control system with limited range and depth in short time. In addition, this system can only further extend and operate more efficiently after the commercialization level is further improved.

B. The relationship between plan and market

The progressive reform and dual systems also add new contents for the relationship between plan and market. In late 1970s and early 1980s, the relationship between plan and market had caused heated discussions in China's economics field, which mainly focused on the disputes over "theory of module combination" and "theory of organic combination". The theory of module combination means that both the production and circulation of products are divided into two modules: one module is regulated by centralized plans, and the other module is regulated by market. The theory of organic combination means that with the entire economic activities developing according to planned direction, enterprises' daily economic activities are included in market regulation; that is, they will be controlled and guided by various economic parameters. According to the reform practice, especially the appearance of dual systems during the transition from direct control system to indirect control system, the paper has reached the following conclusions on the relationship between plan and market:

First, the two different meanings of plan should be clarified: one refers to a mandatory material plan featuring direct control; the other refers to a parameter plan featuring indirect control. According to Kornai, the reason of previous disputes on the relationship between plan and market was partly caused by the ignorance of two different meanings of plan. This is also true in China.

Second, the plan of the first meaning, i.e., the mandatory material plan is mutually exclusive with market. The strengthening of plan functions will weaken market functions and vice versa. The conflicts of dual systems have reflected this kind of relationship between plan and market. Hence, if the transitional stage of module combination between plan and market and the coexistence of dual systems is inevitable, it is infeasible to take it as a target mode.

Third, the plan of the second meaning, i.e., the parameter plan can integrate with the market. The parameter plan features realizing planned targets through the market regulation mechanism. Here plan and market are in an organically correlated relationship, which is also one of the reform targets. Previous disputes on the relationship between plan and market resulted from not only their ignorance of two different meanings of plan, but also the negligence of the difference between target mode and transitional stage. This also explains why those in favor of the theory of module combination deny the necessity for organic combination and those in favor of the theory of organic combination deny the necessity for module combination within a certain period.

Fourth, under dual systems, the relationship between plan and market features not only module combination in forms of coexistence of two systems and conflicts between two systems, but also organic combination in forms of existence and development of economic parameter functions under indirect control.

Fifth, during the process of transforming from direct control mode to indirect control mode, the module combination gradually wanes while the organic combination gradually waxes. Only after the old system is completely transformed into the new system can the organic combination of plan and market be finally realized.

(Published in *Economic Research Journal*, 1986, ninth volume.)

Notes

1 For example, Virlyn Bruce holds that "every economic operational system has its own uncompromising and independent internal logic . . . the eclectic mix of different elements from different modes usually lead to worse results than those low-efficient but consistent systems. Therefore . . . economic operational system should be based on a clarified model within certain period." Bruce. (1981). 社会主义的的政治与经济 [The Politics and Economy of Socialism] (p. 190). Beijing: China Social Sciences Press; Bruce. (1984). 社会主义经济的运行问题 [The Operational Problems of Socialist Economy] (p. 193). Beijing: China Social Sciences Press.
2 Renwei W. Zhao. (1981). 布鲁斯关于社会主义经济模式的理论 [Bruce's Theory on Socialist Economic Patterns] (p. 334). In *Foreign Lectures on Economics* (Vol. 3). Beijing: China Social Sciences Press.
3 David Granick. (1976). *Overview of Enterprises in East Europe* (Chapter 5–7).
4 According to the provisions of the State Council in May 1984, the price of enterprises' self-marketing products can be higher or lower within 20% of state fixed price; the 20% limit was cancelled in January 1985.
5 *Economic Daily* (February 26, 1986). It is said that some materials acquired by local governments from the market are supplied to enterprises through planned distribution.
6 Guoguang G. Liu et al. (1985). 经济体制改革与宏观经济管理—"宏观经济管理国际讨论会"评述 [Economic System Reform and Macro Economic Management: Macro Economic Management International Symposium Review]. *Economic Research Journal*, 12.
7 Xiaodong D. He et al. (September 1, 1986). 对经济增长速度陡跌的两点评论 [Review on Slump of Economic Growth Speed]. *World Economic Herald.*
8 Mengjue J. Guan. (1986). 新旧体制不是一刀两断 [The Old and New Systems Cannot be Severed with One Blow]. *Comparative Economic & Social Systems*, 3.
9 Linru R. Zhao. (1986). 关于价格改革的几个问题 [On Some Issues of Price Reform]. *Learning Materials for Economic Professionals*, 7.
10 Xiaodong D. He et al. (September 16, 1986). 对经济增长速度陡跌的两点评论 [Review on Slump of Economic Growth Speed]. *World Economic Herald.*
11 Jinglian L. Wu (1986). 经济波动和双重体制 [Economic Fluctuation and Dual Systems]. *Finance & Trade Economics*, 6.
12 János Kornai. (1985). The Significance of Hungary's Reform Experience for China's Reform. *Paper provided for Macro Economic Management International Symposium in 1985*, cited from 1986 modified version.

13 Guoguang G. Liu (1986). 我国价格改革的一些情况和问题 [Some Situations and Problems during China's Price Reform]. *Finance & Trade Economics*, 5.
14 Jinglian L. Wu (1986). 经济波动和双重体制 [Economic Fluctuation and Dual Systems]. *Finance & Trade Economics*, 6.
15 Lin Z.R., an economist at the University of Oxford, pointed out this in 1984, see more details in Zhao Renwei. (1984). *Economic Perspectives*, 12.
16 Refer to *People's Daily* (April 15, 1986).
17 Kaixin X. Li. (June 23, 1986). 关于发展生产资料市场的探讨 [Discussions on Developing Production Materials Market]. *People's Daily*.
18 Refer to Renwei W. Zhao & Jingben B. Rong (1982). 我国原来属于什么经济模式 [What Was the Original Economic Mode in China?]. *Economics Perspectives*, 2.
19 Refer to Hua Sheng et al. (1986). 经济运行模式的转换 [Transformation of Economic Operational Mode]. *Economic Research Journal*, 2.
20 Chuanzi Z. Shi. (1986). 社会主义经济和中国的经验—对经济改革的展望 [Socialist Economy and China's Experience: Prospect on Economic Reform]. *Science & Technology Review*, 2.

8 Reflection on the "Bashan Cruise Meeting" in 1985

.

In September 1985, an "International Macroeconomic Management Seminar" that was well known in China's economic system reform history was held on the "Bashanlun" Cruise. This Seminar was jointly held by China's Economic System Reform Board, the Chinese Academy of Social Sciences and the World Bank. It was an important meeting at the turning point of China's economic system reform, normally known as the "Bashanlun Meeting". This six-day meeting began on September 2, when the "Bashanlun" Cruise started its journey in Chongqing and ended on September 7, when the cruise reached Wuhan.[1]

I. The background of the Bashan Cruise Meeting

Readers need to know the economic reform and economic development background of that time before the content of the meeting is introduced.

I want to start with the overall background of the economic reform of that time. By then, rural reform had made great achievements. The focus of reform was turning from rural areas to urban areas. Urban reform was much more complicated than rural reform. It required the government to reform state-owned enterprise and to invigorate the micro-economy. As a result, it had new requests on macroeconomic control and touched the core of the planned economy – the mandatory plan on materials.

It is well known that China's economic system reform at the end of 1978 began with an urgent need for economic activity and a lack of theoretical preparation. Although China borrowed theories and experiences from the reform of Eastern Europe at the beginning of the 1980s, it was not until mid-1980s that China's economic policy makers (known as economic workers) and economics scholars (known as economic theorists) became familiar with the mechanism of and the control over the market economy, especially with the transition from planned economy to market economy. Therefore, this meeting, which gathered Chinese economists and foreign economists together to discuss hot issues in the Chinese economy, was a good chance for the Chinese to summarize their own experience and to draw on foreign experience. Therefore, we can conclude that an important background for the Bashanlun Meeting is the turning of reform focus from rural areas to urban areas.

China's transition from planned economy to market economy is a historical process. As is known to all, the third plenary session of the 11th Central Committee at the end of 1978 emphasized commodity production and a better role of law of value or market mechanism in economic life. Nevertheless, both policy makers and scholars were still exploring how to enhance the role of market mechanism within the boundary of the planned economy. Because of this, the Twelfth National Congress of the Communist Party held in the autumn of 1982 still insisted on "maintaining the dominance of the planned economy and the complementary role of the market". However, this situation underwent big changes in 1984. The third plenary session of the 12th Central Committee held in October in 1984 passed *the Central Committee of the Communist Party of China's Decision on Economic System Reform*. The *Decision* wrote, "The reform of 'planned commodity economy' emphasizes narrowing down the scale of mandatory plan." I believe this is a key step for China to transit from planned economy to market economy. Although the statement in the *Decision* is only slightly different from expressions such as "the central government regulates the market and the market guides enterprises" (1987) and "socialist market economy" (1992), it still provides a broad scope for economic workers and economic theorists to discuss how to transmit to the market economy since it makes commodity economy or market economy as the goal of reform. This is an important reason why the Bashanlun Meeting was able to take place in 1985. If the planned economy and mandatory plan were still in dominance at that time, was it possible to hold such a seminar? People always say that China's reform since the end of 1978 was a market-oriented reform. Now when we look back, we can see that the reform from the end of 1978 to the autumn of 1984 was the trailblazer (or starting point) for market-oriented reform. In other words, the reform at that period had only "embedded" the market mechanism into the broad frame of planned economy, not let the economy run based on the market mechanism. The *Decision* in 1984 started the fundamental change from planned economy to market economy, or provided a turning point.

All of the preceding is the background for Bashanlun Meeting, or broader background. There is also another background – the overheated economy from the second half of 1984 to the first half of 1985, or the smaller background.

The third plenary session of the 12th Central Committee of CPC not only came up with the reform goal of "commodity economy with planning", as was previously mentioned, but also raised the strategic goal of quadrupling gross agricultural output by the end of the 20th century. Under this circumstance, the whole country was enthusiastic about reform and development. All the provinces set forth regulations to expand the scale of investment and competed with each other with regard to salary raises and bonuses; they also adopted expansive monetary and credit policies. By the beginning of 1985, there appeared both investment and consumption expansion, which was manifested by the mounting pressure of inflation. Such a situation hindered the reform and development at the next stage.

As Comrade Xue Muqiao said at the opening speech of the Bashanlun Meeting,

If we want to invigorate micro-economy, we must tighten our control on macro-economy. Right now, we are not good at macro-economy management that is why many loopholes have appeared since we have loosened the control on micro-economy. We lost control on bank credit fund and consumption fund from the fourth quarter of last year to the first quarter of this year, adding difficulties to this year's economic system reform . . . the biggest problem China's macroeconomic control is faced right now is to avoid incontrollable credit caused by the overexpansion of capital construction.[2]

The articles written by the deputy dean Liu Guoguang and I for the conference also made the following summary on the overheated economy of that time. Firstly, the economy grew too fast: economy growth rate rose to 14.2% in 1984, while gross industrial output value in the first half of 1985 saw a year-on-year increase of 21.8%. Secondly, investment expansion and consumption expansion intensified. Fixed assets in 1984 increased by 21.8% and banks' cash spending in salary and bonus increased by 22.3%, much higher than the 12% growth of national income. Third, there was an oversupply of credit and currency. Bank loans grew by 28.9% in 1984, and accordingly, currency in circulation increased.[3] Mr. Lin Chonggen described the situation back then as follows in the seminar: firstly, credit over-expanded while key energy, raw materials and transportation facilities were in short supply, leading to a huge gap between list price and market price. Secondly, the balance of international payments was terribly broken. Thirdly, a wage-price spiral led to mounting inflation pressure.[4]

It should be said that the larger background (the background of economic transit) and the smaller background (the background of the overheated economy) was interrelated, or overlapped largely. A discussion on macroeconomic management against such a complicated background involves not only general issues in a mature market economy, but particular issues in the initial stage of economic transit; involves not only general issues in indirect regulation and control, but also particular issues in the gradual abandonment of direct regulation and the maturing process of indirect control. For the attendees of the meeting, taking part in discussion on these issues not only helped them to study the case of China, but also enriched their international experience in macroeconomic control in the market economy and economy in transition.

Foreign attendees were invited by Mr. Lin Chonggen, who worked for the World Bank. These experts have rich experience and have a say in their respective areas. For example, the Nobel Prize laureate James Tobin conducted an extensive and in-depth study on the macro control over the non-centralized economy. Janos Kornai and W. Brus had unique insight on the maladies of the traditional socialist planned economy and on how to transit from the planned economy to the market economy. Alexander Cairncross not only had rich experience in the macro-management of developed market economy system, but also had experience in the transition from the hard-controlled economy during wartime to the soft-controlled economy in peacetime after the Second World War. Otmar Emminger had unique insight on how macroeconomic control was exercised through monetary policy in Germany's after-war economic recovery. Other foreign experts, such as Aleksander Bait from Yugoslavia, Leroy Jones from the United States, Michel Albert from France and

Kobayashi Minoru from Japan all had rich experience in economic study or economic decision-making.

Experts at home mainly include economic workers in the government decision-making department and economic theorists from the research department. There were older-generation economists such as Xue Muqiao, An Zhiwen and Ma Hong, middle-aged economists such as Liu Guoguang, Gao Shangquan and Wu Jinglian, and young economists like Guo Shuqing and Lou Jiwei. Although they were in different age groups and held different positions, they were all determined to carry out reform and were the trailblazers of reform.

Therefore, we can see that the attendees are basically made up of three groups of people: economists from China, including economic decision makers and economic theorists; economists who came from Eastern Europe or have rich experience in the reform in East Europe; economists from the West, especially economists who have rich experience in the macro-management of the market economy and economic transition. From the make-up of the attendees, we can see that by the 1980s, it was not enough for China's economic reform to merely absorb Eastern Europe's experience and to just bring in the market mechanism under the framework of the central-planned economy. The reform should also absorb experience in how to macro-manage the market economy and how to transit from planned economy to market economy. In other words, the make-up of attendees is closely connected with the aforementioned economic transition.[5]

II.   Major issues discussed in the Bashanlun Meeting

A.   *The goal of economic system reform*

The attendees had shown strong interest in the goal of economic system reform, believing that this reform was the prerequisite for conducting macro control.

Professor Kornai gave his opinions on the target mode of reform at the beginning of his speech in the seminar.[6] He divided the economic coordination mechanisms in macroeconomic management into two categories: one is the administrative coordination mechanism; the other is the market coordination mechanism. The feature of the first mechanism is that there is a vertical flow of information between superiors and inferiors and superior-inferior relationship is in dominance. The economy is centralized. The feature of the second mechanism is that there is a horizontal flow of information between buyers and sellers. Both buyers and sellers are in the same ladder, and there is no superior-inferior relationship. Decision-making is not centralized. Both coordination mechanisms can be demonstrated with two pictures (shown in Figures 8.1 and 8.2).

In these two pictures, there is the flow of commodity from Business 1 to Business 2 and from Business 2 to Business 3. These flows are demonstrated in full lines. The two pictures also reflect the flow of information, which are demonstrated in dotted lines and regulate the actual flow of commodity. In Figure 8.1, information flows vertically from a "center" to businesses, then returns to the "center" from businesses. This represents a form of administrative coordination.

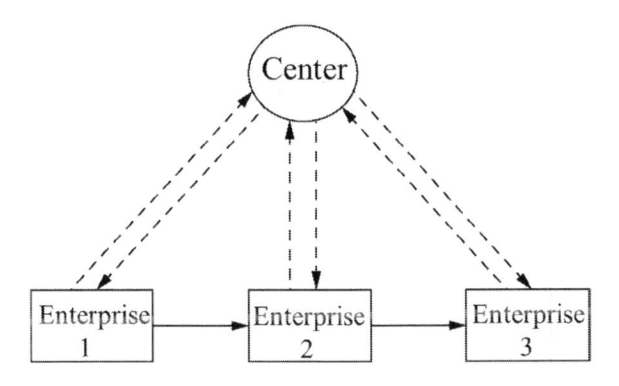

Figure 8.1 Vertical Administrative Coordination

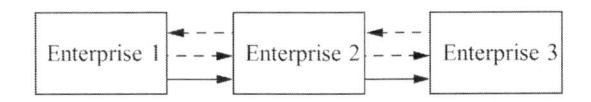

Figure 8.2 Horizontal Market Coordination

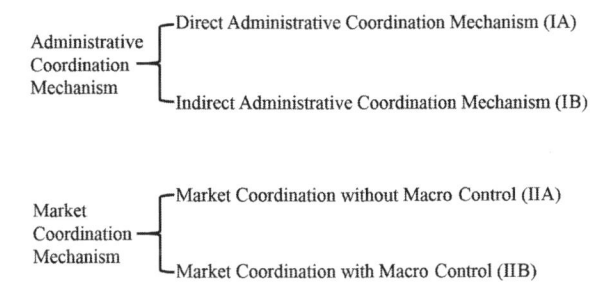

Figure 8.3 Four Models of Economic Coordination Mechanism

In Figure 8.2, information flows horizontally from one business to another, from the buyer to the seller and then returns to the buyer. This represents a form of market coordination.

Each of these mechanisms has two forms. Administrative coordination is divided into direct administrative coordination (IA) and indirect administrative coordination (IB), while market coordination is divided into market coordination without macro control (IIA) and market coordination with macro control (IIB). Professor Kornai believes that reform that is truly effective should make IIB its target mode.

After a simple description of these four modes, Professor Kornai pointed out that the feature of IIA is that after the cancellation of administrative control, the new macro control system is not developed. The economy is totally under the spontaneous and aimless regulation of market mechanism. This mode is not adoptable and does not exist in real economic life in any country. During a reform, once a country passes the stage of IA, it always goes to IB. Professor Kornai says IB can serve as a transitional stage but should not be the destination of reform. Therefore, he believed that China should press on with its reform. It should not forget that its target is IIB, not IB. He maintained that in stage IB, businesses have two kinds of reliance, one is horizontal reliance and the other is vertical reliance. Horizontal reliance refers to the reliance on buyer and seller, while vertical reliance means the reliance on higher authorities. Vertical reliance is the major reliance. To put it in another way, business leaders have two eyes; one is on administrative authorities, the other on the market. But the authorities have more power in this case.[7]

Most experts went with Professor Kornai's classification in their discussion and agreed with making IIB mode the target of reform. Brus also agreed with Professor Kornai's opinion. Despite so, he had unique insight for the starting point of China's economic reform. He said China's started its economic reform not from IA mode, but from half IA mode. At the beginning of its economic reform, China did not even qualify to IA mode in some areas. For example, China did not have a labor market, which is different from Eastern European countries. This opinion was in line with what he said in 1980 when he gave a lecture in China saying that China started its economic reform from a "standard military communist mode" (while the Soviet Union and Eastern Europe started from "typical planned economic mode" or the "Stalin Model"). Therefore, Brus said, the transition of China's economic reform from half IA mode to IIB mode is "a real Long March".[8]

B. The way of system transition and double systems under a progressive system transition

Before the Bashanlun Meeting, economists at home and abroad had already started discussion on the way of system transition. Some people proposed a "package" solution while others advocated a "progressive" solution. With the lessons and experience learned from the reform in Eastern Europe, both Brus and Kornai once believed that instead of adopting progressive solution, which would lead to "a chaos in traffic rules", a "package" solution was the way to take.

After the discussion in the Bashanlun Meeting, economists at home and abroad began to have a better understanding of the issue and fewer disagreements. They seemed to have reached consensus on the following aspects: firstly, China's economic reform would go through a long transitional period under such conditions (a backward economy, a dual structure, a vast territory, an unbalanced development and a low starting point of reform). Secondly, drawing from the experience of the past six-plus years of reform, it was clear that reform could not succeed within a short period. It could happen only in a progressive way. For example, people can gradually extend reform from rural areas to urban areas, from operational mechanism to ownership system, from coastal regions to inland regions, etc. Third, two ways of reform should not contradict each other. The "package" solution should be viewed as a comprehensive reform conducted on a particular day, while the "progressive" solution should be viewed as a complex long-term reform with setbacks.

Some economists went further in their analysis, saying that the ways and steps of economic system reform should not be understood in a simplified way. Kornai maintained, for example, that the reform of ownership structure should be more progressive, while the reform of operational mechanism (such as reform of price, wage, financial and monetary methods and the hardening of constraints on businesses' budget) should think more about "package" solution since it should consider more about how to make these reforms match each other. Cairncross added that if the reform was going to adopt the "package" solution, there must be a prerequisite – a relatively balanced aggregate supply and demand. But a country does not always have such conditions at the beginning of its reform. Therefore, reform should be carried out gradually.[9] He introduced that the control mode on economy that Britain adopted during the Second World War shares many similarities with the control mode of the socialist economy. It took Britain around ten years to transit gradually from a hard-control economy (economy focusing on controlling the supply of materials) to a soft-control economy (economy focusing on controlling aggregate demand). Control on foreign currency was not even lifted until 1979.

As a reform gradually progresses, it is inevitable that dual systems exist for a certain period. China's reform, especially the comprehensive reform on economic system with urban reform its focus after the 12th National Congress went on a track of dual system, of which the major manifestation is a dual price system for the same product – that is, one product having a low planned price and a high market price at the same time.

In the seminar, economists at home and abroad made almost the same analysis as to the pros and cons of the dual system. They believed that the purpose of carrying out dual system transition is to avoid great shock in reform. But a dual system will inevitably bring friction and chaos; as a result, such a situation cannot last too long. As Brus said, other socialist countries had dual price in consumer goods in their transitions from planned system to commodity system. But China also adopted dual price in the means of production, which could be a beneficial invention. It had served as a bridge from the old system to the new, with which administrative, official price system could transit to a market price system in a relatively smooth way. But as it has obvious flaws, the dual price system cannot last for too long.

In their discussion, economists at home and abroad believed that the macro management under the dual system is much more complicated than the macro management under either an old or a new system, which poses a serious challenge to reformers.

C.   *Major methods in indirect control*

Experts at the seminar believed that if a market coordination mode with macro control is to be established, indirect control must be strengthened while the state government's control on businesses' micro-economic activities must be loosened.

The feature of direct control is to allocate materials from top to bottom under administrative order. Then, what are the priorities and methods of indirect control? Tobin believes that there are three targets of macroeconomic management: first is to achieve the balance of aggregate supply and aggregate demand; second is to maintain the stability of the general level of market price; and third is to keep the stability of a country's economic relationship with other countries. Of these three targets, the first is the major one. Since it is hard to carry out centralized management on aggregate supply, the priority of macroeconomic management is to regulate aggregate demand.

There are mainly four methods of indirect control focusing on controlling aggregate demand. Since China is in a transitional process, or changing from direct control to indirect control, the application of these indirect methods is also in a process of development.

1.   Fiscal policy

Some scholars pointed out that people tend to stress monetary policy when indirect control is concerned. But it should be recognized that the fiscal budget is the basis of controlling the stability of aggregate demand. Cairncross pointed out that after the Second World War, Britain did not use monetary policy to avoid excess demand, because using the interest rate to influence investment takes a longer time than fiscal policy. Once there is a financial surplus, the whole picture will not be the same any more. Some experts pointed out those Latin American countries often issue as much currency as their deficit, leading to uncontrollable inflation, which also proves the importance of maintaining a balanced budget from another aspect.

To have a budget with surplus or with deficit while maintaining its balance depends on market conditions. If aggregate demand exceeds aggregate supply, leading to mounting inflation pressure, government should implement a tight fiscal policy and have a budget with surplus; if demand falls short of supply, government should implement expansive fiscal policy. Fiscal policy influences aggregate demand from two aspects: first is to regulate government's demand for commodity and labor, which is to regulate government's expenditure; second is to regulate the spending of businesses and individuals through taxation and subsidy. In other words, fiscal expenditure and subsidy should be increased while tax is reduced to spur economic growth when demand is insufficient, and fiscal expenditure and subsidy should be reduced while tax is increased to rein in aggregate demand to achieve a balanced budget. Experts at the seminar all believed that under no circumstance should the government raise funds by "creating currency" (like overdrawing its bank account). It can issue bonds to control aggregate demand if necessary. What issuing bonds has in common with increasing tax is that they both can subdue aggregate demand, but these two also have obvious differences: increasing tax will lead to a reduction of the wealth owned by businesses and individuals, while issuing bonds can transfer their purchasing power to the government without reducing the wealth of bond owners. Therefore, issuing bonds can be a complementary method to balance aggregate supply and aggregate demand.

2. Monetary policy

Foreign experts at the seminar introduced western countries' experience in using monetary policy to conduct indirect macro control and analyzed the problems China had encountered. Emminger and Tobin mentioned that the core of western countries' monetary policy is to control the aggregate supply of money, and that the central bank controls aggregate money supply mainly through controlling bank loans. There are three methods: first is to stipulate that commercial banks need to deposit reserves in the central bank, second is to adjust rediscount rate and third is to trade securities in "open market".

However, foreign experts believed that it was premature to have "open market" in China given the development of China's financial market. Another important method – interest rate – also plays a limited role in China. Experts believed that the nominal interest rate must be above the inflation rate if interest rate is to play its leverage role; otherwise, people will not be willing to deposit their money when the real interest rate is negative and those taking out loans will squander their loans. Emminger even said that even an increase of 1% to 2% in the real interest rate is not enough to curb excessive demand; only when the increase rate passes 4% can businesses' demand for credit be curbed. The reserve system should set the reserve requirement rate (RRR) of different deposits according to their liquidity. For example, a check deposit that can be paid any time should have a relatively high RRR, while a savings deposit could have a relatively low RRR.

Experts at the seminar believed that in light of China's conditions at that time, means of indirect control such as the bank interest rate and reserve requirement system had not yet played an effective role. Therefore, Tobin and Emminger believed that it is more realistic for China to replace aggregate money supply with aggregate credit supply as the indicator of aggregate demand control. In the meantime, the government should explore how to establish and improve the bank system and financial market as well as how to strengthen control of businesses' budgets so as to gradually transit to an indirect control-oriented currency and credit management system.

Experts also discussed how to match fiscal policy with monetary policy. In principle, there are four match patterns: easy fiscal policy with easy monetary policy; tight fiscal policy with tight monetary policy; tight fiscal policy with easy monetary policy; easy financial policy with tight monetary policy. So which pattern should be chosen in China's case? At that time, tendencies such as "expansionary impulse" and "investment thirst" coming with the old system, coupled with the tendency of "consumption thirst" brought by the invigorating of micro-economy gave rise to a huge pressure of expanding demand. In the discussion, Tobin, Cairncross and Emminger all believed that at that time, China should have a mix of tight fiscal policy and tight monetary policy. That is to say, the government should not only strictly control credit and currency, but also try to have a balanced fiscal budget with a small surplus. They also said that they hope their opinions can attract the Chinese government's attention given that they seldom have a same opinion regarding economic issues, since they came from different schools.

3.   *Income policy*

As has been mentioned before, China was then faced with two urgent problems: out-of-control wage and swelling consumption fund. Therefore, experts began heated discussion on how to employ income policy to control the growth of wage (and bonuses). They generally believed that controlling the growth of wage is an effective weapon to dampen cost-driven inflation. Tobin pointed out that even the most effective fiscal policy and monetary policy can do nothing except cope with demand-driven inflation, and individual income distribution policy is the trump card against cost-driven inflation. Therefore, the Chinese government should never give up its grip on wage growth. The experts introduced respectively the lessons of Hungary, Yugoslavia and Japan in this respect, pointing out that Hungary and Japan had done well in wage growth control and maintained currency value stability; whereas Yugoslavia lacked macro control on income distribution, leading to big inflation. They believed that to effectively control the money supply, the Chinese government must control the amount of wage, which takes a large portion in cash supply.

Experts also discussed the relationship between labor productivity growth rate, inflation rate and wage growth rate. In theory, the change in nominal wage growth depends on the change in labor productivity and inflation. But in practice, it is hard to predict the inflation rate. In the Federal Republic of Germany, the Union always requires that prospective inflation rate be considered in the growth of wage. But this can only set the standard for future inflation rate, leading to a wage-price spiral. That is a mistake that the Chinese government should avoid in its reform. Nevertheless, experts believed that under no circumstance should wage growth exceed labor productivity growth. Emminger even believed that with inflation, excessive demand, trade deficit and lack of construction fund at hand, the Chinese government should make wage growth rate a bit lower than the labor productivity growth rate.

Foreign experts also held different opinions as to the link between wage growth and profit in China's state-owned enterprises. Profit growth in state-owned enterprises is always connected directly with external factors such as the state government's investment and resources. Therefore, if salary increases too fast in state-owned enterprises because of such external factors, there will be a bandwagon effect, spreading this trend to other businesses. As a result, businesses will transfer the increase in salary cost to the price of their products, leading to inflation in the society.

As for how to control salary, experts believed that it is not the total amount of salary, but the average salary or salary per hour that should be controlled. Only businesses or individuals that have made exceptional contributions can enjoy increases in salary that are above the average in society.

4.   *International balance of payments*

An important aspect of macroeconomic management is to control a country's economic relations with foreign countries so as to achieve international balance of payments. Brus said three essential elements in macroeconomic management are the control on investment, income and economic relations with foreign countries. To control economic relations with foreign countries is not to monopolize foreign trade. It is to make sure that a country has the capability to pay and maintain economic independence, so that the change in other countries' economies will not automatically lead to overall domestic economic change while advanced technology and management experience from overseas can be brought in after the evaluation and selection of the government. Tobin believes that it is not urgent for China to turn from direct control to indirect balance in the issue of foreign currency balance. There is no need to sacrifice the balance of domestic macro-economy in return for the balance of foreign currency. Cairncross said that even an international financial center such as Britain did not give up control on foreign currency until 1979. They believed that for a long time to come, China would not be ready to give up foreign currency control or achieve free convertibility of foreign currency.

D. Important conditions for indirect control

Experts pointed out that there is a close connection between macroeconomic operation and micro-economic activities. To establish an effective indirect control system of macroeconomy depends not only on whether there is a reasonable management mechanism or proper policy measure, but also on whether micro-economic entities can give in-time and flexible responses to indirect control as well as whether other conditions for macroeconomic management are in place. Experts believed that essential conditions for indirect control include the following.

1. To harden constraint on businesses' budgets

The concept of soft budget constraint was first raised by Kornai in his *Shortage Economics* and was later used by more and more economists. In the seminar, experts at home and abroad all believed that soft constraint on businesses' budgets is a big drawback in macro-micro-economic relations under the traditional socialist planned economy framework. Under the condition of soft constraint, businesses cannot truly assume sole responsibility for their profits or losses. When businesses cannot make their ends meet, they can always get compensation from the government through soft price, soft subsidy, soft tax and soft credit and transfer their troubles to the government. If the condition of soft constraint will not change, various regulatory means of the government such as tax rate, interest rate and exchange rate will not be able to make businesses improve their management and performance. Kornai compared the relationship of the state and businesses under the condition of soft constraint to the relationship between father and son. He believed that only by changing such "paternal" care and hardening constraint on businesses' budgets, can businesses fix all of their attention on the market and improve management efficiency under the pressure of market competition; and only under such conditions can the aforementioned indirect control play its role.

In the discussion, some Chinese experts pointed out that after the government put the focus of its reform on cities, in invigorating the micro-economy it tended to grant decision-making rights to businesses and allow them to keep more profits but seldom paid attention to businesses' responsibilities; in macro control it tended to send the signal of government control but ignored businesses' reaction to these signals. Therefore, the theory and experience of hardening constraint on businesses' budgets in other countries can provide many inspirations on how to improve the relationship between conducting macroeconomic control and invigorating the micro-economy in China's reform.

2.   To cultivate a market system

Experts all believe that another important condition for carrying out effective indirect macroeconomic control is a mature market system, especially a sound commodity market and a sound funds market (or capital market).

First of all, commodity market, including a consumer market and market of means of production, should be opened completely. Experts pointed out that physical supply of products can be accepted only in wars. In peacetime, the government should focus on demand management instead of organizing physical supply of products. If physical supply of products continues in peacetime, market mechanism and competition would be hampered, depriving economic growth of impetus and leading to a huge cost. In the past, under the guidance of the theory that means of production are not commodity, the commodity market was opened only to consumer goods, while the means of production were subject to government supply. With the gradual abolishment of the mandatory plan, this method should be abandoned gradually.

Next, the factor market should be opened. Experts believed that there couldn't be a normal commodity market without a normal factor market, especially a funds market. Brus said China should establish financial intermediaries in the investment sector to help businesses organize capital flows among businesses. A large portion of investment should be distributed through the funds market. Foreign experts suggested that the bond market should first be established in consideration of doubts over private-owned stocks in China. Tobin pointed that China could first establish a non-monetary government bond market, giving people a chance to make a choice between government bond and bank deposit. Without such a bond, market monetary policy has to comply with fiscal policy and inflation control can be carried out only through cutting financial expense.

The issue of the labor market was also mentioned in the discussion. Brus pointed out that to some extent, there is no labor market in China, which limits the role of market mechanism on the macro-management of state-owned enterprises. He believed that labor flow is more flexible in the Soviet Union, and China can look up to its experience. However, there was no detailed discussion on how to grow labor market in the seminar.

3. *To carry out price reform in a decisive way*

A reasonable price system is essential for carrying out indirect control. Besides, hardening constraint on businesses' budgets and improving the market system require that a reasonable price system be established. Kornai pointed out that without a reasonable price, there will not be correct information; thus it is impossible to find a gauging standard that can apply to different sectors and different businesses. Bait also believed that when price is unreasonable, any enhancement of "budget constraint" would be dubious. Under such condition, the hardening of constraints on businesses' budgets will reduce instead of increasing profits.

Therefore, experts believed price reform should be conducted in a decisive way on the basis of aggregate demand control. The price-forming mechanism should be changed (from administrative price to market price) and a relatively complete market price system should be gradually established. This system should include not only commodity price but capital price (interest), labor price (salary) and exchange price (exchange rate). Only when these prices become market-oriented can it be said that a reasonable price system has been established.

4. *To diversify forms of ownership*

This seminar mainly discussed reform of the operational mechanism. Specifically, it discussed how to play the role of market mechanism in economic operation. Nevertheless, some experts mentioned the reform on the forms of ownership. They believed that a diversified ownership is an important condition for market regulation or indirect control.

Bruce pointed out that while the important role of state-owned businesses in socialist countries should be acknowledged, a diversified ownership is a must in socialist conditions. Traditionally, state ownership is viewed as the best and the most ideal form of ownership. Even though collective ownership is legally recognized, in reality it equals ownership by the whole people. Meanwhile, individual ownership is sidelined. However, it is hard to prove that one form of ownership is absolutely superior to another. Therefore, in economic reform, forms of ownership should be diversified so that the strengths of the various forms can be utilized. The great achievements made by China's agricultural reform and the invigoration of the non-state economy had clearly proved this fact.

Albert believed that the market's role is more important than ownership of the means of production. Although nationalization is necessary in some sectors, it should be carried out on the basis that state-owned businesses take part in market competition and will not impede the functioning of the market.

5. *To establish and improve the economic information and supervision system*

Experts generally believed that an urgent task for managing such a big open economy in China's case is to establish a sound information system. Tobin said that he had given the same suggestion when he visited China in 1972, and after 13 years, he had to mention it again. Without reliable statistics and economic analysis, it is impossible to make an accurate economic prediction or the right macro policy decision. Albert also emphasized that a country's economy develops with the development of information, and any plan made without accurate information will be a plan made blindly.

To make sure that the different means of indirect macroeconomic control are effectively implemented, experts said that economic legislation should be strengthened and a unified national accounting system and an independent auditing system should be established. Without a unified national accounting system, it will be hard to evaluate business performance accurately, and the allocation of social resources will be hard to bring good results. Without a strict auditing system, the cheating and illegal action of businesses will not be prevented, and economic laws and regulations will not be implemented in earnest.

The six-day "International Seminar on Macro Economic Management" was an unusual gathering of experts. China's economic reform can draw many lessons from the aforementioned conclusions. As some scholars have said, the "Bashanlun Meeting" was in fact a high-level seminar on economic system reform and macroeconomic view management.

Notes

1 Liu Guoguang et al. (1985). 经济体制改革与宏观经济管理 – " 宏观经济管理国际研讨会"评述 [Economic System Reform and Macroeconomic Management: A Review of the International Symposium on Macroeconomic Management]. *Economic Research Journal*, 12.
2 Xue Muqiao. (1985). 开幕词 [Opening Speech]. *Selected Works*.
3 Liu Guoguang & Zhao Renwei. (1985). 当前中国经济体制改革遇到的几个问题 [Several Problems in the Current Reform of China's Economic System]. *Selected Works* (pp. 193–203).
4 Lin Zhonggeng. (1985). 与会外国专家的意见和建议综述 [A Summary of Opinions and Suggestions of Foreign Experts Who Participated in the Meeting]. *Selected Works*.
5 Lin Zhonggeng. (September 2008). 中国改革开放过程中的对外思想开放 [Opening of China's Foreign Thought in the Process of China's Reform and Opening up]. *Comparative Studies*, 38.
6 Janos Kornai. (1985). Some Lessons Learned from Hungary for the Reformers in China. *Selected Works*.
7 Janos Kornai. (1985). The Double Dependence of State-Owned Enterprises: The Experience of Hungary. *Economic Research Journal*, 10.
8 Guo Shuqing et al. (1985). 目标模式和过渡步骤 [The Goal Model and Transitional Steps]. *Selected Works* (pp. 16–23).
9 Alec Cairncross. (1985). The Post-War Transition in Britain from a Tightly-Controlled Economy to a Softly-Controlled Economy. *Selected Works*.

References

A. Kane Klaus. (1985). The Post-War Transition in Britain from a Tightly-Controlled Economy to a Softly-Controlled Economy. *Selected Works*.

China Economic System Reform Seminar, Chinese Academy of Social Sciences. (1985). 关于"宏观经济管理国际研讨会"主要情况的报告 [Report on the "International Symposium on Macroeconomic Management"]. In China Economic Reform Seminar. 宏观经济的管理和改革 – 宏观经济管理国际研讨会言论选编 [Macroeconomic Management and Reform: Selected Works of International Symposium on Macroeconomic Management] (hereinafter referred to as *Selected Works*). Beijing: Economic Daily Press.

Guo Shuqing et al. (1985). 目标模式和过渡步骤 [The Goal Model and Transitional Steps]. *Selected Works* (pp. 16–23).

Janos Kornai. (1985a). Some Lessons Learned from Hungary for the Reformers in China. *Selected Works*.

Janos Kornai. (1985b). The Double Dependence of State-Owned Enterprises: The Experience of Hungary. *Economic Research Journal*, 10.

Liu Guoguang & Zhao Renwei. (1985). 当前中国经济体制改革遇到的几个问题 [Several Problems in the Current Reform of China's Economic System]. In *Selected Works* (pp. 193–203).

Liu Guoguang et al. (1985). 经济体制改革与宏观经济管理 – "宏观经济管理国际研讨会"评述 [Economic System Reform and Macroeconomic Management: A Review of the International Symposium on Macroeconomic Management]. *Economic Research Journal*, 12.

Lin Zhonggeng. (1985). 与会外国专家的意见和建议综述 [A Summary of Opinions and Suggestions of Foreign Experts Who Participated in the Meeting]. *Selected Works*.

Lin Zhonggeng. (September, 2008). 中国改革开放过程中的对外思想开放 [Opening of China's Foreign Thought in the Process of China's Reform and Opening Up]. *Comparative Studies*, 38.

Xue Muqiao. (1985). 开幕词 [Opening Remarks]. *Selected Works*.

(The Reflection on the "Bashanlun Meeting" in 1985 was published in the *Economic Research Journal*, No. 12, 2008. Based on the above articles, the author compressed them by deleting some parts regarding the thoughts in the original texts.)

9 China's economic system in reform – retrospect of economic reform in the past decade

China's economic system reform has been going on for ten years since the end of 1978. This ten-year period can be divided into two stages. The first stage spans from December 1978 to October 1984, during which time the reform is focused on rural areas with some urban explorations and experiments. The second stage starts from October 1984 and enters the process of comprehensive reform centered around cities, which is still ongoing.

I. Preface: starting point and goal of the reform

China's economic system reform was lacking in theoretical preparation and practical experience at the beginning. When the concept of reform was raised, people had a strong feeling that we must reform, but there was no clear outline of the starting point and the goal of the reform, so they had to explore these issues along the way of reform.

Concerning the starting point of reform, the initial view was too general, stating that China's original economic system, copied from the Soviet Union in the 1950s, belongs to the traditional mode of centralized management of planned resource allocation system. After years of practice and comparative studies, the understanding of the starting point of reform greatly deepened: First, the economic system learned from the Soviet Union could not cover the entire national economy, with its scope limited to the main part of the national economy. Second, after over 20 years (1956–1978) of serving as the main system in China, this economic system had undergone many changes and the economic system before the reform (1978), compared to the economic system 20 years before the reform in 1978, was more homogeneous in ownership, more centralized in economic decision-making, more materialized in economic processes, more even in income distribution and more closed in foreign economic relations. Third, China's economic system reform was carried out when there was not much economic development and market development; therefore, the process of economic reform was bound to be restricted by such low development and the fact that the starting point of China's reform was lower than that of the Soviet Union and most Eastern European countries was unanimously acknowledged without much controversy.

The goal of reform, however, was a heatedly debated issue. At the beginning of the reform, there seemed to be little disagreement over the market orientation, but opinions diverged on how far we could go in this way. In the first stage of the reform, namely before 1984, much of the economic literature focused on the combination of the mandatory plan, the guiding plan and the market regulation with different proportions. It seemed that the distinctive designs of the reform goal lay in the different proportions of the three pinned together, and the prevailing theory was that only when we maintained the dominant position of the mandatory plan could we maintain the socialist nature of the economy. Obviously, this theory, whether in concept or in method, was relatively obsolete. After 1984, the reform entered the second stage. There was a clear breakthrough in the design of the goal of reform, which gradually formed the idea of the basic framework for "Trinity", or "three actions in one spirit". (1) Make state-owned enterprises independent commodity producers and operators with production rights and their own interests. Enterprises should make sensitive response to the market signals and bear sole responsibility for its profit and loss in the market competition. (2) Establish a relatively complete market system where we not only have the goods market, but also the market for production factors, including the capital market, the real estate market, technology market and labor market; besides, the market rules and market order should also be established correspondingly. (3) Change the governance of the enterprise by the state from the direct and administrative means to indirect control through various parameters on the market; the government can still conduct the guiding plan through the participation of market activities while conforming to market rules. In the economic literature, including the official documents, experts summarized this idea as "the state regulates the market, and market guides enterprises" from the perspective of economic operation. Obviously, such a design for the goal of reform excluded the mandatory plan fundamentally, which, admittedly, represented a major breakthrough in the reform theories.

The design for the goal of the reform involved not only the transformation of the economic operation mechanism, but also the transformation of the ownership of the means of production. However, in the first stage of reform, people seemed to focus on the reform of the operational mechanism, and regarded the public ownership of the means of production as a prerequisite. Only a few economists stressed that national ownership itself needed to be reformed. Nevertheless, as the reform evolves, it became increasingly clear that the reform of the operational mechanism, especially the change of corporate behavior, was essentially intertwined with changes in ownership relations. Therefore, people gradually formed two basic clues on the economic system reform: namely, the reform of ownership and the reform of operational mechanisms. Of course, the change of ownership mentioned here referred to not only the transformation of ownership from sole-ness to diversity (coexistence of economy with different types of ownership), but also, and more importantly, how to extend the reform into public ownership, especially state ownership, and fundamentally solve the malpractice that the property was owned by everyone yet no one was responsible. In recent years, the economic community has conducted extensive and heated discussions on the issue of ownership reform.

In short, when it comes to the goal of reform, the following two major break-throughs stood prominently in the guiding ideology of China's economic reform: (1) changing from defending the mandatory plan characteristic of the original economic system to principally denying mandatory plan; and (2) changing from insisting on making the public ownership of the original economic system as the unchanging prerequisite to conducting reform on the public ownership itself.

II.   Progress and achievements of the reform

China's economic reform made remarkable achievements first in the rural areas. The rural reform generally included the following three aspects. First, the household contract responsibility system was carried out all over the country with the land originally under collective ownership now contracted to the farmer's families. Meanwhile the original people's commune system featuring "integration of government administration with commune management" was abolished, so that political organizations and economic organizations became separate. So far, around 180 million farmers have been involved in the household contract responsibility system, accounting for 98% of farmers nationwide. Second, the policies governing the price and purchase of agricultural products were adjusted. The purchase price of agricultural products increased by 20.1% in 1979 and 8.1% in 1980, which solely resulted in an increase of farmer income by 46 billion yuan between 1979 and 1980. Third, the rural industrial structure was adjusted, and vigorous efforts were made to develop non-agricultural industries. By 1986, the proportion of agricultural output value accounted for 53.1% of total rural output value, while the four sections of industry, commerce, construction and transportation accounted for 46.9%. In the same year, the number of township enterprises reached 15.15 million, employing 79.37 million people, accounting for 20.9% of the total rural labor force. The total annual income was 336.4 billion yuan, making up 48.9% of the rural economy.

There have been significant changes in ownership relations over the past decade. The implementation of the household contract responsibility system in rural areas was essentially reforming the ownership relations. The fact that land could be contracted to farmers resulted in the separation of land ownership and operation rights, and farmers could own certain means of production, which led to the formation of the mixed ownership featuring collective land ownership and private ownership of other means of production. The ownership relations in the urban area was largely transformed according to the following two clues: (1) changing from a single form of public ownership to the coexistence of various forms of ownership; and (2) separating ownership from operation rights in the public ownership. Since the reform, individual industrial and commercial households, and private enterprises, have witnessed significant developments, and the urban individual industrial and commercial households skyrocketed from a little over 100,000 in 1978 to more than five million in 1986. With the progress of reform and opening-up, China introduced all kinds of foreign investment in various forms. By June 1987, 8516 Sino-foreign joint ventures, cooperative enterprises and foreign-owned enterprises were approved for establishment, and the contracted foreign investment volume registered 117.176 billion dollars. In addition to the implementation of the contract management and leasing operations within the public ownership, China also began stock-holding pilot programs in Guangzhou, Shenyang, Beijing, Shanghai and other cities. From 1978 to 1986, the share of output value of enterprises owned by the whole Chinese people dropped from 80% to 68.7% in the total industrial output value, while that of the collectively owned enterprises increased from 20% to 29.2% and the share of individually owned business and other forms of economy sprang from nil to 2.1%. Obviously, the reform of ownership relations so far has been very preliminary in terms of both breadth and depth, but it was undoubtedly a good start.

The reform of enterprise management mechanism constituted an important part in economic reform. Regarding the malpractice of the original economic system featuring overwhelmingly smothering government control, the reform started with the essential link of increasing autonomy for enterprises themselves. Since the reform began, the State Council has issued 13 official documents and 97 provisions to expand enterprise autonomy. With expanded power, enterprises have had certain autonomy in such fields as production plan, product purchase and sales, capital use, labor and personnel affairs, and wages and bonuses, which allowed enterprises to make headway in becoming relatively independent commodity producers and operators, and thus initially changed the status of enterprise being just an adjunct to the government.

As for the state-enterprises relationship, the latter now basically pay income tax instead of turning over all profits to the former. As a result, the enterprises have witnessed ever-increasing profits retained. According to statistics, the proportion of profits retained by enterprises accounted for 3.7% of the total enterprise profit in 1978, 26.1% in 1981, 38.9% in 1985, and 42.4% in 1986. From 1985, the depreciation funds of the enterprises have been left to themselves. In this way, the enterprise began to have the ability of self-transformation and self-development.

Within the enterprise, the director (manager) responsibility system was implemented, and the work of the Party's organization was separated from the enterprise management. The directors of many enterprises came to the fore through recruitment and bidding, which was beneficial for cultivating a cohort of innovative entrepreneurs who understand the market competition rules.

In 1987, various forms of contract responsibility system were widely practiced in large and medium-sized enterprises. Under this system, the enterprises were contacted to individuals or groups according to certain conditions (mainly the quotas for the profit turned over to the state and the added value of enterprise assets). The system had certain advantages in reducing the administrative intervention by the government, ensuring the fiscal revenue of the state, increasing the profits retained by the enterprises and invoking the enthusiasm of the employees. Overall, however, it still features the practice of vertical bargaining between the contractor and those who authorized the contract; while the horizontal competition among enterprises for the contracting eligibility does not really exist, which therefore does not fundamentally change the weakness in the property rights system of the traditionally state-owned enterprises. Therefore, many economists envisage that enterprises should move in the direction of restructuring property rights – namely, go share-holding – so that enterprises can really bear the profits and losses on their own.

In 1987 and 1988, China enacted the Enterprise Bankruptcy Law and Enterprise Law, the purpose of which was to prompt enterprises to gradually be able to assume sole responsibility for the profits and losses, and to provide a strong guarantee that the country's assets can be effectively used by the enterprises and achieve growth in asset value.

To gradually expand the role of the market mechanism, the original planning economic system and the price system went through a preliminary reform. Subsequently, the scope of the mandatory plan in the field of production and circulation was drastically reduced. Industrial products produced under central directives were reduced from 120 varieties in 1984 to 60 in 1986, and its share in the national total industrial output fell from 40% to about 20%. In terms of the circulation of means of production, the raw materials allocated by the central authorities was reduced from 256 varieties in 1984 to 26 in 1987. In the circulation of consumer goods, the prolonged practice of issuing rationing tickets has been basically canceled except for a few varieties.

The price reform was carried out in the following two aspects: (1) prices were adjusted to change the situations where the relative price of various products was seriously distorted; and (2) the government's administrative control of prices was reduced so that prices could reflect the market rules. In China, it was called price reform "combining relaxed control with re-adjustment". With this policy in place, the procurement price of agricultural products has greatly improved, and the price of industrial consumer goods has experienced waving adjustment since 1979. The initial economic reform narrowed the price difference between agricultural products and industrial products. The procurement price of agricultural products increased by 77% in 1986 compared with 1978, while the sales price of industrial products in rural areas increased by 14% in 1986 compared with that in 1978, and the amount of industrial products which could be traded with the same number of agricultural products increased by 54% in 1986 compared with 1978. The reform of the price of the means of production was also focused on the two aspects. First, the planned price of some products was adjusted. For example, the price of raw coal increased from 16.52 to 32.32 yuan/ton, casting pig iron from 150 to 285 yuan/ton, and concrete from 40 to 90 yuan/ton. Second, enterprise products exceeding the planned quota could be sold at a higher price. In this way, there was a "two-track system" not only for the price of agricultural products; namely, part of the products is purchased by the state at a fixed price, and the rest is sold by the producers at the market price, but also for the price of means of production. So far, 65% of agricultural products, 55% of industrial consumer goods and 40% of industrial production have been sold based on market prices and floating prices which reflect varying degrees of market rules.

The finance and taxation system and even the versatile model of the government system also experienced some changes in order to transform the functions and methods of the government's management of the economy and gradually complete the transition from direct control to indirect control.

In terms of the financial system, the local government's financial rights were expanded apart from adjusting the relations of distribution between the government and the enterprises. In the state budgetary revenue, the part controlled by the central government has been reduced from 60% before the reform to about 50%, and the part controlled by local government went up from 40% to 50%.

In the tax system, the first step of tax-for-profits reform was conducted among state-owned enterprises in 1983, that is, in the profits of the enterprises, the government levied an income tax, and the after-tax profits were distributed in various forms between the state and the enterprises. In fact, there was a coexistence of paying taxes and turning in profits. In 1984, the second step was taken to change the profits handed in by the enterprises into regulatory tax paid to the state by the enterprise. The regulatory tax was inconstant and enterprise-specific. Therefore, it could serve as a temporary makeshift.

The banks were freed from its attachment to the state's finance. The People's Bank of China has been identified as the central bank, and a cohort of banks has been restored or newly built. A financial system has taken shape, with the central bank as the core, the four major banks (Bank of China, Agricultural Bank of China, Industrial and Commercial Bank of China and Construction Bank of China) as the pillars, including other financial institutions. The state's for-profit investment been changed from the direct financial grant to bank loan. Banking systems in cities generally carried out lending business with financial institutions; a short-term capital market was initially established, and the bond market began to emerge.

The reform contributed to the development of the economy and the improvement of people's livelihood. If calculated at comparable prices, the gross domestic product (GDP) increased by 102% in 1986 against 1978, 95% in national income and 98% in national revenues, and 3.8 times in extra-budgetary funds of the departments, local governments and enterprises. China's production of electricity, steel, coal and oil has respectively risen from the world's seventh, fifth, third and eighth places to the fifth, fourth, second and fifth places. From 1978 to 1986, the total social output witnessed an average year-on-year increase of 10.1%, of which the highest annual growth rate was 16.5% and the lowest 4.6%, deviating from the average speed by +6.4% and −5.5% respectively. Compared with two decades featuring wild swings before the reform (deviating from the average speed by +24.8% and −41.4% at maximum), the stability of economic growth has increased. Also, employment has significantly improved since the reform: 80 million farmers in rural areas have shifted from agriculture into non-agricultural industries; over 70 million among the urban population have taken jobs. As for people's livelihood, the per capita living expenses of urban residents increased by 82.5% in 1986 compared with 1978, meanwhile the per capita income of farmers increased by 1.7 times if not calculating the inflation. In 1987, the per capita real income of urban and rural residents increased by 1.7% and 5.3% respectively over the previous year despite the high price hike.

Compared with the decades before the reform, the decade of reform (1978–1986) was indeed the most stable period in economic development, and the period when people benefit the most.

III.   Challenges in deepening the reform

However, there still exist a series of problems and difficulties along the journey of reform. To deepen the reform, it is imperative to solve these problems and overcome these difficulties. Due to length constraints, I hereby only put forward a few more prominent issues for a general analysis.

A.   Contradictions and frictions caused by the dual-track system

Since the reform, especially since 1984, China's economic system has embarked on a dual-track system. The planning system featured dual tracks, that is, part of the products were produced according to the mandatory plan, and the rest according to the needs of the market. The system for material circulation also took dual tracks, namely, part of the materials were distributed to the enterprises by the state, and the rest freely purchased by the enterprises. Even the price system also adopted the dual-track system; that is, the planned products were sold at the planned price according to the administrative plan, and unplanned products at market prices (floating price, agreement price, free price) reflecting the market rules at various degrees. Under the dual-track system, the enterprises' behavior and the state's macro-control behavior also took dual tracks. At the beginning of the reform, economists were aware that the dual-track system would cause chaos, but the practice of reform showed that China's reform could not avoid the coexistence of dual-track systems.

Opinions about dual-track systems have always diverged. Some economists believed that, in view of the low starting point and the lofty goal of our reform, the transition from the old system to the new system could not be achieved overnight. The coexistence of the dual-track system was inevitable in the transition from the old system to the new system. Although the coexistence of two tracks would bring some frictions and chaos, it could reduce the risks of reform after all and soften the blows, which make it easier to implement reform, so it could serve as a transitional measure. Some economists believed that the dual-track system not only caused the planned products to flow outside the planned scope and impaired the realization of national economic plan, but also rattled the standards for the measurement of business conditions and provided a hotbed for speculation and other illegal profiteering activities, undermined social atmosphere, and eroded the cadres. It should be immediately ended. How to regard the dual system is a dilemma that has plagued economists for many years. As I have a few papers dedicated to this issue, I will not elaborate on it herein.

B.   The relationship between price reform and enterprise reform

As mentioned earlier, in the process of reform, people have gradually created two basic clues of operation mechanism reform and ownership reform, but as to which is the key and which should be placed in priority, economists diverged in the debate. One side was behind the theory that centers on "enterprise and ownership reform". Economists who held this view argued that price reform could only create the environment for the development of the market economy. They believed that only ownership reform can touch upon fundamental issues such as profitability, accountability and motivation, and that the problem of shortages could not be achieved in the short term; therefore, the price reform should be bypassed, and energy should be focused on ownership reform centered on enterprise property rights system. The other side was in favor of "price and market reform" as the priority. Economists held this view deemed that the reform of the enterprise economic mechanism was aimed at shaping enterprises into the main market players. So, it must take the existence of the market as the prerequisite and a relatively reasonable price system as the guarantee. The new enterprise system cannot be born within the distorted price system. Hence, energy needs to be focused on the market reform centers on price reform.

These two views were justified in terms of logic, but I think there was a certain one-sidedness to both. In fact, these two types of the reform should not be competing for which one should take place first; rather, they were like the two sides of a coin. They were interrelated and mutually reinforcing. In the case of price distortions, the autonomy and self-financing of enterprises could not be achieved, as exemplified by the current difficulties caused by price chaos to contracting enterprises. On the contrary, if the enterprise reform was not carried out, the enterprise was not responsible for its own profits or losses, or the budget constraint of the enterprise was still lax, then the enterprise would not make sensitive and correct responses to the market signals, especially the price signals, even if the signals were not distorted. From the perspective of practice and reality, the former view had a greater impact on decision-making in 1986 and 1987, emphasizing enterprise reform and relaxing the price reform. In recent months, however, price reform has been highlighted. I hope that the future reform can learn from the lessons in the past and better integrate the two types of reform. I think that the long-term freeze on prices and wages (which has basically been the norm in the past 20 years before the start of the reform) is not conducive to economic development, but the drastic changes are also detrimental to economic development, and it is unrealistic to expect the price and wage reform to be completed overnight.

C. *Inflation*

Since 1985, prices have shown a rising trend across the country. According to official statistics, the annual rate of increase in the retail price index was 8.8% in 1985, 6% in 1986 and 7.3% in 1987. The first quarter of this year witnessed a 10% plus year-on-year increase. In terms of varieties, food prices rose the fastest, registering a 10.1% hike in 1987. In terms of regions, the cities, especially major cities, witnessed the fastest rise in prices. The reason for the rise in prices were of course multifaceted. Even changing the distortions of relative price in the original system, namely, the structural adjustment of the price, could also lead the overall

Table 9.1 Growth of National Income, Fixed Assets and Total Payroll between 1985 and 1987

Year	Growth rate of national income	Growth rate of fixed assets investment	Growth rate of total payroll
1985	12.3	38.8	22
1986	7.4	18.7	14
1987	9.3	16.5	12.4

prices to increase. But in the couple of years, no major measures have been taken in the adjustment of the price structure, and the trend of rising prices has becoming increasingly evident. Therefore, many economists believe that the fundamental reason for the rise in prices in recent years lies in the excessive issuance of money, which fundamentally represents a kind of inflationary rise in prices.

As for the excessive issuance of money, it is caused by the overlarge scale of investment and expansion of consumption funds. Since 1985, the growth rates of fixed asset investment and wages have been much higher than the growth rate of national income (see Table 9.1)

The result is embodied by the fiscal deficit and the credit balance. The former is often offset by overdraft from the banks, while the latter was balanced by issuing additional currency, which results in excessive currency issuance. According to statistics, the growth rate of currency circulation over the four years was 49.5% in 1984, 24.7% in 1985, 23.3% in 1986 and 19.4% in 1987, all of which greatly exceeded the growth rate of gross national product (GDP) in each year. Even with the need to monetize the national economy, the money supply was still excessive.

The fundamental way to manage inflation is to eliminate the swollen investment and inflated consumption and to solve the "economic overheat" problem, while also changing the common concept that inflation is good for economic growth.

D.   *Inequity in income distribution*

Before the reform, income distribution in China emphasized equality and ignored efficiency, which resulted in the ills of egalitarianism. Since the reform, the policy of letting some people get rich first has been carried out and reasonably widening the income gap was emphasized in the hope of achieving the goal of common prosperity by enhancing efficiency. This is in line with China's actual situation and resembles the research results of international economists like Kuznets.

But in practice, the implementation of this policy has encountered various difficulties. Recently, the social response to unfair distribution of income has been strong and become a hot topic of people's concern. For example, the income of taxi drivers significantly exceeded that of bus drivers; the income of workers in private enterprises was much higher than that of the employees in state-owned enterprises, and the income from the second occupation was higher than that of the first occupation. The fact that some people reaped profiteering income through illegal means has aroused dissatisfaction among the public.

In fact, the issue of egalitarianism has not yet been solved in China. According to statistics, the Gini coefficient in rural areas has increased slightly since the reform from 0.2124 in 1978 to 0.2636 in 1985, but the Gini coefficient in urban areas has fallen a little, from 0.185 in 1977 to 0.168 in 1984. The initial wage reform in 1985 resulted in a wage system featuring a smaller wage gap. For example, the wage gap between university professors, associate professors, lecturers, and teaching assistants now is much smaller than it was in the 1950s. Therefore, in the current personal income distribution in China, there coexists the following two phenomena: where the state exerts direct control, the old egalitarianism has not been eliminated while the new egalitarianism has emerged; where the state cannot exert direct control and the indirect control system has not been effectively established, some people and some economic activities have generated unreasonably high income. The coexistence of these two phenomena shows that the current situation of income distribution in China deviated from the requirement that the economic system reform should achieve common prosperity by rationally widening the income gap.

The reasons for this situation are found in many aspects, starting with the dual-track system. The existence of the dual-track system makes the income from unplanned economic activity significantly higher than that from the planned economic activities. The contrast between the two represents the contradictions of the dual-track system in the distribution of personal income. Of course, the result of inflation would inevitably widen the gap between planned and unplanned prices, as well as the gap between the income from planned economic activities and the income from unplanned economic activities, which would further strengthen the contrast between the two. As for the prevalence of unequal opportunities, there are more deep-seated reasons. Obviously, it is imperative to tailor the medicine to the root causes of the problems that have emerged in personal income distribution. Meanwhile, attention must be paid to the overall situation and root causes instead of the symptoms.

E. Relationship between economic decentralization and administrative decentralization

The market-oriented reforms are decentralized reforms from the policy perspective. Ten years of reform are tainted with both economic and administrative decentralization. Economic decentralization refers to changing the status of enterprises from being the appendant to the state administrative organization to producers and operators of goods, so that the enterprises are out there in the market. Administrative decentralization means delegating the functions of the central government to local governments. At the outset of the reform, people have recognized from the experience of the Soviet Union, Eastern Europe and China that the economic decentralization with expanded enterprise autonomy is the key to decentralization of decision-making, and that the administrative decentralization divorced from economic decentralization is meaningless. But during the two decentralization processes over the past decade, there has been a tilt towards administrative decentralization. By 1987, industrial products under central direct management were only 50% of the original, and materials under unified central distribution only 10% of the original; but the decision-making power really enjoyed by enterprises was only about 40%, and the reason is that the power decentralized by central government was retained by the local government to a substantial extent. Such a phenomenon originates from the early 1980s when some provinces and cities adopted the Fiscal Responsibility System, which later spurred the Local Responsibility System for investment, materials, credit, foreign trade and foreign exchange, and even the Department Responsibility System for investment, materials, and foreign exchange. The Local Responsibility System strengthened the regional division and mutual blockade as well as the local government's intervention in the enterprises, which hindered the formation of a unified national market. Hence, some economists put forward the "highly centralized-government-plus-commodity-economy" model. In my view, it is necessary to strengthen the economic decentralization of the enterprises and weaken the administrative decentralization of local government for some time at the current stage of reform and development, especially for the purpose of solving existing problems. However, in terms of long-term goals, "highly centralized government" is not appropriate. Particularly in such a large country as China, it is essential to leverage the local government's economic role, which is commonly referred to as giving play to the role of the intermediary bodies. Therefore, the long-term orientation of reform should be the unity of economic decentralization and administrative decentralization, rather than the combination of economic decentralization and administrative centralization.

The aforementioned represents my analysis on some difficulties in reform from the economic point of view. In fact, there are also some non-economic difficulties. For instance, many things are incompatible with the reform requirements in the political system and people's traditional ideas, such as bureaucracy, abuse of power, corruption, etc. They have become obstacles in the reform process, and there is an urgent need to overcome them to deepen the reform.

IV. Conclusion: actively and steadily push the reform forward

Although the ten-year reform has made remarkable achievements, the process of reform is bound to be intertwined with the development process, as the starting point of our reform is so low, and the goal of reform was very high. Therefore, we have covered just a short distance in our path to the goal. The difficulties facing the current reform are so complex that, as some economists have said, reform is now at a new turning point where people can make a variety of choices. First, people can fight against the economic maladies through strengthening and restoring direct administrative control, such as re-freeze prices and widely imposing the rationing system. However, this means backtracking and regressing, which is definitely unadvisable. Second, people can choose to maintain the status quo and just take some remedial measures to reduce friction. This would mean making the transitional state during the system reshuffle become the norm, which is apparently not in line with the direction of the reform. Third, people can create a buyer's market through drastic measures, or even artificial methods, to form a reform environment with generally balanced supply and demand and make a swift shift to the new system immediately. This idea is desirable in in its intention, but it seems to fail to grasp the complexity of the reality in our reform. It should be noted that even the buyer's market can be artificially created; the degree of market development results from its free development and cannot be artificially maneuvered. Therefore, I think the only alternative path is to take active and sound measures to push the reform forward and gradually strive for the early establishment of the basic framework for the new economic system.

References

Dong Fureng. (1979). 关于我国社会主义所有制形式问题 [On China's Socialist Ownership]. *Economic Research Journal*, 1.

Gao Shangquan. (1987). 九年来的中国经济体制改革 [China's Reform of Economic System for Nine Years]. Beijing: People's Publishing House.

Li Yining. (June 9th, 1986). 关于经济体制改革的思路 [Ideas on Reform of Economic System]. *World Economic Herald*.

Liu Guoguang et al. (1987). 中国社会主义经济的改革、开放和发展 [Reform, Opening Up and Development of China's Socialist Economy]. Beijing: Economy & Management Publishing House.

Liu Guoguang. (April 5th, 1988). 正视通货膨胀问题 [Confronting Inflation]. *Economic Daily*.

National Bureau of Statistics, 中国统计年鉴 [China Statistics Yearbook] (1987). Beijing: China Statistics Press.

Shegero Ishikawa. (1986). 社会主义经验和中国的经验 – 对经济改革的展望 [Socialist Economy and China's Experience: Outlook on Economic Reform]. *Science & Technology Review*, 2.

Wu Jinglian. (1987). 关于改革战略选择的若干思考 [Several Thoughts on Choices of Reform Strategies]. *Economic Research Journal*, 2.

Wu Jinglian & Zhao Renwei. (November, 1987). The Dual Pricing System in China's Industry, U.S.A. *Journal of Comparative Economics*.

Zhao Renwei. (1982). 我国原来属于什么经济模式 [What Economic Model China Originally Belongs to]. *Economic Perspectives*, 2.

Zhao Renwei. (1986). 我国经济改革过程中的双重体制问题 [The Dual-Track System in China's Economic Reform]. *Economic Research Journal*, 9.

Zhang Zhuoyuan. (April 25th, 1988). 我国物价上涨的原因与对策 [Reasons and Countermeasures for Price Rise in China]. *Guangming Daily*.

(Submitted to the Symposium on China's Economic Reform and Cross-strait Relations held at the University of California, Berkeley, in August 1988.)

10 Retrospect and outlook of China's economic reform over the past two decades – characteristics, experience & lessons and challenges

China's economic system reform has been going on for two decades. In this article, I do not want to describe the process of reform over the past 20 years briefly; rather, I want to sum up the characteristics of the reform, experience and lessons learned and the challenges to offer some useful insights for further deepening the reform.

I. Characteristics of China's economic reform

Compared with the Soviet Union and Eastern Europe, China's economic reform has distinct characteristics. Dwight H. Perkins, a professor at Harvard University, put forward the Asian pattern of reform of Socialist economic systems. He thinks the Asian pattern of reform has the following three characteristics:[1]

First, economic reform precedes political reform.

Second, the socialist countries in Asia are much poorer than those in the Soviet Union and Eastern Europe.

Third, in the Asian socialist countries of Asia, most of the populations were engaged in agriculture when the reform started, and most of the industrial output came from small and medium-sized industries.

He also points out that these three characteristics are interrelated. Professor Perkins's analysis of these three characteristics is suitable not only for countries like Vietnam in Asia, but also for major countries like China. However, in terms of China's specific socio-economic situations, I think China's economic reform shows three other characteristics (of course, these features are closely linked with the characteristics mentioned previously). These features can be summarized as follows.

First, the economic system borrowed from the Soviet Union exerts different forces on various parts of the national economy, with the most powerful role limited only to the main player of the national economy, namely, the industrialization; and a less powerful role on the decentralized agriculture and small industries. As pointed out by Professor S. Ishikawa, the original economic system in China can be defined as a "system featuring centralized management of planned rationing and resource allocation" in the broad sense; but because of the low income and other conditions, the role of this system is limited only to one part of the entire national economy, excluding the market economy and customary economy.[2] Some economists described this feature as "the low coverage of the planned economy". This feature provides space for China to take the phased approach of overcoming the challenges gradually.

Second, the starting point of China's economic reform is lower than that of the Soviet Union and Eastern European countries. This is because the aforementioned economic system, as the main economic system in China, has experienced a number of variations over the 20-plus years after its establishment. Compared with the economic system in 1956 when it was first established, the economic system on the eve of the reform (1978) was more homogeneous in ownership, more centralized in economic decision-making and more materialized in economic processes (namely, advocating rationing and rejecting the market mechanism in the allocation of resources), as well as more egalitarian in income distribution, more closed in the external relations and more mobilized in economic organization. Therefore, the economic system on the eve of China's reform has more supply factors characteristic of military communism, although it can be referred to as the traditional planned economic system. If the economic system of the Soviet and Eastern European countries before the reform can be called a typical planned economy (the Stalin model), then the pre-reform economic system in China can be called a model of paramilitary communism. It can be seen clearly from Figure 10.1 that the starting point of China's reform was later than that of the Soviet Union and Eastern European countries.[3]

Figure 10.1 evaluated the starting point of China's reform only from the perspective of the economic system itself. If other factors were taken into account, such as the lack of theories on economic reform and the low level of economic development, then the relatively low starting point for China's reform would be even more obvious.

Third, compared with the Soviet Union and Eastern Europe, China's economic reform was closely integrated with economic development. Before the reform, Soviet Union and Eastern Europe, in general, had achieved industrialization, so they were developed countries, while China belonged to the developing countries. As shown in Figure 10.2,[4] China not only went through a transition from the planned economy to the market economy in the transformation of the economic system, but also experienced a transition from the conventional economy or agricultural economy to the market economy and from the dual economy to the

Planned (centralized)   Market (decentralized)

Military Communist Economy	Premilitary Communist Economy	Typical Planned Economy	Revised Planned Economy	Adjusted Market Economy	Free Market Economy

The starting point
of China's
economic reform

Figure 10.1 The Starting Point of China's Economic Reform

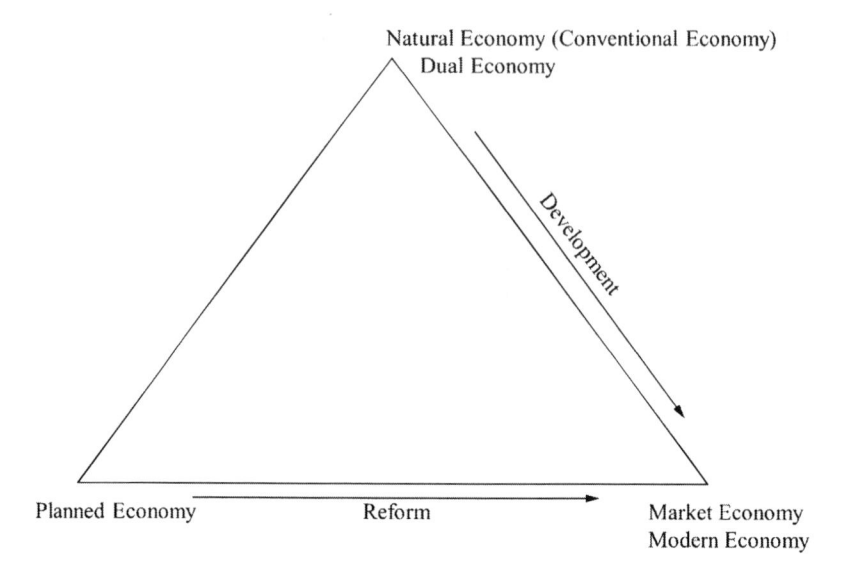

Figure 10.2 Institutional Transformation and Development Transformation of China

modern economy in the transformation of its economic development. With regard to how to combine these two transformation processes, I will further explore the issue in the second section of this article when discussing the experience of China's reform.

Compared with development transformation, institutional transformation is more difficult. This is because the former development is an evolving process, while the latter is a reforming process, which is bound to encounter more artificial obstacles, mainly ideological obstacles and obstacles created by people with vested interests. Of course, people's understanding of this issue is by no means linear. Because of the aforementioned reasons, China's reform over the past two decades has gone through a complicated process of twists and turns and is beset with repeated debates. The debate about reform goals is a typical case.

It can be seen from Figure 10.3 that since the task of reforming the economic system was raised in the Third Plenary Session of the Eleventh Central Committee of the Communist Party of China in December 1978, China has experienced a number of major ups and downs until the 14th Congress of the Communist Party of China, where the reform goal of the socialist market economy was clearly formulated. At the beginning of the reform, there seemed to be no disagreement about expanding the role of the market mechanism, but opinions divided on how far we should go in this direction. Such inconsistency was less pronounced in the 1979–1980 discussion about relations between planned economy and market economy. This is because at that time, even the economists who advocated market-oriented reform did not jump out of the framework of the planned economy in general. They just had different views on the role of the market mechanism. Therefore,

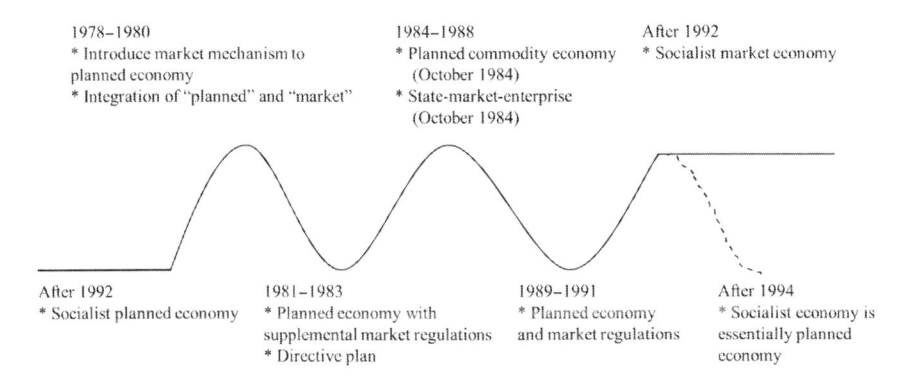

Figure 10.3 Arguments about the Goal of China's Economic Reform

they did not have prominent divergences with the economists who persisted in the planned economy.

However, as the reform progressed, the differences became apparent. From 1981 to 1983, the idea of downsizing the directive plan and expanding the guiding plan was criticized, while the idea of advocating the planned economy, especially the directive plan, supplemented by market regulations, gained the upper hand and was adopted as the goal of reform on the 12th People's Congress of the Communist Party of China. In retrospect, the twists and turns then seem completely understandable now. This is because China was busy putting wrongs to rights in the early 1980s. People strongly demanded a complete change from the chaotic decade of the "Cultural Revolution", and they wanted societal order to be restored. However, the theory of reform was not in place, and even the Eastern European reform theory had just begun to be introduced to China, so the whole country was just making explorations and experiments. According to China's own experience, only the prime time of the planned economy in 1956 and 1965 witnessed relatively good results. Therefore, the prevailing thinking was that the goal of reform should be returning to the orderly state of the prevailing mandatory plan supplemented by certain market regulations. This idea of replacing the reform with "putting wrongs to rights" gave rise to some doubts at that time, and this idea was bound to be challenged in the practice of reform (because even if the typical planned economy were returned, it could not be called reform.) Still, it became a guiding ideology of the reform objective in a not-so-long historical period.

With the progress of reform, the Third Plenary Session of the Twelfth CPC Central Conference in 1984 put forward the goal of "a planned commodity economy", and regarded reducing the mandatory plan as the focus of the reform. Then the idea of indirect regulation featuring state-regulated market and market-led enterprises was raised in the 13th National People's Congress of the Communist Party of China In 1987. These were undoubtedly shaking the foundation of the planned economy, thus marking important steps towards the reform goal of the market economy. It could be said that the five-year period between 1984 and 1988 was one when China's economic reform strode forward.

China's economic reforms were once again at low ebb because of the failure of the price reform in 1988 and the political turmoil at the turn of the spring and summer of 1989. The aforementioned idea of indirect control and regulation died down. Instead, the idea of "planned economy and market regulation", which is similar to the "planned economy supplemented by market regulation", once again became the dominant thinking, with the analogy of "bird cage economy" regaining the front page in western media coverage.

However, this period brimmed with twists and turns did not last for too long, and was reversed after Deng Xiaoping's South Talks in early 1992. Moreover, the detour took place under the premise of unchanged general policy in the reform and opening-up, with limited volatility. According to the spirit of Deng Xiaoping's South Talks and the development of reform, the "socialist market economy" was finally established as the goal of reform at the 14th National People's Congress of the Communist Party of China held in October 1992.[5]

It can be observed from the ups and downs above that although China's economic reform was market-oriented at the beginning, it took 14 years to change the goal of reform from the planned economy to the market economy. Moreover, the debate over the goal of reform did not end after 1992.

During the debate, the ideas still existed that the essence of socialism is the planned economy and that the planned economy is an example of macro control. However, since the "socialist market economy" has been recognized officially, such ideas became somewhat informal. So, for the arguments on these ideas happened after 1992, I present them with a dotted line in Figure 10.3.

II.   Experience and lessons in China's economic reform

China's economic system reform has made remarkable achievements. We do not need to list them one by one in this essay. From a macro perspective, they can be summarized in the following sentences. First, in terms of ownership, the system featuring "large in size and collective in nature" was dismantled and a diversified ownership structure with a variety of economic components was initially established. Second, the market mechanism began to play a fundamental role in some important areas, with remarkable progress in the development of a competitive market system and great improvement in the general adoption of the market principles. Third, in macroeconomic management, important progress has been made in the transition from direct regulation to indirect regulation. Through the reform of finance, taxation and investment, the indirect control system based on economic means has been formed initially. Fourth, the labor employment system and the income distribution system have also undergone major changes. Fifth, an all-around and multi-level pattern of opening up to the outside has been basically formed.

In light of the great progress made in China's economic reform, there are inevitably abundant successful experiences worthy of our consideration. Here, I take the liberty to raise the following two points:

A. Reform and development (growth) move in tandem, reinforcing each other

Many experts argue that, regardless of the ways reform is carried out, the decline in the level of production and the level of consumption is inevitable at the initial stage of the reform; that is, the initial stage of reform comes inevitably at the expense of economic growth. Adam Przeworski, a professor at the University of Chicago, made the argument based on experience of reform in Eastern Europe and Latin America that during reform, whether in a radical or a gradualist way, the decline in production and consumption is inevitable, except that both increase and decrease are sharp when the reform is in a radical way while declines or raises are slow when the reform is in a gradualist way. Figure 10.4 well illustrates this phenomenon.[6] In the table, S represents the starting point of the reform, R represents the radical approach of reform and G represents the gradualist way of reform.

However, China's experience runs contrary to this situation. China has achieved reform and growth simultaneously and witnessed rapid economic growth for a very long period, as shown in Figure 10.5. From 1978 to 1996, China's gross domestic product (GNP) grew at an average annual rate of 9.8%, of which 1991–1996 saw an increase as high as 11.8%. The growth rate of the following two years, however, declined slightly, but the average annual growth rate for the past two decades was still above 9%. With the introduction of each measure, China's economic reform, whether in rural or urban areas, is focused on improving the incentive mechanism to increase the total economy, and promote the reform based on "making a bigger cake". Evidence can be found in the implementation of rural household contract responsibility system, the reform of purchase prices of agricultural products, the development of rural township enterprises (TVEs), the expanding autonomy of state-owned enterprises, the development of the non-state-owned economy, retained foreign exchange of foreign trade enterprises, and the establishment of

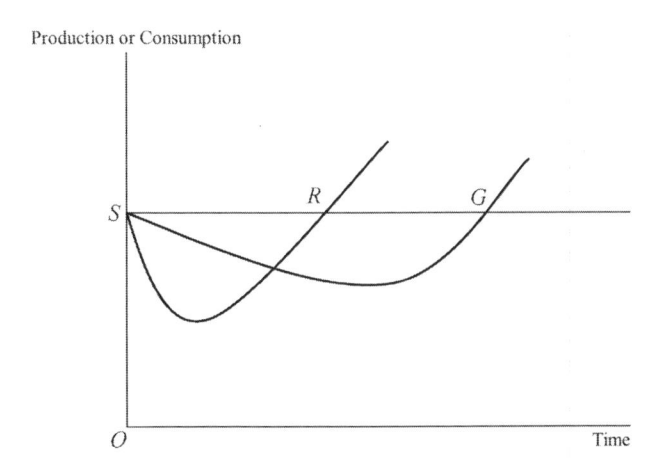

Figure 10.4 Reform at the Cost of Economic Growth

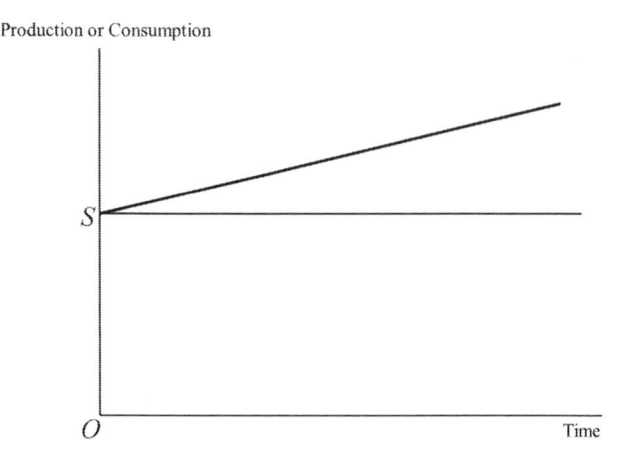

Figure 10.5 Reform Progress along with Economic Growth

special economic zones.[7] If there were no rapid economic growth, it would be impossible to lift about 200 million people out of poverty and raise people's living standards generally and substantially while allowing some people to get rich first (widening the income gap).[8] According to official statistics, China's impoverished population has dropped from 250 million in 1978 to 60 million in 1996.[9] As for the relationship among economic growth, inequality and poverty, the World Bank's report showed this from the perspective of international comparison.[10] It follows that reform and growth mutually advanced each other and formed a virtuous circle, which should be a successful experience in China's reform.

B.   Gradualist transformation is conducive to reducing the cost and the risk of reform

Chinese and foreign scholars hold different views on the advantages of the gradualist way or radical way in reform and even on whether China's reform has taken a gradualist approach.[11] I would like to put forward some opinions on this. I think that China's reform, has taken a gradualist approach generally speaking, except that the rural household contract responsibility in the early 1980s is tainted with radical colors. In September 1980, the Central Committee of the Communist Party of China (CPC) issued "Several Issues Concerning Further Strengthening the Responsibility System of Agricultural Production". Subsequently, the rural areas witnessed the replacement of the three-level system of the people's commune by the household contract responsibility system in the short two years between then and the fall of 1982, which was quite radical. However, this only constitutes part of the rural reform. The rest of the rural reform, especially the price reform, as well as the entire urban reform took the gradualist approach. According to China's national conditions, this transition has so far been successful. Not only many Chinese scholars, but also some foreign scholars who advocate radical reform in general, think that China's gradualist reform is successful. For example, the American professor J. Sachs from Harvard University is a well-known scholar in studying the radical reform (so-called "shock therapy") of the Soviet Union and some countries in Eastern Europe, but he came to China to give lectures in the early 1990s and affirmed the gradualist way of China's reform. Another figure is Professor W. Berns from the University of Oxford. He came to China in the 1980s and advocated that China's reform should take a "package" approach, namely a radical way to avoid friction brought by the dual-track price system. However, when he came to China again in the early 1990s, he thought that the gradualist way of China's reform was suitable for China's national conditions.

So, in what ways is the gradualist reform successful? I think that from the perspective of the two main lines (or two main aspects) of economic reform, the successful experience can be attributed to the approach of combining relaxed control with re-adjustment in price reform and focusing on the periphery first in the ownership reform. In terms of the price reform, such measures prompt the prices in the planned economy system to reach the average market level through continuous adjustments on the one hand and make the market prices which is outside the planned system expand in the proportion continuously on the other hand and finally realize the integration of two tracks. Although this kind of transition inevitably encounters the double-track friction, it is much less risky than the "one-step" price reform or the price break (see subsection 1). In the ownership reform, the battle begins with the periphery and allows the non-state-owned new business to enter the ownership spectrum, which is conducive not only to reforming the ownership structure for expanded proportion of non-state economy, but also to the benefit of economic growth. This is often referred to as the gradualist way of "incremental reform",[12] which is not only in line with the low coverage of China's original planned economic system, but also in congruence with China's transition from the dual-track economy to the modern economy. Moreover, it reflects the simultaneity of reform and growth mentioned earlier.

Although the collective ownership of the land was retained, the contractual tenure was very long (15 years, and then extended for another 30 years), and the rights and responsibilities of the farmers were clear, so it could be viewed as a successful ownership reform. Setting aside some detailed aspects of the reform, Figure 10.6 shows the benefits that rural price reform and ownership reform have brought to farmers. Before the reform, farmers must sell all the surplus grain and other important agricultural products to the country at a planned, very low price, and the benefits covered only ACDF. However, through price reform, farmers increased the benefits represented by HJAC. Among them, HIAB represented the benefits through the gradualist adjustment of the price and IJBC the benefits through the release of prices. The so-called gradualist adjustment of prices means that the state gradually increases the planned purchase price of agricultural products and changes the relative price of agricultural products

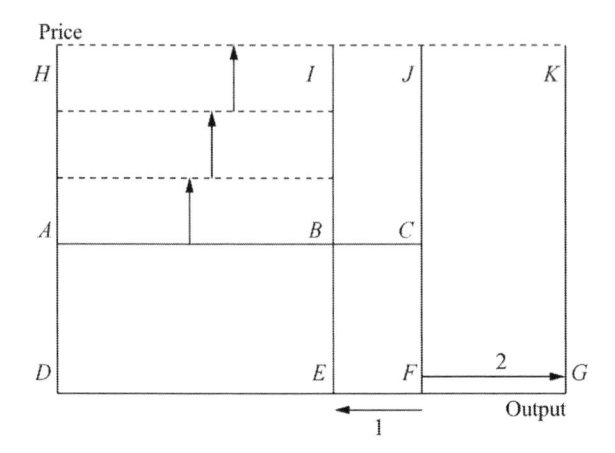

Figure 10.6 Rural Price Reform and Ownership Reform

compared with industrial products, thus narrowing the gap between these two (see the three upwards arrows shown in Figure 10.6). The so-called price liberalization refers to the practice that the state reduces the quota of the purchase or order of agricultural products so that farmers could sell agricultural products on the market beyond the quota (as indicated by arrow 1 in Figure 10.6). Therefore, price liberation was actually changing the mechanism of the price formation, namely the shift from planned price to market price. The experience of "integrating adjustment with the relaxed control" in rural price reform was later extended to the urban reforms. As for the rural ownership reform, the effect has been very notable. For example, between 1978 and 1984, agricultural output increased by 42.23% (as indicated by arrow 2 in Figure 10.6), of which 46.89% came from the increase in productivity resulting from the implementation of the household contract responsibility system.[13] The success of rural ownership reform not only increased the output of agricultural products, but also benefited the farmers because of the high market prices of these products, as shown by JKFG in Figure 10.6. Ownership reform in the city was special, and it was difficult to copy the rural experience. However, whether it was the rapid development of urban non-state economy, or rural non-agricultural industries, especially the rapid development of township enterprises, all could be attributable to the incremental reform.

That being said, what lessons can be learned from China's economic reform? In this connection, I could not agree more with the opinions of Xue Muqiao, who is a highly experienced economist in the economy community. The 1988 "price break" and the contract system of state-owned enterprises from the mid-1980s to the early 1990s were failures to be alerted to. He even called the two actions "errors in reform".[14] Herein, I would like to talk about my views briefly.

1.   *Regarding the "price break" in the summer of 1988*

The radical price reform, known as the "price break" was hastily launched in June 1988. At that time the guiding ideology of price reform was "long-term pain is worse than short-term pain" and "finish it at one go". However, China's macroeconomic situation was quite tense then. There was much pressure caused by inflation (then the annual inflation rate was 18.5%), and the friction between the dual pricing systems was very serious (that year saw the biggest difference between market price and planned price in the 20 years since China's reform and opening-up; for example, the planned price of ordinary steel was 700 yuan per ton, while the market price was 1800 yuan per ton). In this case, it was simply unrealistic to bypass the inflation and the friction of the dual-track price system to implement "one step" price break, as truth would have it. I was invited to participate in the discussion of the price reform program in July. However, upon the release of the "price break" news by the media in August, there aroused a national wave of bank runs and panic buying. This wave washed away the ideas to speed up the price reform.

The failure of the "price break", however, proved once again that the price reform integrating adjustment with the relaxed control of the dual-track transition was feasible. Of course, that we could not achieve the goal at one go did not mean that we could not achieve the goal. The goal of double-track transition was to merge the two tracks and finally become the market track. However, we can learn something from the lessons above, namely what are the necessary conditions for the merger of the dual price tracks. I think the following three conditions are inevitable. First, the planned price should be gradually closer to the market equilibrium level through the continuous adjustment; that is, the gap between the two price tracks cannot be too large, so that double-track friction can be reduced drastically. Second, the ratio of market price expands to a considerable extent through the transformation of the price formation mechanism; that is, the parts with price liberalization has accounted for a large proportion. Third, the macroeconomic situation cannot be too tense; especially the supply and demand of currency should be more moderate.

2.   *Regarding the contract system of state-owned enterprises*

The contract system for state-owned enterprises was tried only in some areas and enterprises before 1986. After the State Council issued "Several Provisions on Deepening Enterprise Reform and Enhancing Enterprises Vitality" in December 1986, the contract system was in full swing nationwide. The basic content was that the enterprises must guarantee to turn over the base quota of profits to the state; they may retain the surplus if any and need to supplement the shortage if any. It had gone through two rounds of contracting (about three years for each). In July 1992, the State Council promulgated the "Regulations on the Transformation of Operating System of Industrial Enterprises Owned by the Whole People", and proposed to bring enterprises to market. In particular, the Third Plenary Session of the 14th CPC Conference held in November 1993 adopted "Decision on Several Issues Concerning the Establishment of Socialist Market Economy" and proposed the establishment of a modern enterprise system. Since then, the contract system of state-owned enterprises also became history.

For the contract system of state-owned enterprises, there are three different types of evaluation in the economics literature: Type A evaluation gives high praise to the system and even regards it as the strategic direction of reform. Type B evaluation holds it common just as a stage of the reform of state-owned enterprise. Type C evaluation belittles it, even taking it as an "erroneous zone" in reform. Mr. Xue Muqiao's evaluation Falls into type C.

I fully agree with Mr. Xue's evaluation for the following reasons. First, in term of mechanism setting, the contract system strengthened the vertical one-on-one bargaining relationship or negotiation relationship between the business and the government, rather than the equal horizontal relationship among multiple market players such as enterprises. This mechanism was fundamentally not in line with the market orientation of the reform. On the contrary, it inherited the bargaining relationship between the business and the government in the planned economy. The only difference is that indicators of the input and output was the contention point in the planned economy, while the basic quota of profits turned in was the question in the contract system. Second, in terms of the relationship between the interests of the state and the interests of enterprises, the state seemed to be able to get stable fiscal revenue in the short term, but the state was at always a disadvantage in the end. This is because, in the businesses' negotiations with government, there was no set of more normative standards for the determination of the contract base. In the negotiations, the interests drove the enterprises, and there was no restraint on the duties of the government department cadres. Therefore, there appeared a common phenomenon of enterprises having no profits and no losses in the process of contracting. This situation was just one of the reasons for the loss of state assets. Thus, the contract system was nominally the separation of ownership and operation rights. It was meant for the preservation of the property of the whole people, but in fact, it deprived the state of its property. Some people commented it was "quiet privatization". Wasn't it contrary to the original intention of preserving the property of the whole people? Later facts also proved that with the loss of state-owned assets and the expansion of the losses of enterprises, the contract system was difficult to continue.

As pointed out by Mr. Xue, "The direction and focus of state-owned enterprise reform should be gradually shifted to the separation of government and enterprises, and the systematic innovation of state-owned enterprises." State-owned enterprises should be commodity producers and operators featuring self-accounting, self-management, self-financing, equal completion and survival of the fittest. However, the use of contract system cannot achieve these goals, thus delaying the timing for the reform of state-owned enterprises. "I think this is a scientific summary of the failure arising from the contract system of state-owned enterprise.

III. Challenges facing China's economic reform

Twenty years into China's economic reform, remarkable achievements have been scored, but it still faces challenges.

First, the gradualist reform itself is faced with challenges. This is because the distinction between progressive reform and radical reform is not absolute, and there is no way to decide which is better. In the early period of reform, we went through a gradualist way with a smaller risk and lower costs to achieve greater results. However, China's gradualist reform has intrinsic connotation of "tackling the easy first" and "approaching the periphery before the core". Therefore, we must soberly realize that the most difficult problem has not yet been resolved and focus on tackling and overcoming the difficulties in the future. For example, the reform of state-owned enterprises, the reform of the financial system, the reform of the housing system and the reform of the social security system are all knotty problems. If we do not press ahead despite the difficulties, and remain satisfied with the achievements of the gradualist reform, even blindly believe in the advantages of gradualist reform, and thus intentionally or unintentionally delay the process of reform, then the cost of reform will rise, and the positive effect of reform will decline. Just imagine this: if we look at the radical reform of those countries that have received economic recovery, can we still rest on the achievements contently?

Second, the challenges of reform are also reflected in how to balance the following aspects.

A. The balance among reform, development and stability

Properly dealing with the relationship between reform, development and stability is a principle we should stick to, but how to apply this principle in practice is a very complex problem. Some economists emphasize stability, put forward the concept of "steady progress", and emphasize the control of inflation in economic policies; some other economists stress development and reform, which is in fact advocating "progressing steadily ", and translates into growth and employment in economic policy. I believe that, based on the reality in China, the major problems in handling the relationship among the three concerns how to combine short-term interests and long-term interests, in particular, how to prevent the pursuit of temporary stability while ignoring reform and weakening development. A case in point would be the question of how to combine short-term stability and long-term stability between state-owned enterprise reform and social security system reform. It has not faded from people's memory that in the early 1990s, the reform of state-owned enterprises set off a boom of "breaking the three irons (iron chair – guaranteed leading post, iron bowl – a secure job, and iron wages – permanent income)". This was supposed to be the righteousness in the reform of state-owned enterprises. However, due to the lack of the necessary social security system, the "breaking three irons" campaign had to be stalled to prevent workers from living on the streets and affecting social stability. In the light of short-term stability, such action was perfectly understandable. However, it should be noted that the problem was not resolved.

A few years later, the problems encountered in "breaking three irons" once again emerged in such manifestations as "lay-off". In order to dispose laid-off workers properly, the social security system reform was up high on the agenda once again. Therefore, we seem to be able to draw the conclusion that the reform of state-owned enterprises and the reform of social security system should try to avoid the trade-offs and on-and-off fights with each other. Rather, a virtuous circle or a benign interaction should form between the two. Only in this way can we not only promote the progress of reform, but also maintain social and economic stability – both short-term stability and long-term stability. In recent years, the concept of "sustainable development" has been recognized by the whole country. Should we also form the concept of "sustainable and stable" to promote the ongoing pace of reform and development?

B.　*The internal balance of economic reform*

The balance of relations within the economic reform is what we usually call the link between the various aspects of economic reform. This is the problem put forward at the initial stage of the reform, but is more practically significant as the reform has deepened. Of course, supporting reform does not mean that the reform in various aspects must mechanically go hand in hand. In fact, there was a certain sequence in the reform of different parts in the past. For example, rural reform preceded urban reform, and price reform preceded ownership reform or property reform. However, this kind of reform is like walking on two legs, so if one leg has taken a step, the other must follow, so we can successfully move forward. The various links of reform also encountered problems of coordination, so one link cannot go too far with other links lagging behind. In the current situation, property rights reform is still lagging behind the market reform in the overall economic reform, and the development of factor market is still lagging behind the development of product markets in the whole market reform. Such problems need to be gradually resolved in the reform going forward.

At present, China's economic marketization has reached a considerable extent. It is estimated that the degree of marketization of price formation is between 60% and 70%, of which the total retail sales of social goods have reached 92.5%.[15] However, due to the lagging of the reform of property right system, it is difficult for state-owned enterprises to get rid of the difficulties, which in turn dragged the financial system reform and bank commercialization. It is estimated that China's state-owned enterprises have bad debts of more than one trillion yuan, of which about 600 billion to 800 billion yuan are distressed debts of state-owned banks. As some scholars have pointed out, "if there is no real business, there is no real bank."[16] There also exists a similar relationship between housing commercialization and labor marketization. The high market price of the houses is too expensive for the employees who cannot sell public housing bought at a lower price. The lack of liquidity in housing resources also constrains the mobility of labor, which in turn constraints the enterprises going to the market. Nowadays, the difficulties of economic reform have actually been in twain and twisted like a basket of crabs. We must break the deadlock in order to promote further development of reform.

C. The balance among economic reform, political reform and other non-economic factors

With the further deepening of economic reform, it will inevitably require a variety of non-economic factors as supporting functions, including political, moral, cultural and other factors. As mentioned earlier, economic reform takes precedence over political reform as one of the traits, and in a certain sense an advantage in China's reform. However, few people believe that the advancement of economic reform does not require political reform, or that political reform can lag behind infinitely.

The relationship between the transformation of the operating mechanism of state-owned enterprises and the conversion of government functions is a typical example of the relationship between economic reform and political reform. An important task of state-owned enterprise reform is to change the enterprises from the appendage of government into the main player of the market. It is obvious that only the unilateral efforts of the enterprise are not enough to complete this task. The transformation of business mechanism and the conversion of government functions are the two aspects of a coin. When the enterprise reform develops to a certain extent, how to convert government functions becomes the main question. If there is no transformation of government functions, then clear property rights, separation of government and enterprises and autonomous management are just empty talk.

Of course, transforming government functions does not mean that the government will do nothing. The World Bank pointed out in the 1997 World Development Report that a good government is not a luxurious product. Without an effective government, economic and social sustainable development would not be impossible; on occasions where market fails, government intervention is inevitable.[17]

In the field where market fails, government intervention and moral regulation are necessitated. The role moral factors play in the economic reform and economic development has attracted more and more attention. How to balance the roles as an economic person and a moral person, an issue rose since the era of Adam Smith, has now attracted more and more attention from Chinese academia. I believe that moral factors will play a more important role in restrictions with the further deepening of economic reform.

Briefly, the challenges facing China's economic reform are quite daunting. Joseph Stiglitz, chief economist of the World Bank, praised the brilliant achievements of China's economic reforms on one hand, and pointed out that China's economic reform faces "daunting difficulties and challenges" on the other hand in his speech during his visit to China in the summer of 1998.[18]

People often say that economic reform is a systematic project, which is true even for the economy itself. If you consider the matching support required from non-economic factors, economic reform is an even larger systematic project. We have been fighting for this project for 20 years. In the future, we should meet new challenges and complete the unprecedented project in Chinese history with greater enthusiasm and perseverance.

(This article was written in January 1999. Its main content was published in the third issue of *Comparative Economic & Social Systems* in 1999 and its summary was reprinted in the ninth issue of *Xinhua WenZhai* in 1999.)

Notes

1 Dwight H. Perkins (1993). Reforming the Economic Systems of Vietnam and Laos. In Borje Ljunggren (Ed.), *The Challenge of Reform in Indochina*. Cambridge, MA: Harvard University Press.

2 Shegero Ishikawa (1986). 社会主义经济和中国的经验—对经济改革的展望 [Socialist Economy and China's Experience: Outlook on Economic Reform]. *Science & Technology Review*, 2.

3 Regarding the starting point of China's economic reform, please refer to: Zhao Renwei & Rong Jingben (1982). 我国原来属于什么经济模式？ [What Economic Mode China Originally Belong to？]. *Economic Perspectives*, 2; Zhao Renwei (1988). 中国经济体制改革目标模式的总体设想 [The Overall Envisage on China's Economic Reform Objective]. In Liu Guoguang (Ed.), *中国经济体制改革的模式研究* [Study on the Mode of China's Economic Reform] (pp. 52–94). Beijing: China's Social Sciences Press.

4 For the relationship in this figure, see Hiroyuki Kato. (1997). *China's Economic Reform and Marketization* (p. 11). Japan: Nagoya University Press.

5 中国共产党第十四次代表大会文件汇编 [Assembly of 14th National People's Congress of Communist Party of China] (1993) (p. 22). Beijing: People's Publishing House.

6 Adam Przeworski (1991). *Democracy and The Market: Political and Economic Reforms in Eastern Europe and Latin America*. Cambridge: Cambridge University Press.

7 For relevant arguments, please refer to: Lin Yifu, Cai Fang & Li Zhou (1994). *中国的奇迹：发展战略与经济改革* [China's Miracle: Development and Economic Reform] (p. 247). Shanghai: Shanghai Sanlian Bookstore & Shanghai Renmin Press.

8 The World Bank. (1997). *Sharing Rising Incomes: Disparities in China* (p. 9). Washington, DC.

9 Zhao Renwei & Li Shi. (1997). 中国居民收入差距的扩大及其原因 [Widening Gap of People's Income in China]. *Economic Research Journal*, 9.

10 The World Bank, *世界银行发展报告(1996): 从计划到市场* [World Bank Development Report (1996): From Plan to Market]. (Chapter 4). Beijing: China Financial & Economic Publishing House.

11 Wu Jinnlian. (1996). 中国采取了"渐进改革"战略吗[Does China Take a Gradualist Approach]. In *渐进与激进—中国改革道路的选择* [Gradualist and Radical–Choices of China's Reform] (pp. 1–10). Beijing: Economy Science Press.

12 Fan Gang (1996). 中国经济体制改革的特征与趋势 [Characteristics and Trends of China's Economic System Reform]. In*渐进与激进—中国改革道路的选择*[Gradualist and Radical: Choices of China's Reform] (pp. 11–20). Beijing: Economy Science Press.

13 Chen Jiyuan (1998). 农村经济体制改革 [Rural Economic System Reform]. In Zhang Zhuoyuan et al. (Eds), *二十年经济改革回顾与展望* [Retrospect and Outlook of the Economic Reform over the Past Two Decades] (p. 81). Beijing: China Planning Press.

14 Wang Yanchen. (1998) *薛暮桥回忆中国改革曲折历程* [Xue Muqiao's Memory of China's Winding Reform]. *Economic Information*, Hong Kong, 42.

15 Wen Guifang. (1998). 价格改革 [Price Reform]. In Zhang Zhuoyuan et al (Eds), *二十年经济改革回顾与展望* [Retrospect and Outlook of the Economic Reform over the Past Two Decades] (pp. 118–130). Beijing: China Planning Press.

16 Yang Jisheng. (1998). *邓小平时代：中国改革开放二十年纪实* [Deng Xiaoping Era: Records of China's Reform and Opening Up over the Past Two Decades] (pp. 466–467). Beijing: Central Compilation & Translation Press.

17 The World Bank, *世界银行发展报告 (1997): 变革世界中的政府* [World Development Report (1997): Government in Change]. (Preface and Chapter 1). Beijing: China Financial & Economic Publishing House.

18 Joseph Stiglitz (October 21, 1998). The Second Generation Strategy for China's Reform (collated by Huang Chenghong), *Ta Kung Pao*, Hong Kong.

11 Brief thoughts on China's economic reform over the past 30 years

China's economic system reform has been going on for three decades with momentous changes and brilliant achievements universally recognized. Regarding the characteristics, experiences and lessons of China's economic system reform, I have already explored them in a separate article.[1] In this essay, I only want to raise some questions that need to be considered from the perspective of problems facing the reform. Therefore, content in this article can only be called some brief thoughts on the economic reform.

I. How far are we from the goal of reform?

During the past 30 years, domestic and foreign economists have been conducting a good deal of research and discussions on the goal of China's economic reform, and the official documents have seen increasingly clear statements for it. The official statements on it were clearest on the following three occasions. The first was on the Communist Party of China's (CPC) 12th Third Plenary Session in 1984, where the goal of China's economic reform was defined as a "planned commodity economy". The second was on the Party's 13th National Congress of the CPC, where the goal was defined as creating a state-regulated market that in turn regulates the businesses. The third was on the 14th National Congress of the CPC, where the goal was defined as "a socialist market economy". The changes embodied in the three statements reflected the transition from the planned economy to the market economy. Foreign economists' research on the goal of China's economic reform culminated in the results of the "Bashan Cruise Meeting" (1985), which divided the economic coordination mechanism in the macroeconomic management into the two types of administrative coordination mechanism and the market coordination mechanism. In the two types of coordination mechanisms, each has two specific forms. Administrative coordination was divided into direct administrative coordination (IA) and indirect administrative coordination (IB). Market coordination was divided into market control (IIA) with no macro control and macro-controlled market coordination (IIB). Real and effective reform should take HB as the target model.

In the process of reform, it is usually very likely to go to IB after coming out of IA. He said that choosing IB mode as a transition was viable, but there was also the danger of staying in IB. Therefore, China's reform should be persistent, even though the IB model cannot be avoided along the way, the real goal of IIB should not be forgotten.[2] Professor Korne made the preceding classification at the meeting. Most of the participating experts explored their discussions revolving this classification and agreed to the IIB model as the goal of reform in principle. Bruce did not make a different view on taking the IIB model as the goal of China's economic reform, but he put forward his own unique insights regarding the starting point of China's economic reform. He held that the starting point of China's economic reform was not IA, and even could be said to be half IA. At the beginning of China's economic reform, there were some aspects that did not even reach IA. For example, China did not have a labor market, which was different from that of Eastern European countries. This point of view was consistent with the "quasi-military communist model" of China's economic reform, as Bruce mentioned in his lectures in China in 1980. (Unlike the starting point of the Soviet and Eastern European reforms, namely the "typical planned economic model" or "Stalin model"). Thus, Bruce commented that China's economic reform from half IA to IIB was "a real long march".

It has been 23 years since the "Bashan Cruise Meeting" in 1985, and it has been 16 years since China established the reform goal of the socialist market economy in 1992. However, we cannot say that the goal of reform has been achieved and that the transformation from the planned economy to the market economy has been completed. We are still at a distance from the goal of the market economy, or the goal of the IB model discussed at the Bashan Cruise Meeting in the following aspects: the use of indirect control means, the establishment of conditions for indirect control, the cultivation of the market system, clarity of enterprise property rights, separation of government and enterprise functions, and the elimination of administrative monopoly and other aspects. Bruce said that China's economic reform started from half IA; today, can we say that we have only covered half IIB? It seems that only by recognizing that "the reform has not yet been successful" can we make more specific arrangements and exert greater efforts for the next round of reform.

II.   How to summarize and appraise the risks of rising costs brought by the gradual way

It should be said that at the Bashan Cruise Meeting, Chinese and foreign scholars generally reached consensus on the coexistence of gradual transformation of economic transition and the corresponding dual-track systems. In other words, the coexistence of the gradual transition mode and the dual-track system was to avoid the violent shocks in the reform and reduce the cost of reform, but it would bring a variety of friction so the coexistence of dual tracks could not be maintained for too long.

In retrospect of the three-decade economic reform, China's overall approach is a gradualist one, and only the rural reform in the early 1980s and the "price break" in 1988 saw some radical elements. Among them, the rural reform was a success;

and the price break in 1988 was a failure. The dual-track system for commodity prices in the gradual reform, including that of production prices, ended around the mid-1990s. Because of the increasing balance between supply and demand in the mid-1990s, coupled with the shrinking gap between the two prices due to the policy of "adjusting price with relaxed control", China was able to integrate the dual tracks for price successfully, which was a remarkable achievement in the transition. The gradual way featuring the dual-track transition was to reduce the cost of reform. Summarizing our experience over the past three decades, we have made significant achievements in reducing the cost of reform, but since the 1990s, we have paid too-high costs on several occasions; in other words, we have suffered some unnecessary losses. Below are just a few examples.

Example 1: It is difficult to say the expanded income gap between urban and rural residents is due to the development; rather, it is more likely to be caused by the system and policy before the reform, such as the household registration system that has been in use today. It was not until recently that there has been a prominent change in the tax policy for the rural residents and the net subsidy policy for urban residents. These institutional and policy factors are not conducive to narrowing the income gap between urban and rural residents.

Example 2: Since the development of real estate in the 1990s, the price for land has gone from almost nil to extremely high, and the practice of rent setting in land sale allowed some people to gain huge profit. As known to all, in the 1980s, the implementation of the dual-track price system resulted in "rent-seeking" activities. If rent losses arise from rent-seeking activities paid a necessary price to avoid excessive shocks caused by price breaks, then the rent losses caused by rent setting in the development of real estates were not only unnecessary but too high.

Example 3: In China, the use of official vehicles has been following the traditional practice. The ensuing waste and privilege is well known. According to gradual reform theory, gradual reform is an "incremental reform", which means the existing pack runs according to the rules of the old system, while the increment runs according to the rules of the new system. Thirty years into reform and opening-up, China's official cars have doubled several times, but the new official cars are still running according to the old system. Although the State Council drafted a scheme for the monetary reform of the official vehicles in 1998, it was too difficult to be implemented. Obviously, the long-term use of the buses used in the old way meets neither the requirements of gradual reform nor the requirements of fair distribution.

Moreover, from a deeper and broader perspective, the problem of the double-track system in the transformation of China's economic system has not been fundamentally resolved.

As we all know, since the 1990s, domestic and foreign economists have made further research on the gradualist reform, pointing out that the connotation of gradual reform is incremental reform. Specifically, it means that the incremental or new wealth adopts the new system, while the stock or the original wealth stays in the old system. With the development of reform and economic development, the proportion of wealth left in the old system will continue to decline, and the proportion of wealth entering the new system will continue to rise, which will help the new system to replace the old system finally. Over the past three decades, however, much of China's new wealth has not entered the new system in line with incremental reforms. The substantial number of new official vehicles entering the old system in the form of rationing is just one example.

If we expand our horizons from the product price to the labor price, that is, the wages, then the problem of the dual-track system is not resolved. Because of China's special national conditions and historical background, for a long time, we have retained the way of supply in the distribution of consumer goods in addition to monetary wages, which means we keep the supply system in addition to the wage system. These supply factors are particularly manifested in the automotive, housing and other higher-level consumer items. It seems that it remains an arduous task to convert those physical supplies into wages and money.

The distortions in labor prices can also distort other prices. In the medical field, the low price of medical services and the high price of medicines (old stuff in new concoctions) and the resulting replacement of medical care with medicines are the specific manifestations.

Rent-seeking activities and rental income are closely related with the gradualist reform and the double-track transition. At present, the academic community has a variety of estimates on the total volume of rental income and gray income. For example, some scholars estimated that the total rent caused by the dual-track price system in 1988 was 356.9 billion yuan, accounting for 30% of the national income of the year.[3] Some scholars estimated that in 2005, the sum of income of urban and rural residents was about 13.5 trillion yuan, compared to 8.7 trillion yuan in official projections, with the former 4.8 trillion yuan more than the latter; and this margin was equivalent to 26% of GDP, of which the clear majority was gray income.[4] However, the academic community raises doubts about the above estimates in reliability and scientificity. So far, no one can prove that their calculations are accurate; but no one can deny that the amount of rental and gray income was astronomical.

The purpose of adopting the gradual way is to reduce the cost of reform, but the gradual approach also has the risks of rising costs. When summing up the experience of 30 years of the reform, should we examine how to prevent and overcome the rising costs of reform?

III. How to confront and solve the problem of the wide income gap

One of the fundamental goals of reform and opening-up is to improve the income and living standards of urban and rural residents based on production development. Since the reform and opening-up, the increasing level of people's income is an indisputable fact. I think that since the reform and opening-up, China has made two major breakthroughs in this regard. The first is to put forward the policy of letting the richer bring along the poorer, which is to break the communal ease and allow some people to get rich first by giving them the incentives, and then it will improve efficiency and achieve the goal of common prosperity. The second breakthrough is to pay attention to the residents' labor income while raising their awareness of property and property income.

However, after 30 years of reform, the wide income gap has become a big problem in economic life and social life. In a nutshell, in the distribution of income, there has been a change from prevailing egalitarian to excessive income disparities; in the distribution of property, there has been a change from almost no private property to high-speed accumulation and prominent polarization of personal properties. I will discuss the income gap in another article.

From the timing sequence, I think the patterns of 30-year-long income distribution can be divided into three stages. The three stages and their main tendencies are summarized as follows.

In the late 1970s to the mid-1980s: egalitarianism. At the beginning of the reform and opening-up – that is, in the late 1970s and early to mid-1980s – the main tendency of income distribution was still the egalitarianism left over from the planned economy. The rural reform during this period achieved remarkable success, but the distribution of its economic interests was more balanced whether in terms of the increasing purchase price of agricultural products or the implementation of household contract responsibility system. At that time, the urban reform was not yet fully unveiled. Whether in the organs, institutions or business units, income distribution still followed the traditional practice of the planned economic system.

From the mid-late 1980s to the early 1990s: the two phenomena coexisted. At that time, due to the coexistence and friction of the dual tracks, the main feature of income distribution was the coexistence of the two phenomena (the egalitarianism within the planned economy and the wide gap between those working in the system and those out of the system). Such complaints as "being a doctor is not as good as being a hairdresser" and "being a scientist is not as good as being a small retailer" were examples of the ramifications on income distribution due to the coexistence of and frictions between dual tracks. At this stage, the greatest concern was the expansion of the income gap caused by the "rent-seeking" activities via leveraging the dual-track system.

Since the mid-late 1990s: the gap has been too large. Since the mid-to-late 1990s, although the egalitarianism exists in certain sectors and enterprises, the wide income gap has become prevalent in the whole society, especially the income expansions or the so-called instant riches, which are unrelated to the incentive mechanism (to promote efficiency) and arouse strong dissatisfaction among the public. If the normal expansion of the income gap caused by economic growth is something that can be universally agreed, then the income gap caused by factors such as the power-for-money deal, corruption, all kinds of monopolies, insider control, rent-setting and other abnormal expansions has become the focus of attention.

Regarding the reasons for the widening income gap, the academic community has made a variety of analyses, the most notable of which should be the analysis of the relationship between the expansion of the income gap and the economic reform. I think that there are two tendencies that we need to avoid when analyzing the relationship between the income gap and the economic reform. One is to simply blame the economic reform for the widening income gap and other problems; the other is to simply attribute the income gap to the price that the economic reform should pay. I think that the expansion of the income gap should be divided into three levels and be treated differently. The first level is the incentive part that is conducive to improving the efficiency and overcoming the results of egalitarianism, and therefore should be acknowledged. The second level is the price that must be paid for economic reform. For example, China's reform can only take the gradualist way of the dual-track transition, which will inevitably result in rent-seeking activities. To a certain extent, this can be considered as the price that the reform should pay, so to speak. The third level is the excessive price paid, or the part that should be prevented, avoided and not paid. Of course, the boundary between the second and third levels is very difficult to tell, especially it is quite difficult to quantify the boundary; but I still think it can be separated theoretically. Excessive costs are often associated with corruption, monopolies, rent-seeking, rent-setting and other activities.

It can be overserved that the excessive income gap is not the inevitable result of market-oriented reform. On the contrary, only by further deepening the reform can China fundamentally solve the problem of unfair distribution of income. Moreover, many problems concerning the income gap and the property gap are related with power-for-money deals, rent-seeking, rent-setting and other activities; in other words, with the lack of power checks and balances. To prevent the use of power for personal affairs, power checks and balances are essential. To strengthen the check and balance of power, it is also essential to continue economic reform while promoting political reform. The reform in China has been advanced for almost three decades, should we calm down to sum up the lessons of reform and continue to push forward the cause of reform?

IV.   How to give play to the functions of the market and government correctly in the transition

At the beginning of the reform and opening-up, the Chinese economists discussed the relationship between the plan and the market extensively. Since the mid-to-late 1990s, quite a few economic literatures have clearly classified this problem as how to correctly divide and handle the functions of the market and the government.

It is quite interesting to follow this idea to examine the new subject of economic reform.

1   In the field of personal products or private products, mainly covering food, clothing, and daily supplies, we have realized the goal of allocating resources through the market mechanism and making individuals take corresponding responsibilities through nearly three decades of reform.
2   In the field of public goods, mainly in defense, environmental protection and basic public services, we have realized the goal of having the government allocate resources and making the state bear corresponding responsibilities.

3   In the field of quasi-public goods, mainly in education, health care and housing for low-income earners, we should let the market and government allocate resources respectively; in other words, both individuals and the state should take responsibility. The difficulty thereof is how to divide the functions of the market and the government. As a result, such a gray area ensues the phenomenon that the government and individuals tend to shove the responsibilities to each other. As mentioned earlier, although our economic reforms have been going on for almost three decades, there are still some areas where the role of the market is not in place and the power of the government is too strong. However, in the field of quasi-public goods, it frequently happens that what is supposed to be in the charge of the government is shoved into the market. Since the 1990s, reforms in the field of education and medical care have led to the imposition of excessive liability on individuals and too much dependence on the market; the reform of the housing system has also led to a similar tendency, that is, too much emphasis on housing commercialization, while ignoring the low-rent housing for low-income citizens.

It follows that unfulfilled market functions and government function are not uncommon in the process of economic restructuring. How to prevent and overcome such situations and let the government and the market play their roles appropriately remains an issue in urgent need of discussion and exploration.

V.   How to further develop the factor market

Over the past three decades, we have made great headway in the cultivation of commodity markets and achieved a market-oriented economy generally in both consumer goods and production materials. However, in the cultivation of factor market, although some progress has been made, there still exists a big gap.

As early as in 1985, Chinese and foreign economists began to discuss how to build the capital market at the International Symposium on Macroeconomic Management (commonly known as the "Bashan Cruise Meeting"). However, many foreign economists at that time generally avoided the stock market and only mentioned the bond market when it comes to the capital market, pointing out that the development of the bond market could make people choose between bank deposits and government bonds. Later reforms and developments proved that people could not only choose between deposits and bonds, but also choose stocks. Although the stock market is still full of uncertainties, this step marks great progress in the capital market.

Hereby, I want to make several points on cultivating the labor market and the land market.

Since the reform and opening-up, China has witnessed great progress in allowing labor mobility, but the problem of tangible and intangible regional blockades of labor mobility and sectoral segmentation still exists. This will inevitably lead to the repulsion of the market mechanism in the formation of wages, generating unequal pay for the same job.

Such situation not only affects the objectivity and rationale for the formation of labor remuneration, but also affects the reasonable relationship between labor remuneration and capital remuneration. We have talked about the relationship between labor income and property income from the perspective of the individuals, and now we encounter the problem of dealing with the relationship between labor remuneration and capital remuneration from the perspective of nurturing the market system. It seems that "increasing the proportion of labor remuneration in the primary distribution," inscribed in the report of the 17th National People's Congress of China, was targeted. This shows that against the backdrop of rapid GDP growth, drastic hike in corporate profits and national revenue, it is imperative that the corresponding increase in labor income should never be ignored. Only in this way can we make the vast majority of working-class people share the fruits of reform and opening-up. Furthermore, it is not in the interest of mobilizing the employees and improving economic efficiency to reduce the wages of workers or in order to reap more profits for the enterprises. Only by building a balanced relationship between the growth of corporate profits and the increase of labor income can we fulfill the requirement of building a people-oriented, harmonious society. To this end, it is imperative to cultivate both the capital market and the labor market at the same time. It can be said that a more robust labor market coexisting with the capital market serves as the premise for workers to obtain their own legitimate rights and interests.

One tricky problem for cultivating the factor market is how to nurture the land market. Since the 1990s, land trade on the land market has encountered a very irregular issue in the development of the real estate industry. In the transition from a planned economy to a market economy, land price has surged from nil to skyrocketing prices. However, farmers, as owners of land (even if collectively owned), have not benefited from land transfer and land appreciation. There is a stark difference between the purchase price and the selling price of the land, thus forming a huge profitable space. If the dual-track system of product price in the 1980s ensured that the profit was generally half the price or just the same as the price, then, since the 1990s, profit margins of land transaction have been several times or even more. As some scholars have said, the dual-track price system for products in the 1980s was a hotbed for rent-seeking activities, and the two-track system of land prices since the 1990s was itself a rent-setting activity. Now that we can integrate the dual pricing tracks for products within an appropriate period of time, Of course we can eliminate as soon as possible the rent-setting activities.

(Adapted from the article published in the issue 9 of *Contemporary Finance and Economics* in 2008.)

Notes

1 Zhao Renwei (1999). 中国经济改革二十年的回顾与展望—特点、经验教训和面临的挑战 [Retrospect and Outlook of China's Economic Reform over the Past Two Decades – characteristics, experience & lessons and challenges], *Comparative Economic & Social Systems*, 3; excerpted and reprinted in *Xinhua Digest* (1999), 9.

2 Refer to Zhao Renwei. (2008). 1985 年"巴山轮会议" 的回顾与思考 [Retrospect and Thoughts on the Bashan Cruise Meeting in 1985]. *Economic Research Journal*, 12.
3 Hu, Heli. (1989). 1988 年中国租金价值的计算 [Calculation of Rental in China in 1988]. *Comparative Economic & Social Systems*, 5.
4 Wang Xiaolu (2007). 我国的灰色收入与居民收入差距 [Gap between the Gray Income and Resident Income in China]. *Comparative Studies*, 31.

12 A summary of positive exploration of provincial economic transition – a book review of *System Changes and Development Trajectory of Zhejiang* written by Fang Minsheng and others

System Changes and Development Trajectory of Zhejiang, written by Fang Minsheng, has been published by the Zhejiang People's Publishing House.[1] A strong impression left by the book is that it is a great piece of work from the perspective of summarizing a province's economic reform and economic development during the past two decades. This book is not a simple narrative of economic evolution in a province during 20 years. Instead, it is a relatively systematic analysis and relatively thorough assessment by reflecting upon such an evolution through the lens of "two transitions". It is known that China's economy is in the middle of "two transitions" on the scale of both a province and a country. Namely, it is transferring from a planned economy to a market economy, and from a traditional agricultural society to a modern industry society.[2] The author of this book further summarizes them as the transformation of economic system and the transformation of social structure. From the economic perspective, I think it can be referred to as the transformation of economic system and economic development respectively, or even more concisely as system transformation and development transformation.[3] Therefore, the system transition and development transition mentioned in this article correspond to the system transition and social structure transition in this book, which also corresponds to the themes of "system changes" and "development trajectory" in the book. I think that it is meaningful to capture the two basic threads of reform and development and summarize a provincial experience from the interaction and the changes of these two transitions. This book is remarkable regarding the study and exploration of both system and development transformations.

From the perspective of system transition, it features distinctive and characteristic exploration for the following questions based on the actual conditions of Zhejiang Province:

I. The extent or depth of system changes

This book uses the extent of marketization to measure the system changes, which is obviously a relatively simple way. Summarizing the various studies by domestic and foreign experts, the author analyzes from four perspectives, including resource allocation marketization and maturing of players in the market, which has led to the conclusion that the marketization in Zhejiang Province reaches approximately 60%, around 10 percentage points higher than the national average level. Given that the maximum marketization in countries with market economy across the world is 80%–85%, Zhejiang has completed 70%–75% of the marketization process. This is no doubt a solid recognition of the marketization progress made by Zhejiang.

II.   The path chosen for system changes

I believe that against the backdrop of the market-oriented economy as the goal of reform, the focus of system innovation lies in the path chosen for system changes. In the 1980s, there were heated discussions regarding adopting a progressive or radical path for reform. The 1990s saw initial fruits of Chinese progressive reform, and the public's attention seemingly shifted to summarizing the experience of progressive reforms. While affirming the merits of progressive reform, the book, with rather special insights, sums up the path chosen during Zhejiang's progressive reform. Besides such paths as growth outside of the system (namely outside of the original planned economy) and the incremental reform featuring gradual changes within the system, the book also summarizes the marginal innovation and non-marginal innovation, as well as exogenous and endogenous changes. Marginal innovation uses the existing system and organizations to conduct marketization reform. For example, many of the township enterprises in Hangzhou, Jiaxing, Huzhou, Shaoxing, and Ningbo have developed by depending on the marginal adjustment of the system in large and medium state-owned companies. Non-marginal innovation, on the other hand, is a kind of innovation which breaks through the existing system and organization to pursue marketization reform. Examples can be found in the shareholding system and specialized commodity wholesale market in Zhejiang. My article will not go into details of the exogenous and endogenous changes. The author of the book also points out that as for choosing the path for system innovation, Zhejiang is characterized by both marginal innovation and non-marginal innovation, as well as exogenous and endogenous changes, with endogenous changes playing the major role. These summaries obviously specify and deepen the progressive reform in China through the lens of a province.

III.   The development of market entity and market system during the system changes

It is clearly pointed out that under the planned economy; there are no true enterprises, entrepreneurs, or market entities in China. Therefore, reshaping the market entities have become the unavoidable road leading to a market economy. During the reform in the rural areas, be it the household contract responsibility system or the development of township enterprises, they all center on reshaping the market entities. In cities, the developments of market entities mainly focus on transforming the company system. Zhejiang has been open-minded in terms of developing private-owned enterprises. By 1998, out of the 500 biggest private enterprises across the nation, 112 of them were located in Zhejiang, which ranked first in China. Through attracting foreign investment, it has built and developed three types of foreign-funded enterprises (i.e. contractual joint ventures, cooperative ventures and solely foreign-funded enterprises), as well as introduced and nurtured a batch of market entities. Another batch was developed through pushing forward reforms of state-owned enterprises as well as urban and township collective enterprises. The book also recognizes the productive role of the shareholding cooperative system on innovating systems and nurturing market entities in Zhejiang in the 1990s. The author points out, "the biggest feature of shareholding cooperative system is the combination of labor cooperation and capital cooperation, thus generating a system which draws clear lines for property right, and which features direct interests, share of risks, and flexible mechanism", "a new system like this is exactly combining the factors in the shareholding system with those in the cooperative system".

As for the development of the market system, in its summary of Zhejiang's experience, this book points out the advance of factor market lags behind the development of the commodity market, which is a common problem in provinces and even across the country. In addition, I find the following two points particularly worth noticing. The first is about Zhejiang's experience on the development of specialized commodity wholesale market. In Zhejiang Province, the annual turnover exceeds 100 million yuan. The specialized commodity wholesale market, whose value is over one billion yuan, has ranked among the top for many years. The volume of business in the "City of Petty Commodities" in Yiwu and in the "Chinese Textile City" in Shaoxing reached 19.68 billion yuan and 18.02 billion yuan, respectively, as the national champion and runner-up. As pointed out by the author, "a specialized commodity wholesale market characterized by spot wholesale and concentrated transactions of a certain type of commodity is a major feature and important achievement in the development of Zhejiang market system", and "the essence of the formation and development of Zhejiang specialized commodity wholesale market is a system change to reduce transaction costs". The book also sheds light on issues such as how such a market relies on industry and gradually forms an economic circle, which centers on such a market. To put it in a nutshell, the experience of establishing a specialized commodity wholesale market in Zhejiang is "to run a market, energize an economy, rejuvenate a group of industries, and enrich local people". The other point is the relations between opening up the market and managing the market. In the market-oriented reform, in order to get rid of the shackles of the planned economy, it's often emphasized that it is undoubtedly correct to let go of the market and liberalize the pricing system. However, the transition from a planned economy to a market economy cannot simply be about "letting go". Instead, it is the balance of "letting go" and maintaining control; that is, the relationship between market liberalization and market management. This book summarizes the role of all levels of governments in Zhejiang during organizing and accelerating market development and clearly states that it will be inefficient and unwise to rely on spontaneous formation and evolution of the market. Instead, giving full play to the role of the government in market organizing, coordinating, guiding and regulating is an effective way to shorten the historical process of market natural evolution and accelerate the development of the market system.

(p. 284)

This is not only a summary of the experience of transition in the past two decades, but also an important measure of how to effectively play the role of the government in the transition to a market economy in the future. It is also in line with the widespread international concern.[4]

IV.   The impetus for innovation in the system changes

This is actually a question regarding the driving force behind the reform. The author points out that according to the actual situation in Zhejiang, the spontaneous innovation by the public is the driving force of system change, and the "first player" for change. Government serves as the "second player" for such changes. Only when these two players make joint efforts, that is, the formation of a joint force between the people and the government, can such substantial changes be realized. For instance, the implementation of the rural contract responsibility system, Wenzhou model, the formation of a specialized commodity wholesale market, the establishment of small towns for peasants (such as Longgang Town) and the advancement of the joint-stock cooperative system, are all the result of such synergy. It can be said that the analysis regarding how the two dynamics are skillfully reconciled is still preliminary so far, but indeed very significant. From the perspective of the development transition and its relationship with institutional transformation, the book's analysis also boasts unique insights.

V.   Estimation or judgment of the degree of development

After two decades of efforts, what is the extent of Zhejiang's economic development? Opinions are divided. Some believe that "Zhejiang has morphed from a small economy to a major economic driver", while some say "Zhejiang is in the middle of industrialization", and others state that "Zhejiang has moved from featuring simply having adequate food and clothing to boasting well off status for its people". It should be said that these statements are judgments made from different angles. This book has absorbed and commented on such judgments. Measured by economic indicators, the most prominent is the extraordinary growth of GDP and increase of economic strength in Zhejiang during the past 20 years, when the growth rate of its per capita GDP has been 13.01%, ranking first in the country. Per capita GDP has risen from 16th in 1978 to 4th in 1997 among various provinces and municipalities across the country. In the assessment of economic strength, the author draws from the research both at home and abroad and designs four schemes on the basis of nine variables. After repeated comparison, it concludes that the economic strength of Zhejiang Province among the provinces in China has changed from ranking 19th in 1978 to 5th in 1997.

VI.   Economic growth cycle and the macroeconomic environment

A province's economy is an integral part of the national economy. Therefore, it is self-evident that the economic growth of a province and its periodic changes are closely linked with the macroeconomic environment in the country. From this perspective, the book summarizes the synchronicity of the fluctuation of the economic cycle in Zhejiang and that of the nation, as well as pointing out that the economic cycle of Zhejiang is also different from that of the whole country. The author believes that since the reform and opening-up, Zhejiang's economic growth has gone through three cycles respectively during 1978–1983, 1984–1990 and 1991–1998 June. It entered the fourth cycle in July 1998. The fluctuation of the four economic cycles is basically in line with that of the whole country and is determined by national macroeconomic environment. After describing the changes of the peaks and troughs and the background during various periodic fluctuations, the author points out that the economic cycle of Zhejiang also has its own characteristics, which is reflected mainly in the following respects: first, since the reform and opening-up, the intensity of the economic cycle in Zhejiang has been higher than that of the whole country. The coefficient of economic fluctuation in Zhejiang before the reform and opening-up was 11.8 in 1951–1977, slightly lower than the national average of 12.56. In 1978–1990, after the reform and opening-up, it was 6.2, much higher than the national average of 3.1. In the past two decades, in terms of the economic cyclical changes in Zhejiang, the peaks were higher than the whole country and the troughs deeper. This shows that the market economy of Zhejiang is very sensitive. Second, the impact of the national macroeconomic policies on Zhejiang's economic fluctuations is relatively small. The proportion of state-owned business in Zhejiang is relatively low, and the state's investment in Zhejiang is also relatively small. When the state adopts a tight monetary policy, it would have a relatively small impact on Zhejiang, where the proportion of non-state-owned economy is larger. Similarly, when the country adopts a policy of reducing capital investment, it will have a relatively small impact on Zhejiang's economy as well. This shows that Zhejiang's economic autonomy and adaptability are relatively strong.

VII.   The process of economic development and the transformation of economic structure

Economic development is closely linked with the transformation of economic structure. Some economists simply interpret development as the transformation of economic structure. This book, based on the actual situation in Zhejiang, offers a detailed analysis of the economic development process during Zhejiang's economic transformation.

As for the structural transformation of the three industries, Zhejiang belonged to the traditional agricultural society structure from 1950 to 1957, and the order of importance among three industries was characterized by "primary industry, tertiary industry, and secondary industry". From 1958 to 1978, the structure prioritized the development of heavy industry, with the order of significance as "primary, secondary, and tertiary". Since the reform and opening-up, the rapid economic development in Zhejiang Province has been coupled with the rapid transformation of its industrial structure. The share of primary industry in GDP dropped from 38.1% in 1978 to 13.7% in 1997 (down by 24.4 percentage points); in the same period, the share of secondary industry rose from 43.3% to 54.1% (an increase of 10.8 percentage points). The share of the tertiary industry rose from 18.6% to 32.2% (an increase of 13.6 percentage points). Specifically, the two decades since the reform and opening-up can be divided into two phases: the first phase is from 1979 to 1986, which belongs to the structure of accelerating the transition to an industrial society. The order of industry importance is "secondary, primary, and tertiary". The second stage is 1987–1998, which is in the middle of the evolution to an industrial structure, with the order of the industrial importance as "secondary, tertiary, and primary".

In addition, the book also contains more specific analysis of the structural transformation within the three industries during the past two decades. In agriculture, for example, it has shifted from simply focusing on the farm production to the all-around development of the four agriculture components, namely farm production, forestry, husbandry and fishery, paying particular attention to the improvement of the structure of grain varieties and the quality of agricultural products. As for the secondary industry, based on the comparative advantages of Zhejiang Province, it has gradually shifted to the direction of light processing. The proportion of light industry with agricultural products as raw material dropped while that of non-agricultural products increased. In terms of the tertiary industry, the initial development is a catching-up development whose achievements are enormous, centering on circulation of trade and commerce, followed by the great development of transportation, postal service, and telecommunications. Later, it boasts comprehensive advance in finance, insurance, real estate, market intermediary agencies and education.

What is worth noticing here is that this book specifically mentions the organizational structure of enterprises when it comes to the transformation of economic structure. The author believes that while nurturing large enterprises, we must also attach importance to improving the organization of small enterprises to become entities which are small but professional, special, specialized, and excellent. These small companies can become "little giants"; in other words, they can exert huge influences on the path of featuring "small product + global market". I think the concept of "Little Giant" is quite insightful. Why Germans can produce Solingen and Adidas in a small town but gain global reputation, while Chinese, or Zhejiang people, haven't achieved such success?

VIII.   Economic development and industrial layout evolution

Economic development cannot be separated from the evolution of industrial layout, which would be affected not only by economic development strategies and policies, but also by the geographical environment and natural resources. The book identifies Zhejiang's features while exploring this topic. The author points out that in line with the principle of regional economics, regional development generally follows the process of advancing from a point, to an axis, and finally a surface. Since the reform and opening-up, Zhejiang's regional development has been basically in the phase of axis development. It is axis development that has been standing out during the past two decades. After 20 years of hard work, the economic development of Zhejiang has formed a pattern of "three zones" and "three belts": (1) Hangzhou Bay zone, which is a V-shaped development belt relying on the Shanghai-Hangzhou line and the Hang-Yu line (Hongzhou Bay V-shape Industry Belt); (2) the coast zone along Wentai, which is a I-shape belt based on Wenzhou and the transportation of Wentai (Coastal I-shaped industrial belt); and (3) the southwestern part of Zhejiang Province, which is a T-axis growth zone based on the Zhejiang-Jiangxi Railway and the Jinhua-Wenzhou Railway (the T-shaped industrial belt). Such a V-I-T layout formed by the regional economy in Zhejiang is in full conformity with the actual conditions in this province. The terrestrial environment in Zhejiang is characterized by "70% mountains, 20% fields, and 10% water". The plains are mainly in the Hangzhou Bay coast, the Wentai coast and the Jinqu Basin, which are also the centers of agricultural resources, population and towns. The focus of industrial development also undoubtedly lies in these areas. This summary of the evolution of the industrial layout over the past two decades undoubtedly contributes to the readjustment of the industrial distribution in the future and further development from line to surface.

IX.   Development paths and system changes

The author attributes the unconventional growth of the Zhejiang economy to the system changes in the first two decades and points out that

> the trajectory of Zhejiang's economic development shows enormous growth within a short period of time, which is the result of its unique mode of system changes. Such changes have released the potential of production, the change of operating mechanism and reshaped a new environment for development.
>
> (p. 11)

The author also summarizes the correlation between Zhejiang's economic development trajectory and system changes from the perspective of time and space. In terms of time, the fastest growing period of Zhejiang's economy is 1979–1982, 1984–1988 and 1992–1995, and these years are also the period of relatively rapid institutional change. In terms of space, in places where the process of system changes is relatively rapid, the economic development there would also be quicker. For example, the rural reforms in the 1980s started with Wenzhou, Jinhua and Lishui, where agricultural production developed rapidly in the early 1980s. Rural reform in Jiaxing and Huzhou lagged behind. Correspondingly, the related development of township and village enterprises was also less competitive there. In the 1990s, the reform of the property rights system under the joint-stock cooperative system was widely implemented in Wenzhou and Taizhou and extended to Shaoxing and Jinhua. Therefore, the four regions witnessed the fastest economic growth in the first half of the 1990s. The author's analysis of the correlation between system changes and economic development clearly helps to raise the awareness of promoting development through reforms at the policy-making level.

In terms of the writing characteristics and background, this book is a summary of experience, offering practical insights. However, it is also heavy on theories and academically professional. This book is an economic book, but also covers a number of social, cultural and historical traditions. In terms of the practice background, experience in this book comes from the practice of Zhejiang. From the theoretical or academic background, this book not only absorbs the academic achievements of the basic theory of economics, but also integrates many branches of economics and even marginal disciplines (such as institutional economics, development economics, industrial economics, regional economics, econometrics and economic geography). Therefore, we can say that this book is a combination of theory and practice, as well as a combination of empirical analysis and normative analysis, and quantitative analysis and qualitative analysis.

As for the structure and methods of analysis, the book uses a structure of comprehensive analysis-classification study-back to comprehensive analysis. This method can zoom in and out on related issues, thus avoiding the lack of coordination among the chapters and lack of cohesion that are epidemic in such collective work. This book features an integrated cohesion among its content. Here, I would like to make a few comments on how to introduce authors in collective works. At present there are three popular approaches: the first is to write the author's name in each chapter or directory; the second is to write the name of the author for each chapter in the postscript or preface of the book; and the third is a list only in postscripts or prefaces, without specifying authors of each chapter. The book uses the second approach. In my opinion, there is no essential difference between the first approach and the second, because both of them state the contribution and responsibility of each author. Although the third approach can highlight the status of chief editor or chief author, it obscures the contribution and responsibility of each author. Such approach is not worth advocating in an era of promoting clear property rights and responsibilities. This book is a summary of a province's economic restructuring experience. Therefore, it is very important to put the experience of a province in a national and even global economic context. This book devotes a lot of efforts in this respect. As mentioned earlier, it is an analysis of the relationship between the cycle of economic growth and the macroeconomic environment in the country. The concept of "little giant" and the term of "small products + global market" fall into this endeavor. However, judging from the high standards, there is still a lot of work to be done in this area. Under the context of large-scale development of the western part of China, facing the question of how to seize the opportunities and meet the challenges, and bring into full play the comparative advantages of the economy of Zhejiang, it is necessary to conduct more in-depth and concrete discussions against the backdrop of accelerating globalization.

This book is based on the two transition issues as the clue, and studies the issue of the market (there are five chapters in the fourth sector which focus on market). However, how to better combine marketization with the two transformation issues is yet to be further explored. In my opinion, the marketization at the present stage in our country can actually be divided into two sides: one is marketization in the process of system transformation; and the other is the marketization in the process of development transformation. The former starts from a planned economy, while the latter starts from natural economy or a semi-natural economy (or from another perspective, from a dual economy). Although this book also refers to "starting from a semi-natural economy" when discussing marketization, and points out that "marketization is always associated with economic development", in general it reckons marketization as a matter of system changes. In my opinion, it makes sense to distinguish between the marketization in the system transformation and that in the development transformation. Because, relatively speaking, the former is a reform process, while the latter is an evolutionary process. The process of reform will inevitably encounter more human-made obstacles, mainly the obstacles of vested interests and ideology. To distinguish between these two different aspects in the process of marketization undoubtedly has a policy implication for guiding marketization in the future. Finally, if the author can make more efforts in data verification and text expression polishing, this book's quality will be further enhanced.

The above comment is entirely my personal opinion, if there is any inaccuracy, I welcome any corrections and comments.

(Originally released in the second issue of *Economic Research Journal* in 2001.)

Notes

1 Fang Minsheng et al. (2000). 浙江制度变迁与发展轨迹 [The System Changes and Development Trajectory of Zhejiang]. Zhejiang: Zhejiang People's Publishing House.
2 See the first page of this book (the pages indicated in this article all refer to the book, unless otherwise stated); see also an article from the World Bank (1997). *2020 年的中国：新世纪的发展挑战* [China in 2020: Development Challenges in the New Century] (p. 5). Beijing: China Financial & Economic Publishing House.
3 Zhao Renwei (1999). 中国经济改革二十年的回顾与展望—特点、经验教训和面临的挑战 [Retrospect and Outlook of China's Economic Reform over the Past Two Decades: Characteristics, Experience & Lessons and Challenges]. *Comparative Economic & Social Systems*, 3.
4 World Bank. (1997). *1997年世界发展报告：变革世界中的政府* [World Development Report: Government in a Changing World]. Beijing: China Financial & Economic Publishing House; the UN Development Program (1999). 中国人类发展报告 *(1999)：经济转轨与政府作用* [Human Development Report (1999): Economic Transition and the Role of the Government]. Beijing: China Financial & Economic Publishing House.

13 Problems for medium- and long-term development plans to draw on international experience – interpreting *Medium and Long Term Development and Transformation of the Chinese Economy*

An international perspective and suggestions[1]

I. Origin

On the occasion of formulating *the Outline of the 12th Five-Year Plan on National Economic and Social Development of the People's Republic of China*, entrusted by the office of Leading Group for Financial and Economic Affairs and the National Development and Reform Commission, an international team consisting of international experts drafted a research report named *Medium and Long Term Development and Transformation of the Chinese Economy: an International Perspective and Suggestions*. The report draft was completed during the spring festival of 2010, as a reference for the Chinese side. After repeated revisions and supplements, this report was finally published by the CITIC Press in Beijing in July 2011. The chief author of this report is Dr. Edwin Lim, the first Chief of Mission of the World Bank's office in China, and Professor Michael Spence, the Nobel Prize laureate in economics. The draft features 100,000 words, along with 20 background articles, amounting to nearly one million words in total.

In the past two years, I participated in the consultation work for this report. When it was officially published, I hoped to interpret and review its content from an academic perspective, which was also part of an exploration, so as to better draw on the international experience and study the 12th Five-Year Plan (the 12th Five-Year Plan, 2011) released in March 2011 in China. If there are any inadequacies in my opinions for the interpretation and review, it should be my liability, instead of the authors'.

II. The background and features

For over 30 years, it has become a common practice for China to draw on international experience during the economic reform and development. Then, what are the features of this report compared with the past international experience?

First, when compared with the international experience provided before, this research report has some unique features in its background and content.

As mentioned earlier, Dr. Edwin Lim and Michael Spence led the editing of this report. Dr. Lim had presided and participated in many reports and conferences providing international experience. Among them, two occasions stood out. One is the investigation report produced by the World Bank Economical Inspection group in 1984, when he was the leader of the group. The report, *China: Problems and Choices of Long Term Development*, was published in 1985 (World Bank Economical Inspection Group, 1985). The other one is the "Macroeconomic Management International Seminar" held in September 1985 (also known as "the Bashan Cruise Meeting") (Zhao Renwei, 2008). Many foreign experts in the conference were invited through Doctor Lim. It's safe to say that the latest report not only builds on the aforesaid two researches but also shows major development.

For example, when compared with the two precious researches, which were conducted a quarter of century ago, they all focus on enhancing market-oriented reform and correctly handling the role of market and government with regard to economic system reform. However, this report puts forward a more demanding requirement on the role of government, especially a more specific and broader requirement on social policy reform. Furthermore, the former two researches mainly look at the way to complete the transition from planned economy to market-oriented economy, whereas this report reminds us to prevent and overcome the resurgence of problems of the planned economic system.

Also, although all these reports made comprehensive expositions and predictions on economic development problems, the latest one puts special emphasis on problems of the transformation of economic development model. The previous two reports discuss how China can transit from a low-income country to a middle-income country, while this research report explores how China can transit from a middle-income country to a high-income country. Correspondingly, the urbanization problem and expanding the middle class become brand new issues of this report

Furthermore, "the Bashan Cruise Ship Conference" mainly discusses the goal of economic reform and the transition model. The aforementioned investigation report and the recent research report discuss the economic development. However, the above-mentioned investigation report mainly has influenced the 7th Five Year Plan, whereas this report is mainly relevant to the 12th Five-Year Plan.

Also, by comparison, this research report gives weight to the status and role of China's economy in the global context. This change is due to the new background of a closer economic tie between China and other economies in the world and that China's economy ranks second across the globe.

Of course, this research report shares one common point with "the Bashan Cruise Ship Conference", in that they all feature a first-class international expert team. Among the participants of "the Bashan Cruise Ship Conference", James Tobin, the Nobel laureate in economics, has a broad and profound insight into the macro control of a non-centralized economy and the methods. Janos Kornai and W. Bruse featured unique insights about the drawbacks of planned economy of traditional socialism and the way to transit from planned economy to market-oriented economy. Alexander Cairncross not only had extensive experience on the macro control of the developed market-oriented economy system but also boasted experience of England's transition from a tight-control economy in during wartime to a soft-control economy in the period following the second war, which can be drawn upon. Otmar Emminger had unique experience about the way to conduct macro-economic control through monetary policy for the post-war German economic renaissance.

Among the participants of this research report providing recommendations for the 12th Five-Year Plan (including the writers of comprehensive reports and authors of background articles): Michael Spence, the Nobel laureate in economics, was once the Chairman of Commission on Growth and Development, and the dean of the Business School of Stanford University. Peter Diamond, who just won the 2010 Nobel Prize in Economics because of theoretical analysis on how economic policies influence unemployment rate, was a professor at the Massachusetts Institute of Technology and an expert in social security. Paul Romer was a senior research fellow at the Economic Policy Institute of Stanford University, with expertise in economic growth. Tony Atkinson was the former dean of Nuffield College of Oxford University and an expert in income distribution and social policy. The fact that the world-class experts accepted invitations to contribute ideas and expertise for China's reform and development implies that China's reform and development attracts the world's attention.

Second, another feature of this research report is analyzing the economic growth and development of China in over 30 years from the perspective of the world's economic growth and development.

It was not surprising that Michael Spence, one of the main authors of this report and chairman of the World Economic Growth and Development Commission, would see China from this perspective. The report pointed out at the very beginning that "Economic growth is a phenomenon that has only appeared recently in human history" (see Figure 13.1; the illustrations cited in this article are all from the comprehensive report). This process started from the Industrial Revolution in Great Britain in the late 18th century, spread to Europe and North America, and gradually accelerated its pace. Ever since we entered into the 20th century (especially the latter half of it), economic growth spread and speeded up again. However, China's rapid growth of economy started from the last 20 years in the latter half of 20th century.

Since the end of the World War II, many countries or regions witnessed rapid growth at least for a short term. However, only 13 economies, including China, maintained an annual growth rate of 7% or even higher for at least 25 years. Up to now, only six of them have developed into the high-income stage. China is still in the transition from low-income stage to the high-income stage. Though there was no reference of "middle-income trap" in this report, it pointed out the arduousness of such a transition from middle income to high income. The report specially noted that China should learn the lessons of some Latin American countries' failure to stride into the rank of high-income countries after reaching the middle-income

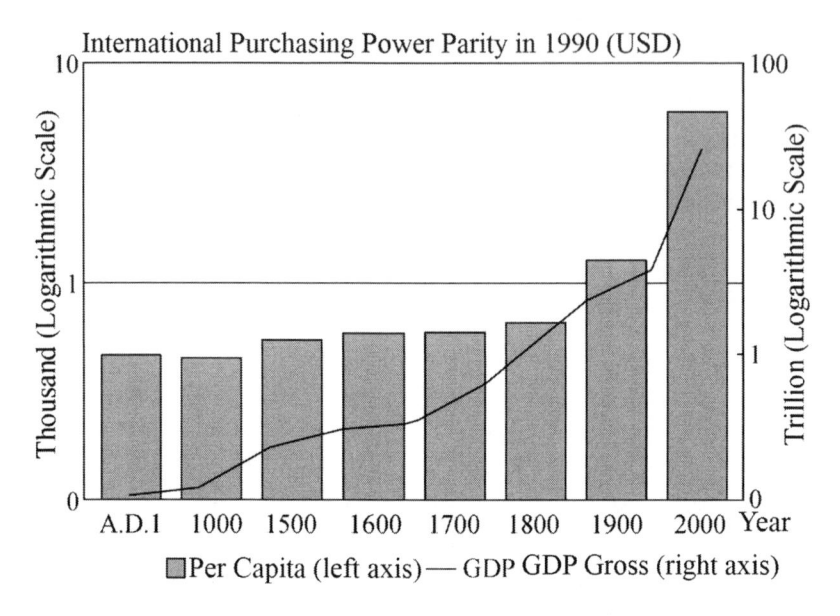

Figure 13.1 Changes of Global GDP and Per Capita GDP during the PST 2000 Years

level. The report stated that the progress of some Latin American countries was intermittent. Its vigorous growth was often interrupted by severe macroeconomic crisis, and then its economy entered into recovery and re-growth. The main reason behind this unstable pattern may be the inequality of income and failure of social policies to address such inequality. Therefore, this report hoped that China could learn from the lessons of Latin American countries and successfully transform itself into a high-income country.

Third, the report also featured analyzing the economic development of China from the perspective of China's role in the world economy.

The report specially included one chapter named "China's role in the world economy", discussing changes of China's economic position in the world economy and China's future role in the development of the world economy. It pointed out that whether seen from the changes of China's share of world GDP or from the changes of China's share in the global export volume, "China's economy is now characterized with overall global influence, and is no more the 'price taker' in the world economy." "From the marginalized position, China has come to the center stage of the world economic and financial development." And, "China has overtaken Japan as the world's second largest economy recently, with the status to influence the whole picture." (Figures 13.2 to 13.5 indicate the changes of China's position in the world.)

This report also hoped that in the future, China can play a larger role in the readjustment of the world economy. China faced not only its own task to rebalance the economy, reduce its dependence on markets of developed countries, and focus

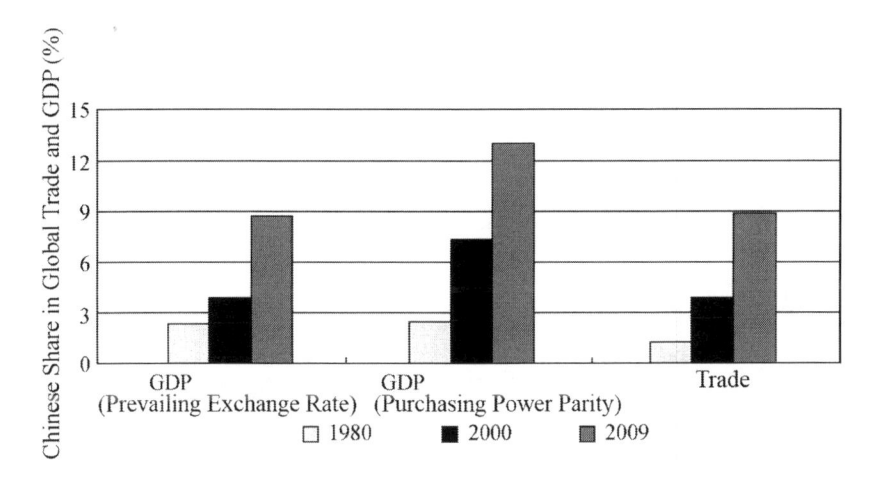

Figure 13.2 Share of Chinese GDP in the World Keeps Increasing

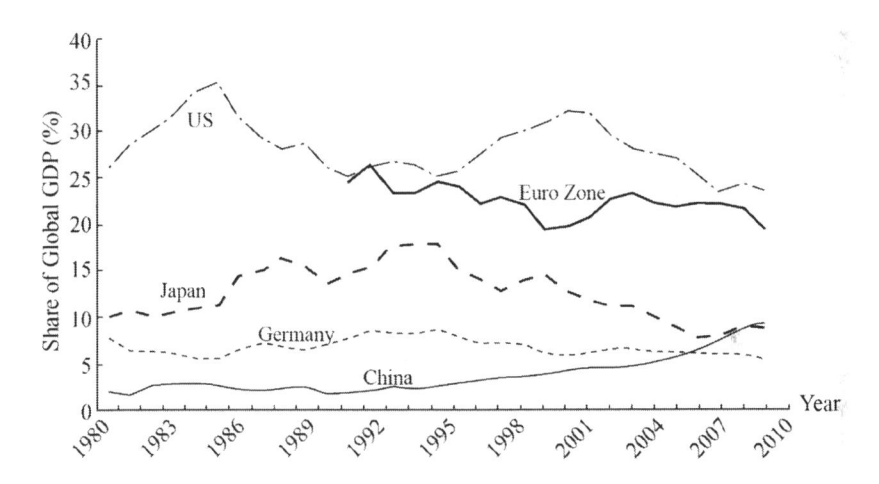

Figure 13.3 Shares of Global GDP through Prevailing Exchange Rate

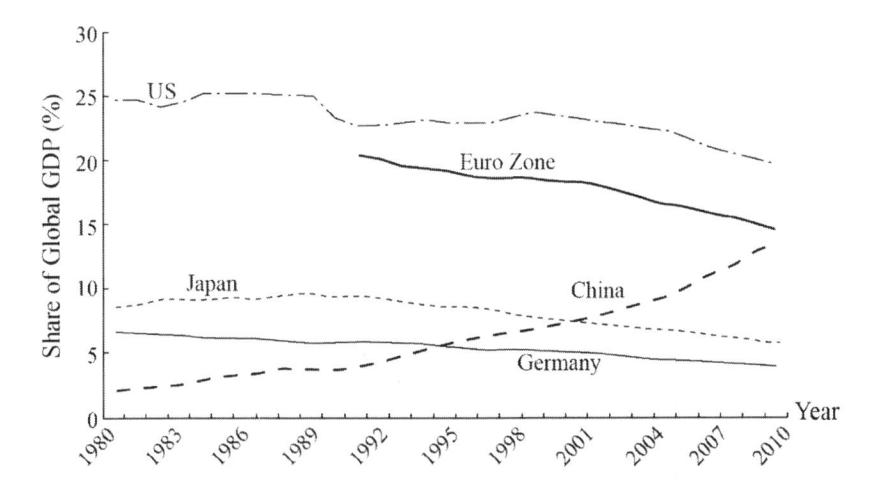

Figure 13.4 Shares of Global GDP through Purchasing Power Parity

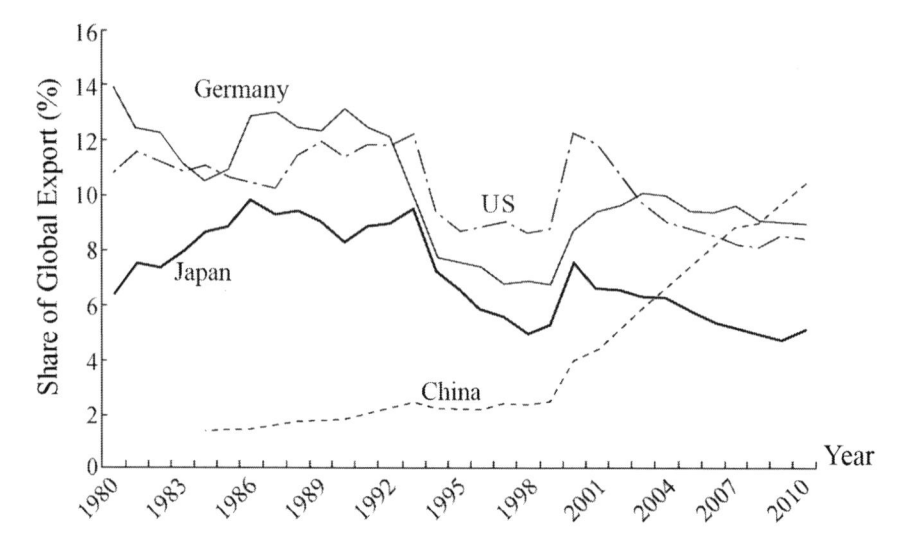

Figure 13.5 Shares of Global Export

more on domestic market, but also the responsibility to make greater contributions to the world economy, including that of the transition to a low-carbon economy.

III.   Highlights and experience

Many highlights and experience were worth learning in this report. Here, we only interpret some major points.

A.   *It defined the connotation of development model transformation*

There had been a long period of discussion and divided opinions about the transformation of development model in the economic community. This report defined the connotation of development model transformation as follows. First, it was a transformation from the investment-driven growth based on the capital and labor accumulation, to growth based on the increase in productivity. Second, the industrial structure transformed its center from the second industry to the service industry. Third, the adjustment of demand structure changed from emphasizing the external demand to the domestic demand.

It is worth noting that this report put special emphasis on linking this transformation to the enormous scale of China's economy when making the definition. It pointed out that though the growth pattern of China in the past 20 years was not much different from that of the "Four Tigers", its influence was greater. China's trade surplus, consumption of raw material, and carbon emission all attracted great attention of the world. The report believed that China couldn't simply imitate the development model taken by the developed countries. Therefore, to accelerate the transformation of development model was also the international responsibility and obligation placed on China as an economic superpower.

B.   It analyzed the correlation among all factors impacting the transformation of the development model

For example, the report pointed out that we needed to turn to a growth model driven by productivity and based on knowledge, and the focus of investment should turn correspondingly from material capital to human capital. This is because the paramount factor impacting productivity was not the stock of material capital, but that of human capital, which were the skills of citizens. The research indicated that the benefits of investment in China's human capital were much higher than that of material capital. The importance of human capital led to the importance of education.

Another instance was that the report did not link the appreciation of exchange rate merely to employment in the export industry. Instead, the report connected it to the upgrading of industrial structure and the transformation of demand structure. The report reckoned that appreciation of exchange rate should be regarded as a method to promote consumption, to give impetus to industrial structure upgrading and to realize internal balance.

Also, the report broadened the relevance of the transformation of development model. It pointed out that turning from expanding external demand to boosting domestic demand was certainly relevant to the changing of industrial structure from centering on second industry to service industry. External demand was mainly industrial products, whereas a large proportion of domestic demand was service industry. It also believed that with the expansion of service industry, it would benefit the reduction of carbon emissions and the rebalance of the economy.

C.   It analyzed the issue of the large gaps or low homogeneity among different parts of the Chinese economy

According to the report, China's economy could actually be divided into three parts, which all featured big gaps in terms of per capita income.

1   Rural economy: It was based on agriculture, with insufficient employment and low income.
2   Coastal economy: It was export-oriented with low salary, which have led the economic growth of the past 20 years.
3   Knowledge-based economy: It will lead China to transition into a high-income country in the next decade.

Therefore, China's macroeconomic policy must seek balance among these three parts. The report also pointed out that the continuing existence of underemployment in rural China meant that we hadn't used up the opportunities of catch-up growth, which was a good thing for the prospect of China's macroeconomy. However, such big gaps also brought obstacles to the construction of a harmonious society.

To narrow such huge differences, the report believed, we couldn't just depend on the power of economy. It specially introduced European experience on "social integration progress". Though the terminology "inclusive growth" was not used in this report, the philosophy was the same. Namely, there should not be excluded groups in the society, and low-income individuals should also be empowered to enjoy the fruits of economic growth, which is more demanding than poverty reduction. Social integration was the same with our development concept of nurturing a harmonious society and people-oriented development, as well as related to the philosophy of enhancing the middle class while strengthening social policy effectiveness, which would be illustrated later.

D.   It analyzes problems existing in China's urbanization

This report regards urbanization as the geographical factor of economic growth. It believes that several problems exist in China's urbanization that need to be solved. They are as follows:

1   The division of city scale lacks efficiency. When compared with the world average level, China's cities with small population scale account for a large proportion, while cities with large population scale account for a small share (see Figure 13.6). Is this problem linked with our habitual mentality? For example, during the early phase of township enterprises in the early 1980s, there was a slogan: "leave the farmland but not one's hometown, enter the

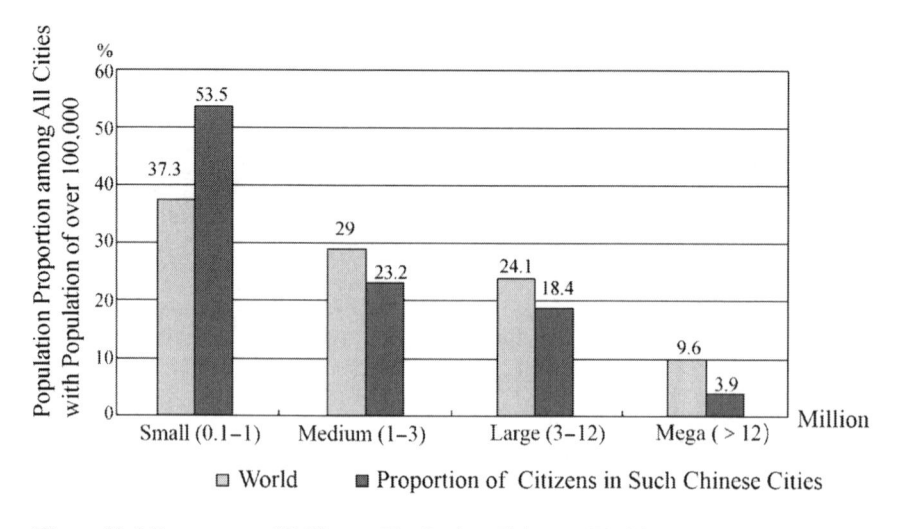

Figure 13.6 Percentage of Different City Scales: China vs. World, Year 2000

factory but not the city". Until today, we use urbanization in the sense of cities and towns rather than metropolis. I think that the international experience of pursuing efficiency in the division of city scale is worth learning from.

2   The urban economy lacks specialized division of labor and efficiency. According to international experience, an urban multi-step system should gradually be formed: small and medium-sized cities focus on the production of certain industry, such as steel, textile and clothes; while the natural economic foundation of metropolis is business service industry and financial industry. However, many big cities in China still rely on its power and resources, enjoying unfair advantages in attracting manufacturing industry. Though these cities have already started to give more attention to the development of service industry, they are still exploring the advantages in manufacturing industry.

3   Urban use of land lacks efficiency, and the development of the urban marginal areas is fragmented. "Village in the city", which is not included in the urban administration, spreads around, in which rural migrant workers without registered permanent residence in the city live. The built-up areas around the city scatter among agriculture lands, and the development of these lands cannot be carried out successfully due to the strict restriction on transforming agricultural land for other purposes.

4   City governments of China rely too much on land leasing as its source of revenue. Government officials with rather short term of office take charge of selling long-term property of the city to maintain recurrent expenditure and part of capital expenditure, which equates to depriving future citizens of the income from these assets. It's a potential "time bomb" that needs to be addressed immediately. On these grounds, this report considers levying a property tax ad valorem on houses, i.e. to levy property tax base on the valuation of property, which will be a great progress. Currently, the urban fiscal revenue mainly comes from value added tax; business tax and land leasing revenue, which all encourage cities to attract industry rather than residents. To levy a property tax on houses not only increases local revenue, but also encourages cities to bring in more residents.

E.   It estimates about the current situation and expansion of the middle class in China

There are all kinds of studies on the middle class, and no consensus can be reached. This report admits that "the middle class" is a rather ambiguous terminology in social category, of which no clear or generally accepted definition can be reached by now, but its importance is universally recognized. For example, China's transforming from strengthening foreign demand to domestic demand requires a large middle class; for China, to build a harmonious society also entails a middle class as the base of social stability. The report points out that one of the important reasons why some Latin American countries have failed to transit into high-income countries is that they can't build a middle class that is strong enough. Therefore,

China must build a middle class which is large enough to realize the transition from the middle-income country to the high-income country. It also believes that the re-balance of world economy also needs China and the entirety of Asia to possess a middle class with strong consumption power. The world growth pattern based on western consumption and resource exploitation of other areas of the world cannot continue any more. To achieve breakthrough, the rapid growth of the middle class of China and the whole of Asia is needed.

Similar to other studies, this report also describes the living conditions of the middle class. It states that from the perspective of economy, the middle class can be defined as a group equipped with a certain amount of income enabling a comfortable life, which will leave some surplus after paying necessities and can be used freely in durable consumer goods. It also features high-quality education, medical care, housing, vocation and other leisure activities. Different from under-privileged people, they have many options about consumer goods; and, different from the wealthy class, their options may be restricted by budget and their sensitivity to price and quality. This class consists of people of different occupations, including government officials, rich peasants, merchants, enterprise employees and professionals.

This report adopts a definition of the middle class that is applicable in any country of the world (which I think is the statement of a school, and I will explain later). The author believes, according to this definition, we can make comparisons between China's emerging middle class with the middle class in the United States, Europe and Japan. This study defines the middle class in the world as a class of people that spend 10 to 100 US dollars per person per day, according to purchasing power parity (PPP). The floor level equals to the average poverty line of Portugal and Italy, and the upper limit amounts to twice of the median income of Luxembourg, the richest developed country. According to this definition, the middle class of the world does not include the poor in the poorest developed countries, nor the rich in the richest developed countries.

Based on this definition, this report cites the estimation in related background articles written by Homi Kharas, who thinks China's middle class accounted for 12% in 2009. Many other scholars consider the estimation to be low, but even we take 20%, a higher one into account, the proportion of China's middle class is still too small. For example, when calculated according to the 2010 statistical bulletin released on February 28, 2011, the GDP per capita of China in 2010 registered 4500 US dollars. Under the same level, the middle class of Korea accounts for 55% (the GDP per capita in 1986 is 4600 US dollars), the middle class of Japan accounts for nearly 55%. The rather small proportion of middle class reflects the large income gap.

The report considers that, with the improvement of income, the number of people crossing the threshold of the middle class will increase rapidly. If the average income of Chinese can maintain a growth rate of 7% from the present until 2030, the proportion of people with daily expenditure over 10 US dollars will surge to 74% (see Figure 13.7).

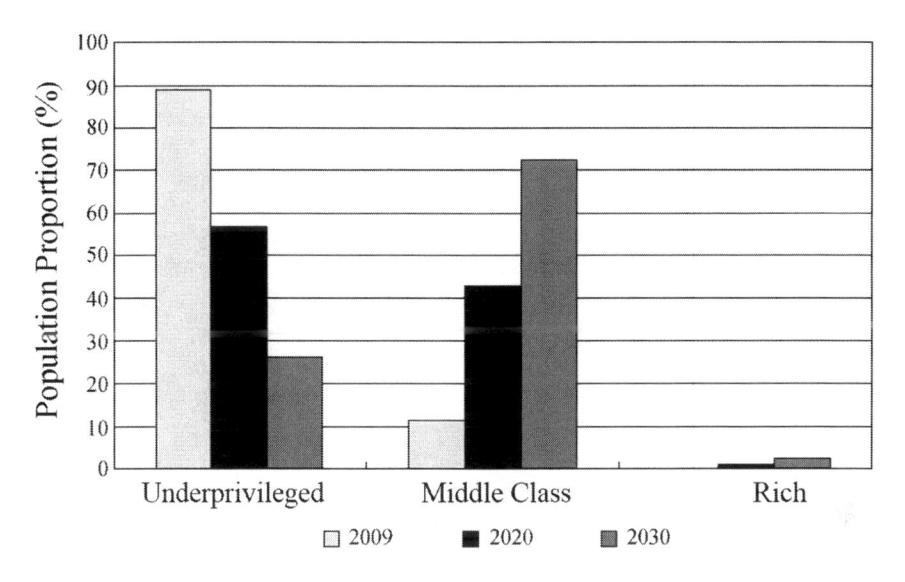

Figure 13.7 The Increase of Chinese Middle Class

F. *China should strengthen social policies*

Apart from economic development issues, the report also focuses on livelihood issues and social development issues, and emphasizes that China should strengthen social policies, including pension, education, health care and a minimum living standard security system. Here, we will only introduce some highlights:

1   The report puts forward some basic principles about social policy reform, including:

- Formulation of social policies should be tightly linked with that of economic policies.
- Seek proper balance between market and government.
- Social projects should ensure nationwide coverage as large as possible.
- Avoid institutional defects, because historical problems are hard to rectify.
- When resources allow, social projects should be promoted more easily.
- Distribute service cost among central government, local government and individuals.
- Provide best personnel for project management and service.
- Ensure projects will get effective surveillance, measurement and assessment.

2   The report suggests, apart from Non-Contributory Basic Pension (pension for citizens) and Mandatory Contributory Pension, China can use the experience of countries such as Sweden as reference, and establish Notional Defined Contribution Personal Accounts (sometimes known as Notional Account).

In this report, it mentions that the pension system is a recent innovation. Countries adopting this system hope to maintain the advantages of a defined contribution system, but not to be fully funded. Both systems, including a Notional Defined Contribution system and a Fully Funded system, can coexist. For example, the pension contribution rate of Sweden is 18.5%, 16% of which will be counted in the Notional Defined Contribution Personal Account, and 2.5% of which enters into the fully accumulation account.

> Chinese scholars have a rather comprehensive discussion about the Notional Defined Contribution system from the perspective of theory. However, how to apply it according to China's actual conditions is still a question that requires further exploration.
> (Find more through Zheng Wei, Yuan Xinzhao, 2010)

3   The report suggests that China should raise the retirement age and believes that the worry that raising the retirement rate will increase unemployment lacks evidence. It points out that with the extension of human life, all countries in the world are considering extending the retirement rate, and so should China. However, many Chinese people worry that raising the retirement age will increase unemployment. The rationale is that the longer employees stay in the work position, the fewer the job opportunities that will be offered to the incoming labor force. The report considers that this point of view is wrong in a general way. In the market economy, the number of employment positions is not fixed, depending on a series of factors related to labor force supply and demand. First, people entering the labor market will bring downward pressure to salary and enable enterprises to find suitable employees, so as to create more jobs. Second, to draw pensions in advance normally will not lead to employees' exiting the labor market. Some employees might draw pensions from the former employer while working for a new employer. What's more, it is the large amount of rural labor force that is the largest source of potential unemployment.

4   China should expand spending on social policy programs. When compared with other countries, the Chinese government investment in this area is markedly low. For example, in the Chinese government's budget, the educational funds expenditure accounts for only 3.2% of China's GDP, far lower than the average amount of Vietnam and that of low- and middle-income countries, not to mention to compare with OECD countries. The public expenditure in the medical field accounts for only 1.8% of China's GDP, also markedly lower than the level of most low- and middle-income countries. Therefore, this report considers that, from the perspective of international standard, China can invest more money in educational, medical and other social programs. (About the public expenditure on educational field, see Figure 13.8.)

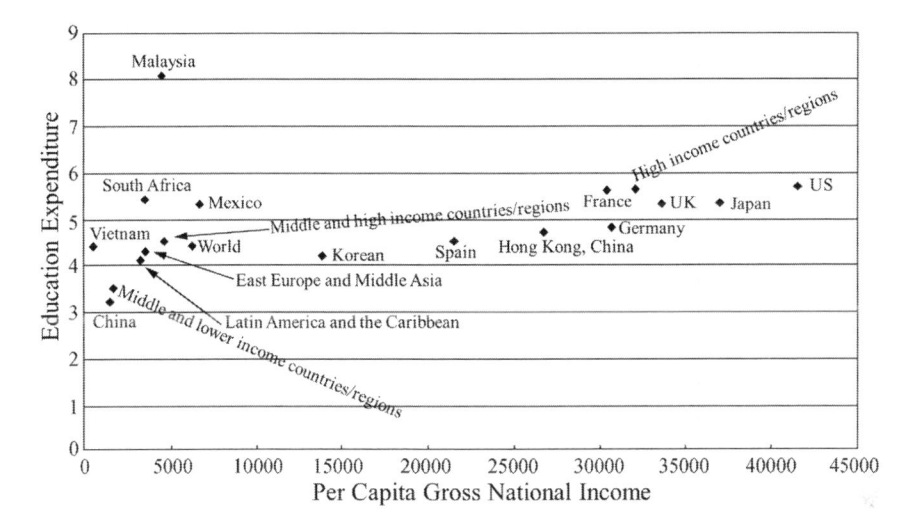

Figure 13.8 Public Expenditure in Education in 2004 (Percentage of GDP, Calculated through Per Capita Income in USD)

Source: Dahlman, Zeng & Wang, *The Challenge of Life Long Learning for Education Finance in China*, a paper provided n a seminar in 2006 for Chinese Ministry of Finance and the World Bank.

G.   It proposes several suggestions on deepening systematic reform

There are many issues about this topic. I will introduce only three points here.

1. Reforming the relationship of distribution among the nation, enterprises and individuals which is reforming the so-called big distribution relationship

First, the proportion of fiscal revenue in GDP shall be increased. In recent years, China's fiscal revenue accounts for only around 20% of GDP, and 25% of GDP after counting in extra-budgetary revenues, far lower than that of the United States (around 30%) and that of the EU (around 40%). The report suggests that the proportion of fiscal revenue in GDP should be raised to at least 30% recently, which is the current US level, but which is still lower than many developed countries.

Second, the proportion of household income (household consumption) in GDP is only 36%, far lower than the world average level of 61% and that of Vietnam (66%), Indonesia (63%), India (54%) and Thailand (51%). Therefore, to increase the proportion of household income in GDP is a major task facing China. The aforementioned growth in fiscal revenue should not aggravate the burden of households (except the few in the high-income class) and avoid any conflicts with the target of increasing the proportion of household income in GDP.

Third, to avoid any conflicts between the aforementioned two targets, profits of state-owned enterprises (with annual profits reaching over 900 billion RMB currently) should be turned in to public finance in principle. This report considers that allowing state-owned enterprises to keep all profits is the provisional measure brought in China in the middle of the 1990s when many enterprises were financially strapped. However, this provisional measure continues to exist today when state-owned enterprises make profitable businesses.

Fourth, residents and households can gain more income from saving and investment. The report considers that China has executed a rather low regulated interest rate for the long term, which damages the earnings of depositors and reduces household income. Therefore, China can consider squeezing on margins of banks through increasing the deposit interest rate and reducing the loan interest rate to benefit households and borrowers.

2.   Promoting the fiscal and tax reform

First, to explore more sources of city revenues, apart from levying property tax on houses, the government can also issue city bonds. The report believes that China will require a bond market with a larger scale and better mobility, including the market of municipal bonds issued because of local government's supporting the rapid development of cities.

Second, apart from property tax, a natural resources tax should also be included in local tax revenues. The value of these immovable properties largely depends on the governance environment created by local governments. A natural resources tax will be particularly beneficial for the underdeveloped areas with rich mineral resources.

Third, China needs to reform its inter-governmental fiscal system. Currently, the proportion of local government in government overall expenditure is only 79%, but its proportion in tax revenues is only 47%. Under this inter-governmental fiscal system, governments at a basic level do not have the resources or motivation to fulfill the responsibility pointed out by the society. This state of unbalance is the unbalance between financial authority and powers and needs to be changed.

3.   Setting up a "reform team"

This report points out that economies with fast growth in the world are usually equipped with "reform teams" consisting of high-level technical officials. For example, there is the Economic Development Board in Singapore, the Economic Planning Board in Korea, the Ministry of Trade and Industry in Japan and the Economic Planning Unit in Malaysia. Based on experiences of countries of the world, this report suggests that China set up a "reform team". This team would be inside the government, but would get rid of daily administrative matters and realistic political pressure. It should be able to coordinate powers among government and overcome the obstruction brought by bureaucratism.

IV. Problems and challenges

After reform and opening-up for 30 years, both Chinese experts' understanding about the outside world and foreign experts' understanding about China are more profound than before, and exchanges between Chinese and foreign experts are also easier than before. However, due to reasons of systematic background, cultural and historical background and even the educational background, the understanding between each other still needs to be strengthened. During the medium- and long-term development and transformation of China's economy, we still face a series of problems and challenges. Here, I can only put forward my opinions by giving examples.

First, how can foreign experts have a more profound understanding about China's reality?

One example is the issue of whether narrowing the income gap can be realized through social policies such as redistribution. Foreign experts live in the market economy and consider that the initial distribution can rely only on the market mechanism. They also believe that the government cannot intervene with initial distribution but can realize social justice through redistribution. However, China had not yet completed the transition from the planned economy to market economy, and labor resource is still in the transition from unified government allocation to market allocation. Up to now, many irrational phenomena in initial distribution are because the transformation of labor resources allocation is not in place and the market mechanism does not play its role. For example, the decrease of proportion of labor payment in GDP can hardly be attributed to the market mechanism; the salary of rural migrant workers in cities is significantly squeezed, which is the result of segmentation of the urban and rural labor market; a large income gap between monopolized industries and competitive industries is because of administrative monopoly; a large income gap between common staff and the management in enterprises is the result of an unsound collective negotiation system on salary. Therefore, there is still much room and need for the government in the initial distribution. Government should not only step out of unnecessary intervention in initial distribution, but also promote the basic role that the market mechanism plays in labor resources allocation, including accelerating the construction of a unified urban and rural labor market, strengthening the reform of administrative monopoly industries, accelerating the construction of collective negotiation and consultation mechanism, and promoting the construction and execution of labor law and regulations (Song, 2010; Zhao, 2010). It is true that foreign experts emphasize realizing the target of narrowing the income gap through social policies. However, it is hoped that they can learn more about the complexities of the interference the market mechanism faces during the initial distribution in China.

Another example is about how we can estimate the current situation of China's middle class in a more comprehensive way. As mentioned earlier, this report uses the absolute standard to estimate China's middle class, i.e. the lowest expenditure per person per day is 10 US dollars. However, experts of Asian Development Bank use its own absolute standard, under which the lowest expenditure per person per day is 2 US dollars. There are certainly great differences between results of these two estimations. The large gap brought up by the absolute standard brings challenges this method. However, Branko Milanovic, an expert of the World Bank, uses the relative standard to study the whole world. He defines the middle class as a group of people with the income between 75% of the median and 125% of the median, and the result of this estimation is that the middle class accounts for only 10% in the world. He further reached the conclusion leading to "A World without a Middle Class" (Milanovic, 2005; Milanovic, 2007). It seems that the conclusion from Milanovic goes too far. Actually, no matter how small the proportion of a middle class is, we cannot deny its existence. Therefore, seen from the global perspective, the conclusion should be "a world with a too weak middle class". And as for the current stage of China, it can be described as "China with a middle class expected to grow". In a word, the research on China's middle class is still in the early stage.

Second, how can Chinese experts further learn from international experience?

Take the issue of how to levy the property tax as an example. This report proposes to levy property tax ad valorem in China in line with international experience. In recent years, in the background of soaring house prices, China's related decision-making departments and economic circles have had a heated discussion about levying property tax and promoting house purchase restriction policies. However, in this discussion, no matter that it's about implementing house purchase restriction policies or levying property tax, few voices of "ad valorem" (as per price) can be heard, but there are many cries about specific duty (as per square kilometers), or even about levying property tax according to the number of houses (the way of dividing houses into the first house, the second house, the third house, is more ambiguous than dividing houses based on its square kilometers). I don't know the scientific basis of this policy that restricts a certain group of people from purchasing a third house, or restricts other groups of people from purchasing a second house. If it doesn't take into account the area of these houses, does it mean to protect the vested interest of owners of large houses? As for properties, there are differences in their areas and also in their locations. But in fact, both of these two differences can be reflected by price. China has gone through 30 years of transformation from planned economy to market economy; when can China realize the transformation from specific duty to ad valorem tax?

How to further get rid of the impacts left by traditional planned economy? In the 30 years of economic system transformation, the two maladies we discussed most in traditional planned economy are the "investment hunger" and the "shortage". It should be mentioned that we have put a lot of effort into overcoming these two maladies and have made great achievements, especially in overcoming the shortage issue. However, once a phenomenon becomes a tradition, it will never be easy to get rid of it completely.

With regard to investment, as the report points out, one great feature of the planned economy is to maintain rather high investment rate by suppressing consumption, and this so-called "investment hunger" is still continuing, especially in local governments that have greater impulsion to invest. Therefore, the next step of reform is to solve this problem, which is to adjust the expenditure structure, suppress investment and increase the household consumption of residents so as to realize the rebalance of economy and to promote the transformation of the economic development model.

With regard to shortage: as early as in the period of "the Bashan Cruise Ship Conference", the problem of how to solve the shortage was already a popular topic. The British economist Cairncross points out at the conference that "Shortage is the function of price" (Cairncross, 1986). The Hungarian economist Janos Kornai's analysis of shortage is also tightly connected with the function of price. *Economics of Shortage* consists of two volumes: the headline of Volume 1 is "adjustment without price", and the headline of Volume 2 is "adjustment in the presence of prices". The implication of Volume 1 is clear, which is that the price doesn't function; the implication of Volume 2 title needs further explanation. There are some doubts about how big a role price and currency can play, so he didn't use the headline of "adjustment through price", but instead merely pointed out the presence of price. On these grounds, I think the analysis of *Economics of Shortage* is based on the background of no price signals (Volume 1) and weak price signals (Volume 2). (Kornai, 1986) All these analyses belong to international experience, whose warning function is to avoid the resurgence of shortage; we should pay attention to the authenticity of price signal. Excessive and long-term price control will result in the signal distortion and lead to shortage. As for the power shortage which appeared recently in China, even it is resulted by multiple factors; we should admit the price control factor is one that cannot be neglected. Under the severe situation of governing inflation, we can understand the intervention of government in price. However, the government should effectively control the time and the level of intensity of intervention. When price of coal, the raw material for electricity, has risen, to implement long-term control on electricity price will inevitably result in a shortage in the power supply, which causes the power shortage. As some remarks point out, "coal under market economy" and "electricity under planned economy" cannot coexist for long.

Third, how can China and other countries work together to solve crucial problems?

Here, I want only to give an example of the crucial problems that need to be solved, which is how to narrow the income gap between urban and rural residents. As we all know, according to official statistics, in 1978 when China just began reform and opening-up, the income ratio between urban residents and rural residents was 2.5; namely, the income of urban residents was 2.5 times the income of rural residents. Thanks to the success of rural reforms, by 1984, this ratio decreased to 1.8. However, ever since the focus of reform turned to cities, the gap between urban and rural residents has been expanding. Despite some fluctuations in certain years, the overall tendency did not change. Entering the 21st century, this tendency of expanding was contained because the government adopted a series of agriculture supporting policies (such as canceling the agriculture tax). In recent years, the income gap between urban and rural residents stands at around the rate of 3.3. It should be noted that the gap rate was calculated according to the disposable

income per capita of urban residents and net income of rural residents released officially. It does not reflect the gaps of public services such as pension, medical care,
education and housing between urban and rural residents. Therefore, the actual gap
is greater than what was officially announced. We all know the gap between urban
and rural areas of developed countries is very small. Even in developing countries,
there are few countries with an income ratio of urban and rural residents over 2.
What's more, when seen from the common sense of a developing economy, the
gap of urban and rural areas should be narrowed in the development transformation
from dual economy to modern economy.

In the medium- and long-term development and transformation of China's
economy, finding the Turning Point to shift the expanding trend of income gap
between urban residents and rural residents should be a challenging task in front
of us. Even according to the regulations of the 12th Five-Year Plan, the average
annual growth of disposable income per capita of urban residents and net income
per capita of rural residents must be over 7% in the next five years, but it doesn't
mention anything about the Turning Point. Therefore, to find this Turning Point is
not only a tough fight, but also an area worth exploring for researchers.

For many years, Chinese academic circles have discussed frequently the Lewi-
sian Turning Point and Kuznets Curve (there is naturally a turning point in this
curve). But I believe that there should be more discussions about the Turning Point,
which is more related to Chinese conditions. Therefore, in my opinion, we should
at least conduct research from the following aspects:

- The influences that the land system brings to income gap between urban
  and rural areas;
- The influences that the household registration system brings to income gap
  between urban and rural areas;
- The influences that labor mobility policies bring to income gap between
  urban and rural areas;
- The influences that transfer payment policies (of pension, medical care,
  education and so on) bring to the income gap between urban and rural areas;
- The influences that industrialization and urbanization policies bring to the
  income gap between urban and rural areas.

If we can quantify the degree of influences of these factors and conduct static and
dynamic analysis so as to find this Turning Point, it will no doubt facilitate the
integration process of China's economical society and accelerate the construction
of a moderately prosperous society and a harmonious society.

Note

1 Edward Lim and Michael Spence. (2011). 中国经济中长期发展和转型：国际视角的
思考与建议 [Interpreting Medium and Long Term Development and Transformation of
the Chinese Economy: An International Perspective and Suggestions]. Beijing: CITIC
Press.

References

Alexander Cairncross. (1986). 战后英国从硬控制经济到软控制经济的过度 [Transition of UK Economy from Hard Control to Soft Control after II World War]. In China Society of Economic Reform. *The Management and Reform of Macroeconomy: Selected Speeches on the International Seminar of Macroeconomy Management*. The Economic Daily Press.

Branko Milanovic. (2005). *Worlds Apart: Measuring International and Global Inequality* (pp. 128–135). Princeton: Princeton University Press.

Branko Milanovic. (2007). 世界的分化：国家间和全球不平等的度量研究 [Worlds Apart: Measuring International and Global Inequality]. Beijing: Beijing Normal University Press.

Janos Kornai. (1986). 短缺经济学 [Economics of Shortage] (Vol. 1 & 2). Beijing: Economic Science Press.

People's Daily. (March 17th, 2011). 中华人民共和国国民经济和社会发展第十二个五年 (2011–2015年) 规划纲要 [The Outline of the 12th Five-Year Plan (2011 to 2015) on National Economic and Social Development of the People's Republic of China].

Song Xiaowu. (2010). 政府应在调解一次分配中发挥作用 [Government Should Play a Role in Adjusting the Initial Distribution]. *Comparative Studies*, 49.

World Bank Economical Inspection Group. (1985). 中国：长期发展的问题和选择 [China: Problems and Choices of Long Term Development]. Beijing: China Financial & Economic Publishing House.

Zhao Renwei. (2008). 1985年 "巴山轮会议" 的回顾与思考 [Review and Reflection about the Bashan Cruise Meeting in 1985]. *Economic Research Journal*, 12.

Zhao Renwei. (2010). 收入差距过大的原因从哪里找 [What Are the Reasons for the Large Income Gap]. *Tong Zhou Gong Jin*, 9.

Zheng Wei, & Yuan Xinzhao. (2010). 名义账户制与中国养老保险改革：路径选择和挑战 [Notional Defined Contribution System and China's Pension System Reform: Path Selection and Challenges]. *Comparative Economic & Social Systems*, 2.

(Originally published in the eighth issue of *Economic Perspectives* in 2011.)

14 Viewing China's social security system reform from the perspective of economic transition[1]

I. Major issues in economic transition

Social security reform is a major subject in China's economic transition. This reform was still in exploratory phase in the 1980s and later ushered into the implementation stage in the 1990s. The establishment of the socialist market economic system as a major reform goal has greatly promoted the process of social security system reform. In 1993, *The Decision of the CCCPC on Some Issues Concerning Establishing the Socialist Market Economy System* of the Third Plenary Session of the 14th Central Committee pointed out that the social security system should, in line with the modern enterprise system, the unified market system, the macro-control system and the income distribution system, be regarded as an major component of China's socialist market economic framework. This statement marked that the reform of China's social security system had become an integral part of the entire market economic system. Since the 1990s, a number of progress and phased achievements have been made during the reform. In addition to the progress made in the reform of endowment insurance, medical insurance, unemployment insurance and social assistance, there have also been advances at different levels in the reform of work-related injury insurance, maternity insurance, social welfare and special care and placement. What's more, with commercial insurance playing a role, improvements can be seen in terms of enterprise supplementary insurance and personal savings insurance.

So far the progress of the social security reform in our country has been deemed gratifying, but with the special context of economic transition, reform can be said to be in its infancy in this respect. According to the internationally accepted expression, the reform of the social security system can be described as the transition of the welfare system, which is based on the economic transition. The economic transition in our country at present stage can be divided into two aspects: the transition from a planned economy to a market economy and the transition from a dual economy to a modern economy (or from a rural agricultural society to an urban industrial society) We often refer to the former as the system transition, the latter as the structure transition. In the context of these transitions, the complexity and difficulty of the welfare system reform are very clear. In fact, there are actually three kinds of transitions going on in China at this stage, respectively aimed at economic system, economic structure and welfare system. However, in some Eastern European countries, there is no dual economic structure, for they have achieved industrialization; therefore, they have no need for transition of economic structure. But they also have to face that of the economic system and welfare system. Similarly, in those well-developed market economy countries only exists the transformation of the welfare system. Among these three kinds of countries, the transition of China's welfare system is the most complicated. Given such background, China's reform of its social security system would surely meet difficulties, not to mention the complexity of the current system itself.

For instance, in China, the dual economic system is accompanied by an institutional segmented labor market. Within such phenomenon coexist the "overplay" and the "underplay" of the welfare-related arrangements. The social security system runs rather differently in China's urban and rural areas, with the majority of resources being allocated to the former. Even so, the urban welfare system is still faced with issues concerning the institutional segmentation. The dual or even multiple structure of the welfare system will inevitably lead to wastage in the well-resourced areas and insufficiency in the under-resourced ones. Such a structure will not only cause a lack of fairness but a loss of efficiency.

In terms of the trends of social security system reform, there is another hard nut to crack; that is, whether or not to establish a unified system at this stage. Furthermore, how should we restructure the rural social security system?

Considering the significance of system transition and structure transition to the social security system reform, we title the book (the outcome of this research project) as *China's Economic Transition and Social Security Reform.*

In addition to analyzing the context of transitions, this project (and the book) possesses some other features as follows:

a   Based on reality. To achieve this, the command of information is of foremost importance. Considering the difficulty to master a large amount of systematic firsthand information of this project, we mainly use indirect data and conduct some small-scale surveys, such as that on the social security for migrant workers in Beijing. In order to make up for the lack of systematic data, we paid more attention to the case studies. For instance, when illustrating the reform and reconstruction of the rural medical security system, we select Zhen'an County of Shaanxi Province as a case of shrinking cooperative medical care; while Nong'an County of Jilin Province is used as a case for its unsuccessful cooperative medical care resuming project. And Jiangyin County of Jiangsu Province is mentioned for its relative success in establishing a rural medical insurance system.

b   Focusing on the research and analysis of related issues. To avoid the universal tendency to overlook related researches on the social security system, we lay much emphasis on this aspect during the design stage. Our project covers, to varying degrees, the researches on the impact of factors such as employment status, labor market, human capital investment, population structure and redistribution of income (taxes and transfer payments) on social security. However, our practice is only an attempt but should be widely acknowledged.

c   Conducting comparative analysis. We take Sweden and the United States as two kinds of extreme examples of the developed countries in a comparative analysis. Hungary is selected as a model for a system-transitioning country, whereas China is a case with both system transition and structure transition. These comparative analyses have enabled us to see not only the great difference between the reforms of the social security system in China and that of other countries, but also many common grounds and points for our reference.

d   Presenting academic and topical studies. There are many domestic publications on social security issues. However, a large number of them are teaching materials and government documents. This project highlights both academic research and thematic design. We arrange and present our findings and results in accordance with the requirements of thematic design, such as the parts referring to relations between income redistribution and social security, human capital investment and social security, women's employment and social security, social security of migrant workers and the dilemma of "SP&IRA" public pension system. Of course, our efforts in this regard are also an attempt. Some of the topics just raise questions, and it is hard to say that we have reaped the desired results.

e   Integrating the policy implications with the independence of research. We aim not only at exerting influence on the government's policy-making, but also at not compromising the research's independence. Issues like implicit pension debt and its repayment have long been avoided in the relevant documents so far. However, our research touches on this issue and offers several recommendations on decision-making. We hope that the independence of our research will not impede the government's decision-making, but rather, help pool wisdom for it.

II.   Preliminary results and major findings

Considering the current state of the studies on social security reform, the work done by this project can be described as a drop in the bucket. Nevertheless, we think it is worth summarizing even the preliminary findings and initial consensus reached during the discussions. Here, we would like to share some ideas as follows.

A.   Basic principles of social security system reform

The basic principles summarized in this book include "combining personal responsibility and social mutual assistance", "keeping the social security level in accordance with the economic level", "putting people first "and "possessing a holistic view". Not only do we draw upon the international experience, but we also take China's actual conditions into account. These principles are the common spiritual wealth of all countries undertaking social security reform. But applying these principles to various countries must be integrated with the specific conditions of each country. For example, based on the principle of keeping the social security level in accordance with the economic level, the status quo of China's social security is still at a relatively low level considering our economic development. In addition, the principle of putting people first should be implemented differently in different contexts. In a developed country, it should be interpreted as the nationwide universality of welfare standards. However, in view of China's current state, putting people first should be materialized as expanding welfare coverage.

The most difficult part of social security reform lies in how to achieve balance between individual responsibility and social assistance. Almost all countries undergoing the reform of the welfare system have to deal with the problem as government bearing excessive responsibility and risks. Individuals should contribute more to the public welfare undertaking. Many reforms require that one's welfare benefits should correspond to his/her contributions to the society. However, in the field of social security, given the reciprocal and risk-sharing nature of welfare, it is hard to achieve complete equivalence between one's rights and obligations. Therefore, it asks for great effort, wisdom and tactics to not only enhance the autonomy and responsibility of individuals, but also promote a caring, mutual-aiding and united society and a responsible government. Here then emerges a crucial problem. Since social security issues have both economic and moral implications (so-called ethical principles, according to Kornai), the promulgation of related measures requires the decision-makers to consider from economic and moral perspectives. The beneficiaries of social security measures should be moral people in need of financial aid.

B.   General idea of the reform and construction of China's social security system

Among the discussions on overall vision, the most debated one is over whether or not to establish a unified national social security system at this stage. In this regard, public opinions vary. Many chapters of the book also touch on the related issues. It seems that there is a great deal of disagreement in the society while the authors' views in this book are relatively close. Based on some authors' studies in this book, we may well conclude that, although a unified national social security system has various benefits such as helping advocate fairness and being easy to manage, it does not meet the complicated background and national conditions under the two transitions at this stage. The homogeneity of our society as a whole is very low, with huge disparities existing between urban and rural areas and between regions. Even in urban areas, pension insurance can be implemented only on the provincial level. Hence, it is obviously unrealistic to establish a unified social security system in China overnight. Moreover, there is no reason to exclude peasants and marginalized urban groups from the social security system for a long period. Blindly emphasizing that "the land is the guarantee" or "the family is the guarantee" is anything but the objective of the transitions. Instead, these improper measures would only ossify the existing structures of the economic development and system.

Despite the fact that it is impossible for China to establish a unified national social security system at this stage, we should still gradually make changes to the dual and multiple structure of the welfare system. Therefore, the basic direction of reform and construction of China's social security system should be to expand the coverage progressively and at the same time stick to multi-level development, which is a widely discussed topic in many chapters of this book.

Some Chinese economic literature argues that, after more than 20 years of hard work, especially the reform and construction since the 1990s, the basic framework of our social security system has come into shape. However, in terms of coverage scale, the existing framework still has much room to improve. Until 2002, the pension, medical and unemployment insurance covered only 18.3%, 10.7% and 13% of the total population respectively, all three figures lower than the international minimum standards set by the International Labor Organization in 1952 that the three insurance policies each should cover at least 20% of all residents. It can be said that the further expansion of coverage is a long-term task of China's social security reform.

It is necessary to insert the multi-level concept throughout the design of the reform and construction of the social security system. If to achieve broad coverage requires us to solve the issue of fairness, then multi-level development asks for the recognition of differences.

Even the countries with an urban-rural integrated or unified social security system are moving toward a multi-level reform. For example, they divide the pension and medical insurance respectively into two categories: basic insurance and supplementary insurance. The basic part is to meet the general needs and demonstrate fairness, whereas the supplementary insurance is to meet the higher needs of some people and reflect differences. It is clear that our country's reform is also moving in this direction.

Multi-level concepts can be presented in many ways. The most prominent is that the development of social security between urban and rural areas will remain at different levels for quite a long period, though the gap will be gradually narrowed. In rural areas, the most pressing issue now is to aid people whose income is below the minimum standard of living. Therefore, the current emphasis should be set on establishing a subsistence security system in rural areas. Of course, meanwhile, we must actively promote a new cooperative medical system, focusing on overall planning for serious illness in rural areas, and steadily carry out a rural endowment insurance policy. Multi-level concepts can sometimes be reflected in a certain insurance project. For example, some authors propose that the unemployment insurance scheme can be divided into the following three levels: the first level is constituted by the urban SOE workers, the second level by employees with urban hukou and the third level by migrant workers employed by state-owned enterprises.

C. Learning from comparing different welfare systems

Reforms of the welfare system presumably sweep out across the world, which China should consequently draw lessons from. Due to subjective and objective limitations, this project mainly makes some comparative researches about reforms in European welfare states represented by Sweden and the United States (comparisons with other countries are scattered in other chapters). The question is, therefore, can we draw lessons from the reform of the welfare system in countries such as Sweden and the United States with desperately different national conditions from those of China? The experience is that from a purely operational aspect, we can indeed draw lessons from countries with similar national conditions. From the perspective of the operating mechanism of the welfare system, however, we can still get a lot of valuable experience from the transformation of the developed welfare state.

For example, almost all countries that carried out the reform of the welfare system are confronted with excessive responsibility and crises, including crises in the payment of welfare spending. Even in countries like Sweden where the previous public expenditures mounted to 70% of GDP before the reform was stricken by a batch of payment crises. Therefore, it is a main task for countries, which need to reform their welfare systems, to achieve a moderate restraint of demand and remove obstacles for payment.

Likewise, before the advent of welfare system reform, many countries had the problem of welfare fraud and welfare overdependence. The reason is that the so-called "same big mess pot" welfare mechanism itself is flawed by practicing a one-way demand inflation mechanism, lacking an inversive supply constraint mechanism, which will not only lead to economic problems in short supply but also trigger moral problems such as "dawdling with an excuse of illness" and other welfare frauds. Evidently, the establishment of the welfare system depends not only on the improvement of the economic development and the soundness of the economic system, but also on the cultivation of the moral sentiments of the citizens.

Another example is that problems of counter-incentives for labor enthusiasm and implicit transfer of income also existed in the well-developed welfare state before reforms. Their reforms of welfare systems, to some extent, resemble the "equal pay for equal work" evolving into "equal share regardless of the work done". Therefore, we can draw lessons from the reforms with regard to solutions to the aforementioned problems.

In the welfare states such as Sweden, one prominent case of welfare dependency is the over-socialization of family functions. Sweden's experience shows that over-socialization of family services will diminish efficiency. The experience of the United States also shows that the establishment and development of the social security system should not affect the family's functions. In the case of China, however, the problem lies in how to cope with poverty incurred by illness and senility due to inadequate family functions and social functions (lack of social compatibility). Thus, given the economic development and cultural traditions, it can be seen that it will be a top priority for China to design a plan featuring combination and complementation of family functions and social functions in different stages of social security reform and development.

Social security systems in developed countries have contributed to the progress of national basic education, from which we also can draw lessons. The proportion of education and welfare spending in the United States stands at 24%–34% in total social security spending. Thanks to its social security system, which highlights education security, the United States has taken the lead in the popularity of elementary education and higher education participation rate in the world. In social education welfare spending in the United States, elementary and secondary education account for about 69%, higher education for 20%, vocational and adult education 7%, other miscellaneous spending about 4%. This kind of social security system, for one thing, has provided a big chunk of educational subsidies to poor or middle-class families, which lifts their overall living standards as well as lays a solid foundation for the next generation to strengthen their income-generating capacity. For another thing, it has provided generations of indispensable manpower capital accumulation for sustainable development and for the enhancement of international competitiveness. The practice of supporting education through social security is of referential value in building a fair and harmonious society.

III.   Issues to be further explored

As mentioned earlier, whether theoretically or practically, the reform and construction of the Chinese social security system are still underway, where there remains a host of problems to be solved. Hereby, several examples are explored in the following parts.

A.   How to solve the problem of malfunction and vague responsibilities in the "combination of social pooling with individual accounts" model

In the choice of the target model for the pension system, most countries and regions have implemented the Three Pillars model to different extents in accordance with the recommendations of the World Bank, embodied by the model of "combining social pooling with individual accounts", referred to as unified account mode in China, which evolved from a fully pay-as-you-go system and an fully funded personal account system. The model is characterized by the fact that part of the pensions of retirees roots in pay-as-you-go financing and partly from fully funding. It can learn from the advantages of the previous two modes as much as possible, and form complementary advantages. At the same time, it can also reduce the risk of relying solely on a certain model. On the one hand, this model retains the function of redistributing personal income among generations under the pay-as-you-go system. On the other hand, to some extent, it generates incentives for people to work and pay under the fully funded system, which not only can ease the payment crisis brought by the welfare rigidity under the pay-as-you-go system but also can overcome the flaws of the uneven annuity under the fully funded system. This model can be a better manifestation of the combination of individual responsibility and social solidarity, fairness and efficiency, current interests and long-term interests. Therefore, the model of "combining social pooling with individual accounts" proposed in the "Resolution on Several Issues Concerning the Establishment of a Socialist

Market Economic Structure" of the Third Plenary Session of the 14th Central Committee of the CPC in 1993 is considered as a more realistic target mode. In 1997, the State Council promulgated the "Decision on Establishing a Unified System of Basic Endowment Insurance for Workers", which eventually resulted in the establishment of a pension system that combines social pooling with individual accounts.

However, there are some flaws in the design and operation of the "combination of social pooling with individual accounts" model. The first is that the standard of basic old-age insurance prescribed by the government is too high. Internationally, the standard is based on the ability to meet the basic livelihood of retirees. China, however, exceeds the international standard, triggering the over-size of first pillar and payment crises. Second, the model did not solve the problem of implicit pension debt, thus giving rising to "empty accounts" of individual accounts. Furthermore, the lack of institutional arrangements for enterprises to supplement pension insurance and individual deposit care for the aged makes the second and third pillars less attractive to enterprises and individuals as well as difficult to regulate their operations, which results in disorders between the redistribution function and the saving function, vagueness between government responsibility and individual responsibility. Therefore, it will be a major challenge to solve the plight in the reform and construction of the social security system in the years ahead.

B. How to solve the problem of implicit pension debt and its repayment

Many authors of this book explored the issue of implicit pension debt from different perspectives. In a fully funded pension plan, each generation saves money for the sake of retirement, free from the implicit pension debt problem. However, during the transition from the pay-as-you-go system to the partial-funded pension system, employees' contributions should no longer be utilized to pay for the existing retirees' pensions, which means that alternative sources of funding should be sought to pay for old-age pensions that occurred prior to the establishment of the new system and the pensions that were accrued for the employee's working years. Otherwise, the existing staff members must pay two generations' (their own generation and the previous generation) pension costs. This out-of-pocket pension, which is not incorporated in government public expenditure plans and embedded in future welfare commitment, has been referred to as implicit pension debt. Many scholars believe that this type of implicit debt is actually the "transition cost" that should be paid during the transition from pay-as-you-go system to partial-funded system.

There are various measurements and estimates of the scale of implicit pension debt, ranging from one or two trillion of RMB to more than ten trillion RMB. Although the scale of implicit debts or transition costs is sizable, some authors are still optimistic about this issue. The reason is that the burdensome transition cost does not need to be completely paid in cash within a year or a few years. Only when the old-aged and the middle-aged who are alive in the reform launched in 1997 all pass away in 2050 or so can the transition period terminate. In other words, the transition costs can be divided in 50 years. In this way, the annual transition cost is limited when it is allocated into individuals. The annual transition cost required to be allocated in 2000–2035 is about 0.6% of GDP in the year, which will reach 0.3% of GDP by 2050. Some scholars also explored methods of funding for the implicit debt such as issuing treasury bonds, increasing fiscal expenditures and selling state-owned assets.

C.   How to find a modest substitute rate of wage and contribution rate for pension

Substitute rate of wage and contribution rate for pension are two sides of a coin. In the sight of funding, the substitute rate depends on the contribution rate. Currently, the prevailing voice is that both the replacement rate and the contribution rate are relatively high. After in-depth analysis, it can be found that both the substitute rate and the contribution rate have been calculated inaccurately and unreasonably high. There-fore, it remains further study to set an appropriate substitute rate and payment rate.

Some scholars argue that most countries set pension substitute rate at 40% to 50%, with 60% at the highest level. The substitute rate of wage of current old-age insurance in China, however, is as high as 80% or even 100%, an explicit trend of welfare. In China's current revenue structure, the proportion of extra-wage income is fairly high. The substitute rate of wage will be high if the pension is only com-parable to the wage, but it may be low if compared with the actual income. The substitute rate in China is inaccurate in that the wage regarded as a denominator when calculating the substitute rate does not fully represent the total income, so there is no comparability with the international counterpart. Therefore, to make a comparatively accurate calculation of the substitute rate of wage, we must first solve the problem of high extra-wage and the exorbitant substitute rate.

Some scholars believe that the basic social insurance premium paid by enter-prises is generally around 10% of the total wage internationally. The contribution rate of enterprises in China, however, reached 25% by the early 21st century. Excessively high contribution rate has become a heavy burden for enterprises. However, if the contribution rate is linked to the premium-paid base, problems such as false pay base and "dodging charges" will occur, thus triggering the exces-sively high contribution rate. The perennial problem remains the high proportion of extra-income in the revenue structure of the employees. These extra-wages are excluded in the premium-paid base, causing the false pay base a prominent issue of the loss of the pension fund. Therefore, it must firstly address the issue of exces-sively high extra-wage and high contribution rate so as to calculate a relatively accurate contribution rate.

D.   How to give full play to the government's redistribution function in improving the social security system

The first is to change the pattern of "regressive redistribution" left over from his-tory. The so-called "regressive redistribution" actually indicates that redistribution tools such as taxation and payment transfer employed by the government has widened the income gap rather than narrowed it. China's extremely large income disparity and the uneven allocations of social security resources between urban and rural areas are partly the result of such "regressive redistribution."

Apart from the "regressive redistribution" between urban and rural areas, attention also should be paid to the widening income gap between urban and rural areas caused by external factors under the new situation. For instance, after China's entry into the WTO, farmers' income will be diminished if produce is imported from developed countries where farmers often receive government subsidies. It will be a complex issue for the Chinese government to take countermeasures against "regressive redistribution" caused by such external factors.

During the implementation of each social security policy, we must also guard against the re-emergence of the "regressive redistribution". For example, in resolving the aforementioned false pay base problem, "regressive redistribution" will also arise in honest if some enterprises still falsify while other enterprises do not.

Government also needs to gradually narrow the gap in allocating social security resources among various departments through redistribution policies. In addition to the aforementioned imbalance between urban and rural areas, there are also gaps between formal sectors and informal sectors, public institutions and enterprises. Certainly, there is a long way to go before these problems can be addressed. However, it is doubtless that the redistribution policy needs to be formulated with a view to reducing such imbalances.

According to international practices, a proper redistribution should not merely be an idea, but a policy goal. An appropriate redistribution policy should definitely be instituted when levels of economic development and cultural traditions of various countries are taken into account. For example, many countries adjust their tax rates when reform their welfare systems. Both Sweden and the United States have adopted measures to reduce the top marginal tax rate, but top marginal tax rate in Sweden is still higher than in the United States. In addition, the appropriate proportion of transfer payments in GDP varies from country to country. It remains an unexplored problem to determine the proper scale of transfer payment in consistent with the different stages of economic development in China.

(Originally released in the third issue of *Economic Perspectives* in 2006.)

Note

1 This is a commentary on the achievements of China's social security reform research project I chair. The results of the entire project can be found in *China's Economic Transition and Social Security Reform*, co-edited by Zhao Renwei, Lai Desheng, Wei Zhong and published by Beijing Normal University Publishing Group in 2006.

Index